THERE IS MORE!

THERE IS MORE!

RECLAIMING THE POWER OF IMPARTATION

RANDY CLARK

GLOBAL AWAKENING

There is More!: Reclaiming the Power of Impartation
First Edition, January 2006
© Copyright 2006 Global Awakening
All rights reserved

Global Awakening
1075 Lancaster Boulevard, Suite 201
Mechanicsburg, PA 17055

Unless otherwise noted, Scripture quotations are taken from HOLY BIBLE, NEW INTERNATIONAL VERSION®. Copyright © 1973, 1978, 1984 by International Bible Society. Used by permission of Zondervan Publishing House.

Scripture quotations marked (NASB) are taken from the NEW AMERICAN STANDARD BIBLE®, Copyright © 1960, 1962, 1963, 1971, 1972, 1973, 1975, 1977, 1995 by The Lockman Foundation. Used by permission.

Scripture quotations marked (NKJV) are taken from the New King James Version®. Copyright © 1982 by Thomas Nelson, Inc. Used by permission. All rights reserved. NKJV is a trademark of Thomas Nelson, Inc.

Disclaimer: Website references given are correct at time of publication, but may change over time. We cannot guarantee their continued accuracy or availability.

Fifth Printing: June 2008

ISBN: 0-9740756-2-0
ISBN: 978-0-9740756-2-4

ENDORSEMENTS

"Your heart will cry for 'More!' as you read this book. Randy's unique combination of thorough research and passionate hunger will stir you to receive more of your inheritance in Jesus Christ. Randy wisely cuts through the controversy and confusion that often surround the subject of 'impartation.' The truths contained in these pages are not theory. They are life-changing realities."

Dave Hess, Pastor
Christ Community Church
Camp Hill, Pennsylvania

"I have been a 'Randy-watcher' for almost a dozen years and am prepared to say with solid certainty that no one on the renewal/revival scene today is more qualified to write a book such as this. No one speaks with greater credibility and integrity than Randy Clark. He is a son and friend! I have read enough of the manuscript to feel its spiritual pulse and will digest it immediately!"

Jack Taylor, President
Dimensions Ministries
Melbourne, Florida

"Randy 'Mr. Impartation' Clark is without doubt the most qualified to write such a book. His classic messages on impartation have affected thousands of lives around the world and I am one of those who have been profoundly touched. This book is filled with amazing stories of those who received an impartation and then did mighty exploits in God's kingdom. It will create in you a spiritual hunger for more impartation to thrust you into your God ordained destiny."

Gary Oates
Author, **Open My Eyes, Lord**
Gary Oates Ministries
Dallas, Georgia

"Randy Clark's passion and enthusiasm for loving the church and blessing the nations is contagious. 'There Is More!' is the cry of an increasing army of world changers that by seeing the invisible can do the impossible. Randy Clark is leading the way toward the twenty-first century slugfest the Holy Spirit is doing around the world today!"

Leif Hetland, President
Global Mission Awareness
Killen, Alabama

"Listening to Randy, soaking up Randy's writing, and just being with Randy talking about the things of God has meant rivers of refreshing to me in recent years. It is easy to be moved to tears over and over in the company of a man with whom Heidi and I can so identify. He longs for all the passion and compassion of the Kingdom of God with a childlike abandon that obviously delights God as much as it encourages us. And he pursues the unrestrained power of God just as God wants to reveal it—in holiness, freedom, and joy. This book will make readers reach out and always find more!"

Rolland and Heidi Baker, Missionaries
Authors, **There Is Always Enough**
Iris Ministries
Mozambique, Africa

"Randy Clark's latest book is stirring reading. If you hunger for more of God, this book will increase your hunger. Randy lays a Biblical foundation, shows the reality of the doctrine's outworking in Church history, and then brings us to the present moves of the Spirit and the fruit they are bearing. Those who have asked the appropriate question, "Where's the fruit?" will find ample evidence that the current move of the Spirit is producing a harvest in the nations. The work of Heidi and Rolland Baker in Mozambique in this regard is particularly moving. Many other examples of the lasting effect of laying on of hands and prophecy are given. This book will make you cry out for more of God. Be warned!"

Joe McIntyre, Pastor
President, International Fellowship of Ministries
Author, **E. W. Kenyon and His Message of Faith: The True Story**
Word of His Grace Fellowship
Kirkland, Washington

TABLE OF CONTENTS

ACKNOWLEDGEMENTS

I want to thank the Global Awakening staff for the production of this book: my son Josh and daughter-in-law Tonya for keeping the project moving and encouraging me to write, Dennis McCormick for his work on the footnotes, Deb Martella for her future work in overseeing the bookstore and ensuring quality in all our products, Ryan and Jackie Adair for their advice and help—you gave valuable advice regarding the book's present form, and Dennis Valen for encouraging me to write.

I also want to express my deep sense of gratitude to my editor Linda Kaahanui. Linda had the vision to edit this book even before it had been written. Thank you for making the message of impartation available in print. You helped organized my disorganized thought processes into a coherent whole. This book would not be what it is without your valuable help.

Most of all I thank my wife, DeAnne, for the tremendous sacrifice she has made for me to be able to travel these eleven and one-half years. God only knows the price you have paid for this ministry. I recognize your sacrifice and hope to make the next eleven and one-half years easier for you. There is no way to make up for my past absences in our family, but I honor you and love you. I will strive to work smarter, not harder, as long as God's grace is upon our ministry.

My children, Josh and his wife Tonya, Johannah, Josiah, and Jeremiah, you too have paid a high price for me to take this gift of impartation to leaders around the world. I look forward to more time spent imparting my love and gratitude into your lives in the future.

I want to thank all the people who allowed me to use their testimony in this book and to the scores of others who received not just a blessing or refreshing, but a commissioning in our meetings. You have helped spread the fire and equip the saints around the world, and I express my gratitude for your faithfulness and willingness to pay the price to give away what we freely received. To the pastors of churches who have partnered with Global Awakening, thank you for your prayers and encouragement—you are a source of strength to me.

I want to express my appreciation to Pastor Bill Johnson. You are continually a source of revelation and inspiration, but more importantly, a good friend. Thanks for being willing to become my Apostolic Overseer as I oversee the Apostolic Network of Global Awakening. I always enjoy when we get to minister together.

Finally, and most importantly, I want to thank the great God we serve who has made Himself known in the unity of the Trinity. Thank You to the Father, Son, and Holy Spirit. You are the One behind all that happens and without Your breathing into us the breath of life, we would have no hope. Thank You for Your gifts and callings and that they are irrevocable (Romans 11:29). You are worthy of all praise, honor, and glory.

Randy Clark
Mechanicsburg, Pennsylvania
November 2006

FOREWORD

Few people in modern history have had the effect on the church around the world as has Randy Clark. His humble approach to ministry and his abandonment to the move of God have kept him on the cutting edge of revival.

I first saw Randy Clark on *a copy of a copy* of a video from a service at Toronto Airport Christian Fellowship. When I watched him minister, I was heavily impacted by his humility and his gift for knowing what the Holy Spirit was doing. During the playing of that video I said out loud, "I must meet that man!" Through a mutual friend, a meeting was arranged. My wife and I flew to St. Louis where Randy graciously gave us fifteen minutes between appointments to share our hearts even though he was in the middle of a very busy schedule due to the conference he was sponsoring. Before we finished, he agreed to come to Redding, California, to minister to our church family.

His first visit with us was for about five days. There were around 400 people healed during that time. While miracles had become more common for us, even weekly, we had never seen a breakthrough of that magnitude. A definite increase in the flow of signs and wonders started that week that has never subsided since. It has only increased.

There are times when God gives an impartation to an individual. I have received that when Randy has laid hands on me. And yet there are times when it is given to a whole church. Such was the case during his visit to Redding. Hundreds were impacted from the impartation that he brought. And we have never been the same since.

Perhaps the area of greatest failure in past moves of God has been the tendency of individuals to use a personal breakthrough with God as the platform to draw people around themselves. God doesn't give us, as individuals, "a spike in human experience" so we can gather people around us to admire our gifts. On the contrary, He gives us a breakthrough in personal experience so we will use the elevated position of favor to equip the saints until our high point of experience becomes the new norm for the body of Christ around us. Randy continues to increase in anointing and impact on the nations because this is his heart. And this book on impartation is the result of over two decades of study and experience on the subject. The evidence is irrefutable. It has not only *survived* the test of Scripture and time, it has *flourished*, with no end in sight. He has made a major contribution to what I believe is the beginning of a Reformation.

This is the book that Randy Clark was born to write. Although I'm certain more great works will follow, this is to date the most important book he has given to us. In it you will see that his skill as an apologist is stunning. He has a brilliant mind, a rich background as a student of the Word and church history, and most of all a God-given wisdom to sort through the stories of the past that actually set a precedent on God's present work in the earth today. I know of no one who has a clearer understanding of revival, what it costs, and how it plays out in day-to-day life. His knowledge of the church's past mistakes has not paralyzed him with fear, nor has it tarnished his vision of the future. Instead it has graced him with wisdom to help lead us through the maze of confusion caused by those who would rather throw stones than join what I believe is the beginning of the greatest move in all of history.

One of the greatest privileges in my life has been my friendship and partnership with Randy. I have watched these truths applied firsthand. I have seen the impact on cities and nations. Some of those who were unknown often rise to the surface of their generation because they were humble enough to hunger, and humble enough to receive. These are real people, with real stories, who are affecting the course of world history. And it all started when Randy became hungry enough to cry out to God for more, no matter the cost. The impartation that he received has been passed on to countless others who are changing their world. As I tell our young people, "At least four other giants were killed in the Bible besides Goliath—and they were all killed by men who followed David. If you want to kill giants, follow a giant killer." And that is the story of impartation.

Bill Johnson
Pastor, Bethel Church
Redding, California
October 2005

INTRODUCTION

During a meeting at the Toronto Airport Christian Fellowship on January 5, 1995, I stepped up to the microphone and announced a call to pastors and leaders. I said, "There are pastors and leaders here who feel fire on their hands and feet or they are being doubled over by the presence of God. I believe you are being invited by God to take the revival to the nations. I want you to come forward." When they had come forward I said, "I want you to count the cost of this ministry. This anointing will cause you to be gone from your family and church for up to half the year while you are traveling to the nations. If you are not willing to pay this price go back to your seats."

Many went back to their seats—but not "John Doe." (This pastor and his staff prayed a lot about writing a testimony for this book, but felt they were to remain anonymous. Only after I told him I wouldn't mention his name or city did he give me the permission to tell his story.) During this time, I was praying from the platform for apostolic power. The Spirit of God came upon "John Doe" in a powerful manner and, hours later, men had to help him back to the room as he was so undone by the experience with God.

His hands and feet were so hot they were very uncomfortable. His feet had such heat on them that he put them in the shower, but they still had tremendous heat in them. Prior to this meeting, he had been suffering for two years with serious problems in his feet. He had thirteen wounds on his feet four inches long and about three-eighths of an inch wide. He had been to the best doctors and they couldn't help him. When he woke up in the morning after the impartation, his feet were totally healed.

Since that impartation for apostolic work, he has been to all the continents, has ordained 300 people into ministry, holds eleven conferences per year, and travels 180 days per year in many nations and pastors a large, growing church.

They have seen many healings and miracles, even major financial miracles in the ministry of their church. (John Doe emphasized that he has received several deposits—impartations from various other leaders—that today make up the composite of who he is.)

John Doe also attended the Catch the Fire Conference hosted by Global Awakening in St. Louis, Missouri in April 1995. Shortly after that conference, his church experienced a glorious visitation of the presence of God. This anointing has not ended, but continues to this day.

When I asked him what they have done to sustain this impartation and anointing he stated, "I have passionately pursued the Lord and lived the book of Acts. I have determined to continue to live and move in the anointing." He said they have services every day of some kind at the church, and they send out teams to minister to other cities in the United States or around the world every week. He didn't tell me because he is a humble man, but I know he oversees a network of over one hundred churches today.

There Is More!

This statement expresses the confident realization that the greatness of God's grace and His salvation far exceed what we have come to expect. For the majority of Christians, the understanding of grace has been limited to not getting the judgment we deserve through the forgiveness of sins, and receiving what we don't deserve—eternal life. This understanding of the effects of Jesus' death on the cross on our behalf, called "substitutionary atonement," brings great comfort to our souls and peace to our minds. It is the wonderful basis of our salvation.

But grace is more than this; it includes even more than forgiveness and eternal life. This understanding alone is not enough to reveal the full benefits of the death of Jesus on the cross. He not only died in our place, but in His death and resurrection He also became victor over death, demons, disease, the devil, and damnation. He descended into Hades and in His victorious ascent, He led the captives free (Ephesians 4:7-9). Jesus proved His dominion over all the destructive power of the curse. He promised us that the gates of hell would not prevail against His church. He now invites us to share in His victory and continue advancing His kingdom throughout the earth until He returns.

This understanding of the work of Jesus on the cross has been historically known in the church as "Christus Victor" and it was the predominant view for the first 600 years of Christianity. Whereas the "substitutionary" view is often limited to our forgiveness and future state in glory, the "Christus Victor" view encompasses the impact of the cross upon our lives in this world. It has a strong emphasis upon Jesus' defeat of the devil and it includes our ability and privilege to share in that victory by participating in His continued ministry through the gifts of the Holy Spirit. I believe both views are true and complementary to each other and that both are needed to fully understand all Jesus did for us.

The primary way Jesus advances His kingdom is through the continuation of His ministry through the church. The message of the church is to be the message of the kingdom and it is to be accompanied by signs and wonders, miracles and healings, and deliverances. Like the first disciples, all the continuing disciples of Jesus throughout the history of the church may be endued with power to enable them to continue His works. Since Jesus came "to destroy the devil's work" (1 John 3:8), the purpose of the church must encompass this purpose as well. This is the full meaning of discipleship. It is not just a new morality, which is the mark of discipleship; it is also a new empowerment for joining the exalted Lord Jesus in the advancement of His kingdom by displacing the work of Satan, sin, sickness, and slavery to evil spirits.

The "more" in the title of this book is the empowerment sometimes called "the anointing" to work the works of God through the gifts of the Holy Spirit. The gifts are divine, grace-based enablements that do not rely upon natural ability or training. Without this "more," the church's work is reduced to the level of any other social endeavor that could be accomplished by human effort. It is this divine

3

enablement that makes Christianity different from Hinduism, Buddhism, Islam, and the other religions and "isms" of the world.

This "more" is the reality of God drawing near, of God rending the heavens and coming down. It is the difference between times of revival and times of decline in the church. Revivals are led by people who have been touched by the "more," whether that experience is described in the language of "entire consecration," "sanctification," or "baptism in the Holy Spirit." Periods of revival are characterized by people who believe the life they are experiencing or the church is experiencing, falls short of what is possible and available. This belief causes them to seek God for an impartation of more.

This book is about the impartation of that "more." But what exactly is the "more"? It is many things: more love for God and humankind, more power, more anointing, more joy, more burden of the Lord for the lost, more revelation from God regarding the needs of others, more conviction over sin, more faith in prayer, more conversions, more gifts, more healings, more deliverances, more churches planted, and more of the culture being leavened by the kingdom of God.

People who have received impartations of God's enabling graces become "history makers." They may not become national or international history makers, but they do change their personal history and the history of those around them at the local church level or the community level. A powerful impartation does produce fruit for the kingdom of God. It is not a matter of talk, but a demonstration of power. The "impartation" experience that I am speaking about is not just receiving a "blessing" from God. Neither is it a matter of being strengthened by the Holy Spirit or an angel of God; it is more than that. There is destiny connected with the "impartation." Many times it is accompanied by a prophetic word that reveals this destiny. At other times, a person's destiny has already been revealed to them. Later, they receive an "impartation" which enables them to accomplish their God-given destiny.

4

The following pages are full of testimonies and stories that attest to the title of this book, *There Is More!* However, the stories alone would not persuade some readers because they have been taught that the "more" ended about 1,800 years ago. Whenever stories about miracles, healings, or deliverances are told, they are rejected as either self-deception or worse, demonic in source.

It is my desire to remove barriers that people have against moves of God by doing three things throughout this book. First, I want to appeal to the reader to be a Berean and study the Scriptures to see what they teach without a preconceived idea that miracles ended with the close of the canon of Scripture. This is crucial because the anointing for impartation is directly connected to the issue of the continuation of the gifts of healing and prophecy as well as other gifts of the Holy Spirit. For this purpose, I recommend the articles written by Dr. Jon Ruthven of Regent University School of Divinity and posted on his website, "Can a Charismatic Theology be Biblical?" and "The 'Imitation of Christ' in Christian Tradition: Its Missing Charismatic Emphasis."[1] I want the reader to see from Scripture the role that gifts, power, healing, and miracles play in the character of God, the message of the kingdom of God, and how God receives glory.

Second, I want us to see how the history of the church contains many illustrations of men and women who received power from heaven. With this impartation of power, they were then used to impart to others mighty experiences of the presence of God. In fact, in the early church, the practice of impartation was such a foundational element of Christian discipleship that it became a part of the earliest baptismal rites.

Third, I want the reader to come to understand the price that is paid for moving in the anointing or the power of the Spirit, once a heavenly impartation is received. I want them to see that, most frequently, this impartation comes to those who have been serving God faithfully for years and that it often comes at a time of brokenness and crisis. The kingdom is the "pearl of great price"–worth going and selling everything in order to purchase it. Before we quickly say this is something we want, have we considered the cost?

If you are already convinced that the experience of impartation is still for today, you might already be familiar with the material in chapters 3 and 4 which discusses the continuation of powerful impartations throughout the history of the church. Chapter 4 tells the powerful way God used the nineteenth century as a century of prayer for a "New Pentecost." This prayer was answered at the beginning of the twentieth century. Though I find the information fascinating and faith building, I realize that many readers place little value on the history of past moves of God. These chapters may be skipped since they serve an apologetic purpose for those who come from a cessationist position, but who are open minded and would want more of God if they become convinced the "more" is not only biblical but beneficial for the carrying out of the Great Commission.

In writing this book, I hope to stir up a greater hunger for this "more" of God. Many Christians, especially in the western church, do not even know there *is* more beyond the routines of their church culture. I hope that you, the reader, will desire to experience more of God's empowering presence; desire to receive a personal impartation; and desire to be more powerfully used of God in your local church, your community, your city, or the world.

PART I: RESTORING THE LOST DOCTRINE OF

IMPARTATION

"DO NOT NEGLECT YOUR GIFT, WHICH
WAS GIVEN YOU THROUGH A PROPHETIC
MESSAGE WHEN THE BODY OF ELDERS
LAID THEIR HANDS ON YOU."

1 TIMOTHY 4:14

"FOR THIS REASON I REMIND YOU TO
FAN INTO FLAME THE GIFT OF GOD,
WHICH IS IN YOU THROUGH THE LAYING
ON OF MY HANDS."

2 TIMOTHY 1:6

CHAPTER 1: THE BIBLICAL FOUNDATION FOR IMPARTATIONS

Since the "Toronto Blessing" started in 1994, the fire of renewal has touched people on every continent. Millions have come to renewal meetings hungry, even desperate, to encounter God in a more tangible way. Millions have been regenerated after experiencing a strong impartation through the renewal that became a revival. More than eleven-and-a-half years later, the Holy Spirit is still moving, stirring up an intense desire in the Bride to move beyond an intellectual, religious knowledge of her Groom, to an all-consuming heart of passion for Him. This passion has brought scores of thousands to the prayer altars for an impartation of anointing for ministry.

As the manifest presence of God has touched them, many have experienced physical and highly emotional responses. But what has the long-term spiritual impact been? Has it lasted? Anyone concerned with true revival will ask the question, "What's the fruit?" Even more important questions for some are, "Is there a biblical precedent for the impartation of anointing?" and "Is this doctrine and practice a part of our orthodox Christian heritage or just a bizarre blip on the timeline?" These questions stir up a whole range of opinions and controversy that still swirl around today's renewal movement. It is my heart's desire to provide some common ground of scriptural and historical understanding with the aim to "make every effort to keep the unity of the Spirit through the bond of peace" (Ephesians 4:3).

THE BIBLICAL FOUNDATION

> "Therefore let us leave the elementary teachings about Christ and go on to maturity, not laying again the foundation of repentance from acts that lead to death, and of faith in God, instruction about baptisms, **the laying on of hands**, the resurrection of the dead, and eternal judgment. And God permitting, we will do so." (Hebrews 6:1-3, emphasis added)

9

The writer to the Hebrews clearly considers "the laying on of hands" to be so basic to the Christian life, it is referred to as foundational, an "elementary teaching" of the apostolic church. The Bible teaches in both Testaments the principle of a person receiving an "anointing" from God. This anointing may be a gift or gifts of the Spirit, a filling of the Holy Spirit—especially for power, or the baptism in the Holy Spirit. This idea of "impartation" or "transference of anointing" is a strong biblical concept. (In Brazil, where I minister frequently, the best translation of the English word "impartation" is the phrase "transference of the anointing" and I believe this understanding is helpful also for those who are not familiar with the term.)

As we look at biblical examples, we see that this anointing often came through the laying on of hands. Now, let me make an important clarification; the laying on of hands is certainly not the ONLY way of receiving an impartation from God. It is simply one of two ways seen in Scripture, the other being waiting on God through prayer. It is, however, a means often forgotten and neglected by the church and, therefore, an important part of the subject of this book. Let us take a look at some Old Testament passages documenting this idea of impartation.

We find the first reference to the concept of impartation in Numbers 11:16-18:

> The Lord said to Moses: "Bring me seventy of Israel's elders who are known to you as leaders and officials among the people. Have them come to the Tent of Meeting, that they may stand there with you. **I will come down and speak with you there, and I will take of the Spirit that is on you and put the Spirit on them.** They will help you carry the burden of the people so that you will not have to carry it alone." (Emphasis added)

In this passage there is no mention of Moses laying his hands upon the elders for them to receive, but the concept of a transference of the anointing that is on one man to others is clearly present. Equally evident from this text is the principle that this is not something man can do, but it is an act of God, totally dependent upon *His* calling and anointing.

10

Again, we see transference of anointing in Deuteronomy 34:9a:

Now Joshua son of Nun was filled with the spirit of wisdom **because Moses had laid his hands on him**. (Emphasis added)

This time, there is a specific mention of receiving or being filled with the spirit of wisdom *because* Moses laid hands on Joshua. With or without the actual laying on of hands, the transference of anointing is clearly a biblically-documented, God-initiated event.

Another example is found in 2 Kings 2:9-15, the famous passage that tells of Elijah's anointing being transferred to his spiritual son, Elisha. This passage indicates that it is possible to receive an anointing similar to that of another person. When Elisha begged, "Let me inherit a double portion of your spirit" he was not asking for the power of Elijah's human spirit, but for the Spirit of God to work through him as He did through his teacher. Likewise, when the people said, "The spirit of Elijah is resting on Elisha," they did not mean that Elisha had received power literally from the spirit of the man, Elijah, but that the Spirit of God was indeed working through Elisha in a powerful way, similar to what they had witnessed in Elijah.

Examples from the New Testament again reflect two ways that one receives power, gifts, anointing, fillings or baptisms in the Holy Spirit. One way is through praying and waiting upon God, and the other way is through the laying on of hands. In Hebrews 6:1-2, what did the "laying on of hands" refer to? It spoke of several things:

The Act of Ordination

1 Timothy 4:14 is most likely a reference to Timothy's ordination: "Do not neglect your gift, which was given you through a prophetic message when the body of elders laid their hands on you." Another reference most likely speaking to the laying on of hands for ordination is 1 Timothy 5:22, "Do not be hasty in the laying on of hands, and do not share in the sins of others." The same thing is found

11

in what many consider the ordination of the first deacons in Acts 6:6, "They presented these men to the apostles, who prayed and laid their hands on them."

The first commissioning or ordaining service for missionaries is recorded in Acts 13:1-3, especially see verse 3: "So after they had fasted and prayed, they placed their hands on them and sent them off." As we will later see with Timothy, these services were not mere rituals but were the occasions when the Holy Spirit imparted gifts and empowered for ministry. Also, these gifts were often accompanied by prophecies.

Healing and/or Blessing

The laying on of hands was not just for ordination, but also for healing and/or blessing. Matthew 19:13-15 states:

> Then little children were brought to Jesus for him **to place his hands on them** and pray for them. But the disciples rebuked those who brought them. Jesus said, "Let the little children come to me, and do not hinder them, for the kingdom of heaven belongs to such as these." When he had **placed his hands on them**, he went on from there. (Emphasis added)

This particular reference doesn't say if Jesus placed his hands on them for blessing or healing, but we know Jesus did both. A clear passage that refers to blessing is Mark 10:16, "And he took the children in his arms, put his hands on them and blessed them." Another clear passage, this time referring to healing, is Mark 5:23, "[Jairus] pleaded earnestly with him, 'My little daughter is dying. Please come and put your hands on her so that she will be healed and live.' So Jesus went with him."

Although Jesus healed in many ways other than through the laying on of hands, many New Testament Gospel references connect the laying on of hands to the ministry of healing. (See Mark 6:5, Mark 8:23-25, Luke 4:40, Luke 13:13-14.) The disciples were also to follow the example of Jesus and lay their hands upon the sick for healing. "…they will place their hands on sick people, and they will get well." (Mark 16:18c)

12

Paul followed the practice of laying on of hands for healing, as in Acts 28:8:

> His father was sick in bed, suffering from fever and dysentery. Paul went in to see him and, after prayer, **placed his hands on him** and healed him. When this had happened, the rest of the sick on the island came and were cured. (Emphasis added)

Paul not only ministered healing, but also received healing through the laying on of hands:

> Then Ananias went to the house and entered it. **Placing his hands on Saul**, he said, "Brother Saul, the Lord—Jesus, who appeared to you on the road as you were coming here—has sent me so that you may see again and be filled with the Holy Spirit." Immediately, something like scales fell from Saul's eyes, and he could see again. He got up and was baptized, and after taking some food, he regained his strength. (Acts 9:17-19, emphasis added)

Although it isn't expressly stated, this passage seems to imply that Paul not only received healing, but also the infilling of the Holy Spirit when Ananias laid hands on him.

Impartation

Another aspect of the doctrine of "laying on of hands" is in connection to impartation. The impartations we see in the Bible were both for gifts of the Spirit and for being filled or baptized with the Holy Spirit. I can't emphasize enough that the laying on of hands is only one way to receive impartation, the other being waiting on God in prayer.

Luke is the historian of the Holy Spirit. His Gospel and the record of Acts are history written with theological significance and considerations. He recounts in Acts 2:1-4, 4:29-31, and 10:44-47 where people are filled with the Holy Spirit without the mention of the "laying on of hands."

According to John 20:21-22, the disciples received the Holy Spirit when Jesus breathed upon them on the evening of the day of His resurrection. Therefore, the Day of Pentecost wasn't when they first received the Holy Spirit, but the day they were, according to Luke, "filled with the Holy Spirit." In Acts 2 and Acts 4, the Holy Spirit came upon believers who were looking to God for enabling power. As Peter preached for the first time to Gentiles in Acts 10, "the Holy Spirit came on all who heard the message" even as they were being saved through the message.

More pertinent to our topic, however, are Luke's accounts of where the Holy Spirit or gifts of the Spirit were imparted with the laying on of hands. In Acts 8:14-17 we read about the revival in Samaria:

> When the apostles in Jerusalem heard that Samaria had accepted the word of God, they sent Peter and John to them. When they arrived, they prayed for them that they might receive the Holy Spirit, because the Holy Spirit had not yet come upon any of them; they had simply been baptized into the name of the Lord Jesus. Then Peter and John **placed their hands on them**, and they received the Holy Spirit. (Emphasis added)

Apparently, the giving of the Holy Spirit was accompanied by some visible manifestation because Luke continues in verses 18-19 to describe the reaction of Simon the sorcerer:

> When Simon saw that the Spirit was given **at the laying on of the apostles' hands**, he offered them money and said, "Give me also this ability so that everyone on whom I lay my hands may receive the Holy Spirit." (Emphasis added)

The second passage in Luke's theological-historical account is found in Acts 19:6-7 where Paul, rather than Peter and John, places his hands upon newly baptized believers in Ephesus:

> When Paul **placed his hands on them**, the Holy Spirit came on them, and they spoke in tongues and prophesied. There were about twelve men in all. (Emphasis added)

In both of these stories, Samaria and Ephesus, it is significant that the experience of receiving the Holy Spirit came *after* the experience of believing. Some teach that the baptism of the Holy Spirit happens at salvation, but one is hard-pressed to prove this from the writings of Luke. It didn't happen that way in any of the six passages discussed so far. These are all references from the earliest history of the New Testament church dealing with when and how people received the Holy Spirit or indicating what it looked like when the Spirit "came upon" or "filled" believers. The focus of these events is a distinct impartation of the Holy Spirit rather than the regeneration of the Holy Spirit that occurs at salvation.

In Romans 1:11-12, we again find the concept of impartation. This time it is for the impartation of some spiritual gift to the Christians at Rome:

> I long to see you **so that I may impart to you** some spiritual gift to make you strong—that is, that you and I may be mutually encouraged by each other's faith. (Emphasis added)

The activity of the Holy Spirit was vital to Paul's understanding of his role as an apostle. At the end of his letter, Paul emphasizes the connection between his proclamation of the word and the empowerment of the Spirit. He states in Romans 15:17-19:

> Therefore I glory in Christ Jesus in my service to God. I will not venture to speak of anything except what Christ has accomplished through me in leading the Gentiles to obey God by what I have said and done—**by the power of signs and miracles, through the power of the Spirit**. So from Jerusalem all the way around to Illyricum, I have **fully proclaimed the gospel** of Christ. (Emphasis added)

In this passage, Paul seems to understand that the effectiveness of his ministry was not simply the result of what he preached, but what he did as well—the "power of signs and miracles, through the power of the Spirit."

I am indebted to Dr. Gordon Fee who brought to my attention that the Apostle Paul's most foundational doctrine was the experience of the Spirit as the basis for certainty of one's salvation.[2] The basis for assurance of one's salvation is the realization of God's empowering presence in one's life. This was even more foundational for Paul than "justification by grace through faith." With such an emphasis upon receiving the empowering presence of God through His Spirit, and the realization that the presence and activity of the Holy Spirit was the true source of his own fruitfulness as a minister of the gospel, it should not surprise us to see Paul wanting to come to the Romans to impart to them some spiritual gift. Nor should it surprise us to see Paul in 2 Timothy 1:6 reminding Timothy, his beloved son in the ministry, to "fan into flame the gift of God, which is in you through the laying on of my hands."

For Paul, Timothy, Peter, John, and by logical inference the entire early Christian church, the impartation of anointing through the laying on of hands was an important catalyst for effective ministry characterized by the manifest presence of God and for operating in the complete gifts of the Holy Spirit. It was this newly-born church—small, despised and poor—that changed the world! God has promised another final and radical outpouring among the nations before His Son returns. Again, He will bring it about through His people. Jesus said, "As the Father has sent me, I am sending you." (John 20:21) If we are to walk in this high calling, we cannot forget nor neglect the resources of heaven made available to those who are humble and hungry enough to receive. God is not looking for the well-financed, the well-educated, nor even the well-experienced in "ministry." He is simply looking for those who are willing to yield their hearts and lives to all that God wants to work through them, for those who are willing to believe for more because "There is more!"

Having briefly established scriptural testimony to the reality of impartation (and before we survey the powerful effect of impartation in church history), I want in the next chapter to share with you how God brought me personally into such an understanding of impartation, and how He powerfully touched me and changed my life. I was not raised in a Charismatic or Pentecostal church or denomination. It is the grace of God that has made this possible in my life. I did not enter into these things because of my will, but by His grace.

As you read on, I pray that the Lord will create in you an intense hunger for the "more" of impartation of His Spirit and His gifts. I pray that He will create in you faith both to receive gifts and also to receive a new and possibly stronger "filling" of His Spirit through impartation.

Chapter 2: A Man Made Ready – My Testimony of Impartation

My understanding of the concept of impartation came relatively late in my ministry. Trained at The Southern Baptist Theological Seminary in Louisville, Kentucky, I had been a pastor for fourteen years before I witnessed the reality of this principle. Since this discovery I have had four significant times of impartation—January and March of 1984, October 1989, and August 1993.

In the summer of 1983, I was sitting at my desk saying, "Oh, Lord, I'm glad I'm not a liberal who doesn't believe You did the miraculous things in the Bible. I'm glad I'm not a cessationist who believes You did the miraculous in the past, but that You've quit doing them now. I thank you for that." (I was becoming quite the Pharisee.) Then I heard an impression in my head, very clear and strong. It said, "So what?" It shocked me so much so that I began to listen. Another thought which came on the heels of that question was, "You might as well be a liberal or a cessationist to say that you believe I do these things, and believe in the gifts, but don't know how to move in them." At that point I was so shaken I said, "Lord, I'm going to learn." I went out and bought $700 worth of books (back in 1983 that was a lot of money for me!) and began reading everything I could on spiritual gifts and the baptism of the Holy Spirit.

A week later, a young man came to preach at my church. He spoke on the woman with the issue of blood. I'd heard sermons like this before. In fact, I'd even preached this sermon, but I had always spiritualized it. I dealt with faith and how, by faith, God meets your other needs. I never focused on the healing. As he preached about her faith—not for healing, as he also spiritualized the passage—I began to cry. Hot tears just gushed out of my eyes as I was thinking, "What's going on? What's happening to me? This is not an emotional sermon! God, what are You doing?" I had three strong impressions that hit me right in a row—bam! bam! bam! "I want you to teach this church that I still heal today. I want you to have a conference on healing in this church. I want you to preach differently." I felt like God wanted me to preach a series of messages on everything that Jesus did. Instead of preaching with three points and a poem, the Lord was asking me to take a big passage of Scripture and just tell what was there.

In order to fulfill this mandate, I contacted a friend of mine who at that time was Chaplain of Oral Roberts University, Dr. Larry Hart. He told me I should invite John Wimber to come teach on healing. I had never heard of John Wimber and was reluctant to invite someone to the church I had never heard teach or preach. The next day I heard a preacher on television articulating everything that was stirring in my heart. "Who is this man?" I thought. "He's the one that needs to come!" It turned out to be John Wimber! I knew this wasn't a coincidence so I contacted his office. He was not available to come but agreed to send one of his teams for a conference in March of 1984. The team would have come earlier but I wanted six months to teach and prepare my congregation for something that was sure to be difficult for some to accept.

About a month later, a woman in our church was diagnosed with cancer. We were praying for her but nothing was happening. This made me realize we couldn't wait until March—we needed to learn about healing NOW! I called Yorba Linda Vineyard in California (the church of the team coming to teach us in March), and I reached Lance Pittluck, who was an intern at the time, and asked him what to do. He asked, "Do you know how to receive words of knowledge?" I had no idea, but carefully wrote down what he said about the five ways that people often receive a word of knowledge and tucked the paper away.[3]

The following Sunday night I had my first word of knowledge. We'd been praying at the altar and my left eye started hurting severely for a split second. I thought, "God? Is that a word of knowledge? If it is and I don't give it, somebody could miss the healing. If it's not and I missed God, I'm going to lose the respect of these people that I've worked so hard to get." What a dilemma. I really struggled there for a few minutes trying to figure out what to do. Then I thought,

"Well, if I give the word and I'm wrong, I'll just look foolish. All I'll lose is my pride. But if I give it and I'm right, God could really heal somebody. So, I'll take the chance."

Being the man of faith that I am, I got up in the pulpit and said, "I think—uh—there may be—uh—somebody here who—uh—possibly—uh—may have—uh—something wrong with their left eye. If you will come forward, we will pray for you." A woman I knew came forward. Ruth was an older lady, known for being strong willed and not given to emotion. None of us had any training in praying for the sick so we anointed her with oil, gathered around her, laid hands on her and began to pray. We prayed until we all ran out of something to say and then quit. Immediately when we quit, she said, "Whew! Brother Randy, if you hadn't stopped praying I think I would've fallen on the floor. I was getting so faint I thought I was going to fall down!" I made a mental note that from now on, if we prayed for people, they needed to make sure their knees weren't locked because I had been taught in second grade not to lock my knees so that I would not pass out.

I didn't understand that the Spirit of God was on her. The good news was that she was actually healed! She never had trouble with her left eye again. Ruth had tunnel vision. The eye had a small square of sight, surrounded by darkness. After we prayed, she had no problem seeing with the entire eye. That was the first word of knowledge that resulted in a healing in the history of our church. I had been activated in this gift through hearing the simple teaching. I had received an impartation through a phone conversation.

Realizing you have received a word of knowledge really puts you under the gun. You're sweating bullets. Is it God or not? I decided I would teach the whole church about what I had just learned the week before about words of knowledge. This way rather than just me perspiring, we could all sweat together!

The following Sunday I taught from 1 Corinthians 12 on words of knowledge, as well as what I'd learned from Lance the week before. During the testimony time, a woman stood up in the back of the church and said, "Brother

Randy? I think I had one of them there things you was talkin' about 'cause I ain't got nothin' wrong with my right wrist, but it's a killin' me!" She held her hand up and moved her wrist and said, "It just hurts!" I thought to myself, "*Oh, no! What have I gotten myself into now? It was just the power of suggestion. I've really opened up Pandora's box this time.*" I decided to wait to see if anyone else would respond.

No one seemed to have a wrist problem so I just ignored the situation, passed it off as lightly as I could and sat down. We continued through the remainder of the service and right before the benediction, my best friend's wife, Barbara Gooch, stood up crying. She said, "Randy, I've had pain in my wrists for years, and I can hardly do any of the work I should. I've got three little kids and I can't knit, I can't hold things very long and my wrists just kill me. I've had surgery on them twice and I've got these plastic pieces in them but they've been hurting. I don't want to have surgery again!" As we prayed for her all the pain left and Barb was completely healed!

That was the first time I ever taught on words of knowledge and someone was activated in the gift—someone received an impartation through the teaching. That was twenty-one years ago and I have never taught on words of knowledge since without someone being activated who heard the teaching. From my experience, it is usually about 10% of the crowd that is activated in this gifting.

In January of 1984, two deacons from the church and I attended the James Robison Bible Conference in Dallas, Texas. Up until this time, I had only had one dream in my life that I would absolutely attribute to God. That is why the dream I had the night before the conference really caught my attention and I have never forgotten it. Through the dream, I knew God was telling me (and my congregation) that He wanted to take us into a closer relationship with Him and into a higher realm of His Spirit. With each phase there would be a higher accountability and there would be things in my own life that I'd have to surrender to Him—things which He would reveal to me at the time of transition.

The next day, John Wimber was teaching a session for about 500 pastors and I was amazed. He had all these words of knowledge, and I loved what he was saying. He had many people come up on the stage and there I was sitting on the front row. As a Baptist I knew how to recognize when someone was under conviction but I had never before seen the power of God move visibly and physically on people. I saw a woman he started to pray for, and John said, "Watch her. See what the Spirit's doing." So my deacons and I watched and we began to see the hem of her dress begin to shake. I said, "Did you see that? Do you see that? Her dress is shaking." I know now it sounds funny to be excited about something as small as a lady's hem shaking, but this was all new for me. The woman began to shake even more. She touched somebody else and they began to shake. People were getting healed and it was a wonderful experience.

That same day, God used David Yonggi Cho's message to convict me of a need for more intimacy with God and a relationship with the Holy Spirit. All afternoon I didn't want to be around anybody as the Lord dealt with my heart. I went back to the meeting that night, and David Wilkerson spoke. The pastors came forward and were on their faces repenting, crying out to God. There were TV cameras there from Trinity Broadcasting Network. I didn't want to kneel or put my face on the ground. Everybody was weeping and crying, but I thought, "Man, this is being beamed back to Marion, Illinois and they'll see it." I knew it was just pride and I finally knelt down and prayed a little bit. Then I stood up and began singing a song. I felt like the Spirit of the Lord said, "Raise your hands up!" Now, I was a Baptist and we didn't do that! But I raised them up and as soon as I did, the Spirit of God hit me. I knew I was in trouble and was getting ready to lose it emotionally. I looked around and saw a big projection screen and headed for it because I knew I could hide behind it. As soon as I got over there, the Spirit hit me. I fell against the wall, tried to grab hold and slid down it. I ended up lying on the floor. The bottom of the screen was about three feet off the floor so I was visible to everyone. I lay there shaking and crying for about a half hour. Then I got up and started to go back to my chair. Before I could even take two steps, the Spirit hit me again, and I slid back down the wall into a heap on the floor and wept and cried and shook.

One of my deacons told me later that they were asking, "Where's Randy?" Finally one of them pointed up to the front and saw me lying underneath the screen in front of about 8,000 people.

The next night I went up to John Wimber. I didn't feel worthy of asking for prayer for myself, so I asked him to pray for my deacons. As I turned to get them, he caught my hands and said, "No. I want to pray for you." He looked into my eyes, and I knew he'd been having words of knowledge. I felt so exposed, expecting the worst to come out of his mouth. It was the first time we'd ever met, and he didn't know anything about me. He said, "I want to pray for you, but first I want to pray for your heart because you've been wounded lately in your church." It was the truth. A couple of months before I had been terribly hurt by the church, so I knew this was from the Lord. John then spoke to me several things, including, "You're a prince in the kingdom of God." I didn't know what to do with that. I felt like anything but a prince in the kingdom of God. Then he said, "There's an apostolic call on your life." I didn't learn until ten years later (1994) that for John, when he used that term, all he meant was that I would end up one day having a ministry that involved traveling. He shared many good prophesies with me, and I went away encouraged. I also went away with a new impartation in my life for words of knowledge, as well as a greater hunger for God than I had known in years.

March rolled around and it was time for the healing conference at our church. The Vineyard team arrived from California and Blaine Cook shared the first night. My wife, DeAnne, did not want to attend the meeting, but God worked on her heart and she showed up late— just in time for the "clinic."

In response to a word of knowledge, a pastor named Bob Shimmon from another Baptist church came forward with a spinal injury. We didn't have "catchers" back then, and when the power of God hit Bob, he fell right at my wife's feet. DeAnne's disgruntled response was, "Well, it's not as bad in reality as it is when you see it on television." That was a significant thing for her. When she and I would watch Christian TV and someone was slain in the Spirit, my wife would jump up, look at me and point her finger to say, "If you think that's real, you're the biggest fool I've ever met!" Then she'd run out of the living room and slam the door behind her. You might say she wasn't too accepting of that falling stuff! However, the real life version didn't scare her; it got her attention. There was an afternoon session and during the worship the people from the Vineyard would kneel down and raise their hands up. When I first saw it, I got aggravated at them, thinking, "Who do they think they are? Why are they doing that? They're just trying to draw attention to themselves." I was angry on the first song, but by the second song I was envious. I realized it was my pride reacting and I knew I had too much pride to get on my knees and raise my hands up.

What excited me most during the three day conference was the intimacy of the Vineyard worship. I loved the way they sang *to* God, instead of just *about* Him. That afternoon, many people in my church, including Sandy Simpson the piano player, were trying to get away. They had never seen God's power come in this manner, and were quite uneasy with the manifest power of His presence. Watching people receive impartations was scary; we weren't used to seeing the power of God touching people. The team caught up with Sandy in the back of the church and prayed for her, and she was slain in the Spirit. There were many other people slain in the Spirit. As I was watching I said to a friend of mine, Tommy Gooch, "You know, I feel like a kid who's got the flu and has to stay inside the house and look out the picture window watching everybody else play. I'm just watching and nothing's happening to me. I really wanted to be touched by God."

I didn't really know what was going on and understood very little about the spiritual gifts. I had given my authority to Blaine and told him to go for anything that he thought was of God. I felt like too much of a novice to know what was and what wasn't right. Blaine promised to protect the church and, interestingly enough, I did see him shut a couple of things down.

At the first evening session, Blaine said, "Randy, the Holy Spirit is on you." I didn't feel a thing and thought he must have the wrong person. Blaine continued, "Randy, just hold your hands up." Now, I was on the front row, and this was my church—my Baptist church. We just didn't hold our hands up in the Baptist church, but I went for it. I raised my hands up. As soon as I raised them up, it felt like a giant vacuum sweeper in the sky sucked them all the way up, and then it felt like I got hooked into an electric fence. I was shaking all the way down, from the top of my head to the bottom of my feet. There was a powerful current of electricity coursing all through me. I was moving my feet to keep from falling on the floor. In the middle of that, I heard Blaine say, "DeAnne, the Spirit of God's on you." I heard her begin to cry and I wanted to turn and watch, but I was frozen in this position. I couldn't turn my head to watch her. Later she told me that she felt like a whole bunch of people were pushing on her and she fell down. In reality, no one was even touching her. She felt hot in her chest and it turned out that she received a healing. She'd taken a leave of absence from work because of physical problems that never plagued her again after that night. Together we had received an impartation from God that night that gave us boldness and activated the gifts of words of knowledge and healing in our lives in a much greater measure.

The same night, a man in the church named John Gordon received an impartation for words of knowledge. His first word of knowledge was about an eye. The pain he felt as a word of knowledge was so bad that he thought it was a problem in his own eye. After praying five times for a girl named Tammy, her eye was totally healed by the power of God. More of John's testimony and the healing of Tammy are contained in chapter 12.

Many more wonderful healings occurred the next night, but I want to share with you one that is the most significant for me. I didn't know it then, but Tammy had been born with spina bifida and was subject to seizures. She was hydrocephalic and had endured twelve surgeries. A shunt in her brain drained fluid into her stomach. Tammy did not have control of her bladder so she wore diapers.

That second night, Tammy's eleven year-old sister, Samantha, went into the ladies restroom, kneeled right next to the commode, and began crying out to God to heal her sister. We started praying for Tammy, full of faith because of her healed eye, but after several attempts with no results, we felt quite discouraged and ready to quit. I determined to give it one last shot and then interviewed her:

"Feel anything?"

"Well," she offered, "I just felt a little heat go down my spine."

We prayed again with great expectation, but again, nothing happened. As they were walking home, Tammy asked her mother,

"Mommy, do I have to wear diapers tonight?"

Out of compassion, her mother answered,

"No, not tonight, honey."

We don't know when God touched Tammy, but from that time on, Tammy has never had to wear a diaper and her seizures stopped! She is no longer hydrocephalic, and the fluid is draining naturally. She'll never have to have another surgery and is now a self-supporting young lady. She has an apartment and drives her own car. That was over twenty-one years ago.

People sometimes ask me, "Has all the change in your life been worth it?" I tell them, "Go see Tammy."

Many amazing things happened over the next eighteen months as God taught us to walk in a whole new realm of the Spirit. We learned about demonic deliverance, all manner of healing including mental and emotional healing, and much about trusting God for finances in a way that we had never learned before. But the next few years also taught me a lot about the cost of following Jesus. The costs are not just economic. There are costs in relationships and allegiances as well, even among family members when they don't understand what you feel God is calling you to do. I learned that not everyone who prays for a revival to come to their church will like it or bless it when it actually comes, especially if it comes in a new manner. In spite of the opposition we faced, these were truly what I would call the glory years, but they were soon followed by the desert years.

When God called us to St. Louis, the Holy Spirit stayed in Illinois. I know that's not the truth, but it sure felt like it was. I can say, however, that the rain of the Spirit was like a flood in those first eighteen months; then the flood went to an occasional shower. Once in a while we'd see somebody healed. On occasion we'd see even a terminal disease healed, but for the most part it was extremely dry my first years in Missouri.

Three years after starting the church in St. Louis I experienced the strongest impartation of my life. I was fearful that I would die from the experience if God increased the power coursing through my body. This impartation had a sanctifying aspect as a result—breaking me free from a powerful temptation that had a demonic influence behind it making it almost impossible to resist. I was set totally free by this impartation of power.

Once, when I was sharing this at the "Founder's Inn" at the 700 Club, the Dean of the Divinity School, Dr. Vincent Synan, who is ordained with the Pentecostal Holiness denomination told me, "That is the most powerful sermon on sanctification I have heard in a long time. My wife came home and told me I had to come hear you. You aren't even aware that you are preaching a holiness doctrine of the power of God to break the power of sin. You don't have the doctrinal background and training of this tradition, but you have the experience of the reality."[4]

This was definitely an oasis in the middle of years in the desert. Interestingly, except for the newfound freedom from a certain sin, little else changed. Life was still lived in the spiritual desert.

Even those occasional showers vanished after a while and we were in the Sahara! I mean, when we prayed we couldn't get an eyelid to flutter. Over the next

28

three and one-half years my life and church became so dry I began to move away from power-based ministry because I didn't see any power. John Wimber had often told us that he would cry out to God like a desperate animal when he needed help. I didn't do that. It was easier for me to go to the Fuller Institute of Church Growth seminars. There was nothing wrong with that, but I was beginning to look to the ways of men. I thought, "If God isn't going to do anything, I will." The church continued to grow but one day I realized I didn't care if I ever grew a big church. I was miserable!

The Bible didn't speak to me anymore, and I felt like God didn't hear me anymore. My heart seemed to be hardened, but I didn't want it to be. I didn't know what to do. Yet, the church was doing all right. We had the Vineyard liturgy—we did everything the right way. We even had words of knowledge occasionally. The problem was that nobody had the faith to respond to the word. We had seen very little happen. I'd say, "Would the ministry team please come forward?" At this time I would pause for a moment. "Would part of the ministry team please come forward? I don't think we're going to have that many people to minister to. Could I get one of you to come forward?" No one wanted to come forward to minister when they didn't think God was coming, so they became as discouraged as I was.

In my desperation I watched the videos of the visitation we had had in my last church when Blaine Cooke had come nine years earlier. I prayed to God, "God I am so desperate. I want You. I want the power of the Holy Spirit to flow through my life again. I want the church I pastor to experience the Holy Spirit. I am returning to my first love. I am going after You. I am going to return to emphasizing the ministry of the Holy Spirit. Even if half of the church leaves when You come, I want You to come.

Then, in my weakness, God stepped in. I cannot take any credit for what happened next. Within one week of my desperate prayer, a call came at midnight.

"How you doin', Randy?" the voice asked. It was an old friend, Jeff.

"I'm doing fine," I lied.

As Jeff told me his story, I realized this call was no accident. Jeff talked about burn-out, back-sliding, and his battle with suicidal thoughts. He had become so discouraged with empty, powerless Christianity, he had completely quit going to church. As Jeff went on to share how God had supernaturally intervened in his darkest hour, I began to cry. I knew help was on the way! By three in the morning, Jeff had convinced me to go hear Rodney Howard-Browne, an evangelist I had never heard.

I called the evangelist's office. When the lady on the phone told me his next meeting was two weeks away and was in Tulsa, my heart sank. Tulsa! I had always appreciated John Wimber's ecumenical spirit of loving the whole church, but this was me, and God knew there was one group I felt critical and bitter towards. Afraid of the answer, I gulped, "What church?" Now, I had this great appreciation for Naaman and Elisha and the river situation. I was thinking, "Oh, the waters in the Vineyard are so much clearer." I felt like the Holy Spirit said, "Randy, how desperate are you for Me?"

"Rhema Bible Church," came the answer.

I thought, "Lord, you know in my heart that is the last church in America I would have personally chosen to go to." I don't mean to be derogatory in that statement, that's just where I was. I still don't agree with some of their ideas, but I knew it was a test so I decided to go.[5]

Three others from the church went with me to Tulsa. The church held 4,500 people. The evangelist, Rodney Howard-Browne, was teaching. While he was teaching, a woman was laughing with the most false-sounding laugh right below me in the balcony. I was thinking, "Why doesn't he get an usher to shut her up?" By the time he finished teaching, I was on edge and was also quite upset. I was thinking this meeting was really out of order, and that ruined my whole evening. Even though many people fell and a lot of "stuff" happened, I still wasn't sure if this was real or not. I didn't know any of these people and for all I knew, they could have just been the overly emotional type. I wasn't convinced at all.

The next morning, Rodney got up and said, "You know, sometimes people laugh out of hurt or immaturity or because they need attention. Sometimes they laugh and it's not the Holy Spirit. They may laugh in the flesh because they need help. If things get too bad, we'll take them out of the meeting. If they are really laughing in the Holy Spirit, they'll keep it up and they won't care who is watching. But if it's in the flesh, they'll soon stop. Now I want to say something to some of you who got angry last night because of what was happening. You moved into anger and judgment and that's your flesh. From God's perspective, your flesh stinks more than that flesh, because yours is the flesh of superiority and judgment." I sat there trying to remove the knife from my back as I realized that God was really out to get me!

"Lord, I just want to know if this is You!" I cried. What finally got my attention was a three year-old boy who went out in the Spirit for forty-five minutes. I knew that couldn't be faked! At the next day's meeting, I asked my companions, "You guys want to go down there for prayer?"

"Nope," they answered, "this is close enough for us!"

We went anyway. One of the guys was powerfully touched; I felt nothing. During the next meeting, when Rodney prayed for me, I fell because I just couldn't stand up! I lay there thinking about the previous two times I had felt God's tangible touch, the heat and electricity that had made me think I would die. This time, apart from not being able to stand, I felt NOTHING. I thought, "This is all the flesh. It must be psychological suggestion because I'm not shaking." I felt really confused, but decided to press in. All of a sudden, people around me started laughing. I started laughing in the natural but, before I knew it, I was laughing in the Spirit and couldn't stop. Due to my Baptist background and the covenants we took saying that we'd never drink, I have a problem with drunkenness—but I was spiritually drunk!

One of the people who went with me that weekend never felt anything. That was a pastoral problem for me and a real problem for him. I remembered when the

31

Vineyard team came to our church—God didn't do things then the way I would have done them. I would have poured out the Spirit on the deacons and the people who had all their doctrine and disciplines right. God did touch a few, but He also poured out His Spirit on those who had one foot in the world and one in the church. People got angry and said, "This can't be God. Why would He touch a person like *that*, and not touch this guy? He's the most spiritual person here!"

In answer to prayer, I understood. If God did it that way, it would be too easy for us to be like the Pharisees. It would also be too easy for us to fall into works and law. God wants to do this as an object lesson to help us see that His workings are *charismata*. *Charis* is the Greek root word for "grace." God doesn't want us to turn his *charismata* into "worksamata"!

I had to fly home the next day, right after the morning service. I felt frustrated because Rodney had been saying there was really going to be a Holy Spirit blowout the next night—and I was going miss it. I wanted more! I didn't just want God to touch me, I wanted Him to touch me so that I could give it away and touch others. In the morning service, Rodney said he would pray for everyone who wanted prayer. Guess how many raised their hands? All 4,500 people. "Just great," I thought, "this is going to take too long!"

Now, I'd only fasted a few times in my life, but this was one of them. I don't think fasting gives a person any brownie points with God, but it does focus you on God. I'd come to the conference saying, "God, I want to be touched so desperately. I'm not going to give up on You. I'm not going to eat until You touch me." If you try to fast and it's not God, it's a bad deal, but if it's God, He'll give you grace in it. I believe His grace was putting this desperation in my heart. Revival always follows the desperation that God gives. The flesh hates desperation for God; it's only the Spirit that gives that.

I hate lines, but I got in that line of 4,500 people thinking, "I've got to get all I can!" I could hear Rodney on the loudspeakers, "Fill! Fill! Fill!" Rodney didn't quite touch me; he more or less slapped me gently on the head and I went down.

There I was thinking, "Nothing happened again. This is not fair, God! What have I got to do? I'm getting hungry, you know. I want to eat!" I asked God, "Why don't you shake, rattle and roll me? Let me feel that electricity again, God!" I was frustrated and thought I would just get up but when I tried to, I found that I was stuck to the floor. I remember thinking, "Uh oh! I don't feel any electricity, but something's going on!"

I lay on the floor for about thirty minutes. Then I got up and went to a line in another part of the building. He prayed for me again and down I went, only this time I wasn't stuck as long. I got up and went to the end of the line in another section of the building! After the fourth time, I decided I wasn't going to do this anymore because I might get caught.

I remember John Wimber told me, "You've got to learn to see what the Father's doing." So, remembering that, I started following Rodney all over the place. He walked, I walked. I was watching and thinking, "What's he seeing? What's he doing?" I studied him closely because I wanted to learn.

The usher stopped me and said, "Can I help you?"

I said, "No, I'm just watching him!"

Five or six times they stopped me and asked, "Sir, can we help you?" Out of respect for their authority, I moved to a less bothersome distance. I was watching from the stage when Rodney's brother and bodyguard, Basil, approached me.

"Sir, would you like to receive prayer?"

"I've already had prayer four times!" I said.

"That's okay," he answered, "you look thirsty."

I received prayer again!

At these meetings God changed my heart, and I repented of my mean spirit towards the Faith Camp and asked them to forgive me for the harsh words I had spoken from my pulpit. I didn't agree with all the doctrinal positions of the Faith Camp, but I realized how precious God's children are in His sight. I realized how much God was displeased with the attitude of attacking brothers over issues which wouldn't be considered heresy.

Back to St. Louis we went. It was like a bomb went off. The Sunday after Tulsa, we taught first and worshipped second. We began to worship and suddenly one of the women on the worship team, Susan Labroad, fell with a loud THUD. Now Susan was a relatively wealthy woman from a Lutheran background. This sophisticated woman took a guitar stand down with her and, when she hit the floor, began laughing and hitting her right thigh with her right hand. She did this through our forty-five minutes of worship. Susan had seen the Shekinah Glory Cloud come into the building right before she fell. Needless to say, God had come!

I said, "Would anybody like to have ministry today?" Immediately, an unusually high number came forward. We simply went up to people, touched their foreheads, and said, "Bless you," and BOOM! "Bless you!" BOOM! . . . BOOM! BOOM! BOOM! We'd get to a hard one and might have to pray a little longer. We were going down the line and it was so wonderful I couldn't believe it! The second service people came in and saw the aftermath of the first service. Everywhere they looked, people were laughing. My wife got upset because she thought this behavior was out of order. We had been discussing what behavior was out of order for three weeks. I told her God was giving an object lesson about what I was teaching, but it still made her nervous.

After that we went to our regional meeting of Vineyard pastors. I asked the Lord to touch the pastors there who were as desperate as I was. The second night, God moved sovereignly and everybody got blasted! People were running around dancing, slapping each other, rolling around, and generally acting drunk. Happy Leman, my Regional Overseer, was laughing hysterically! When I saw Happy do that, I knew this was God!

Then my Area Pastoral Coordinator, who was already drunk in the Spirit, asked me to pray for him. I agreed even though he had already been prayed for twice. I touched him and it was like the Spirit of God hit him and knocked him into some chairs. He said it felt like a truck had hit him. I didn't know he had a severe spinal injury that caused him to wake up in tears every morning from the pain. I also didn't know there was no hope for correcting it surgically. When God came upon him, he said it felt like a hot hand went down in his stomach and pulled something out and he was healed. The anointing of God was on him and he couldn't talk for months without stuttering. He stuttered all the time when the Spirit of God would come on him. In spite of this, God had done a wonderful thing for him.

A pastor in Toronto, John Arnott, heard about these meetings and invited me to come speak at his church. That made me really nervous. What if the same thing didn't happen? John said he realized we couldn't know if the same thing would happen, but he wanted me to come anyway. I agreed to come for four nights, but still felt nervous about the expectations. Anni Shelton, my associate worship leader's wife, had a vision of a map of Toronto being set on fire. The blaze of fire was going out all over the map. She told me, "I think God's going to start something there and it's going to go all over North America." That encouragement still didn't help my faith.

Deep down, I still struggled with my faith that God would do for me what He did for others. Sure, He would show up for someone like John Wimber or Blaine Cook, but why would He bother with me? I knew theology. I had a Masters in Divinity degree. But what I knew about my heavenly Father in my head was not what I felt in my heart.

The night before I was to leave for Toronto, I received a phone call from Richard Holcomb. Richard knew absolutely nothing about what had been happening in my life or what I was about to do. Richard told me he had a clear, prophetic word for me.

I did not place a high value on prophecy at that time; I thought it was too messy. I did not want my church contaminated by the prophetic activity at the Kansas City Metro Vineyard, so I did not encourage them to go over there!

(Shortly after, I came to have the highest estimation for Mike Bickle and his church, because my life had been changed by prophecy.)

So I said, "What is it?"

He replied, "The Lord says to you, Randy, 'Test me now. Test me now. Test me now. Do not be afraid. I will back you up! I want your eyes to be opened to see my resources in the heavenlies for you, just as Elisha prayed for Gehazi's eyes to be opened. And do not become anxious because when you become anxious, you can't hear me.'"

It was this prophetic word that did much to change my life. It gave me the faith to move in the anointing I had received when John Wimber prayed for me ten years earlier and when Rodney prayed for me. I would lead forty-two of the first sixty days of the outpouring in Toronto. What happened for the next eleven and one-half years in Toronto is now a part of church history and has been written about, positively and negatively, in countless books and articles.

I just want to say, it wasn't something Randy Clark did; God did it all. It was God in Jeff's telephone call. It was God reminding me in the vision of Dr. Smith's words, "Do you love the church enough to serve her when she hurts you?" It was God giving me the desperation to even be willing to want to go to Tulsa. It was God who gave the prophetic word to Richard the night before I left for Toronto. God wanted to take failure and turn it into His strength. I had pastored in St. Louis for eight years and my church was only at about 400 people, averaging 300. Some people, including myself, saw this as a failure. I was not a successful pastor. I was a broken man. I had a black mark against me because of the divorce when I was twenty-two. In spite of all this, God chose to use a simple man like me. God chose a manger, humble surroundings, and a poor mother and stepfather for His only Son, too.

This is the story of how God was preparing me, putting values in me, healing me of doubt and fear, and empowering me for the work which was to break out into something bigger than I ever expected. I am grateful to the men of God who believed that their anointing was something to be given away. It is my sincere conviction that all God has entrusted to me is to be given away to others, until the whole church is built up, equipped, and empowered by the fullness of the Spirit to the glory of God.[6]

In the next chapter we will consider obstacles that have kept many from desiring an "impartation." I will attempt to remove the obstacles and build a bridge of understanding that will allow them to come out of the land of skepticism and unbelief regarding the present day ministry of the gifts of the Holy Spirit. The bridge that I'm attempting to build is a bridge over which I hope many will cross to enter the land of God as the "I Am," to the land where "Jesus Christ is the same yesterday and today and forever" (Hebrews 13:8).

CHAPTER 3: BUILDING BRIDGES SO OTHERS MIGHT RECEIVE IMPARTATIONS

In 1994, I heard the still, small (non-audible) voice of the Lord speak to me ever so clearly, "You are to be a fire-lighter, vision-caster, and a bridge-builder." I understood the "fire-lighter" to represent the beginning of outbreaks of the presence of God in power in a church or area, the "vision-caster" to be the lifting of the understanding of a group of people to believe God for great things—miracles, healings, deliverances, and powerful manifestations of God's presence in our midst. I understood the "bridge-builder" to be removing barriers that kept people from entering into these blessings of God, and/or building relationships between key leaders around the world to bring greater unity between them for the purposes of revival. I have tried to accomplish one or all of these goals in every invitation I have received since hearing this word over eleven and one-half years ago. This chapter is written in the hope that it might be used to accomplish the last of the three statements of my purpose, to be a "bridge-builder."

During my M. Div. program at The Southern Baptist Theological Seminary, I took a class that studied the history of revival. My professor, Dr. Lewis Drummond, was a man I greatly respected and an excellent teacher of past revivals. In his lectures I heard what God had done in the First and Second Great Awakenings, the 1858 Prayer Revival, and the Welsh Revival of 1904. He also taught us about the greatest revival of Southern Baptist history, the Shantung Revival of northern China in the 1930s. It was this training from my Southern Baptist seminary that gave me great courage not to be scared when some of the phenomena began occurring in my meetings in Toronto. During the first days of Toronto I called Dr. Drummond to tell him what was happening. He was excited to hear what God was doing, but also gave me caution to keep it biblically focused. I tried to heed those words. For me, keeping it biblically focused meant not focusing upon the phenomena or lack thereof; instead it meant focusing on the content of the messages. I have strived to do so even to this day.

One of the earlier messages I preached in the "renewal" that began in Toronto was called "Come Out Of the Bunkhouse," a message based upon the parable of the Prodigal Son. I was overwhelmed when God gave me insight into this parable of the Father's love—love not only for the *Prodigal Son*, but also deep love for the Elder Brother, especially when the Prodigal Son seems oblivious to the fact that the older brother is missing from the party (Luke 15:11-32). Yet, this absence does not escape the Father's notice. He goes out from the party to find the Elder Brother. When he finds him, the Elder Brother smarts off to his dad complaining about how he had never disobeyed any of his orders and had slaved for him all these years. Then in jealousy over the Father's extravagant redemptive love for the Prodigal, the Elder Brother states, "Yet when this son of yours comes home, after running through his inheritance on wild women and partying, you kill the fattened calf for him. And you haven't even given me so much as a kid goat." I noted that the Father didn't say, "Listen to me son, if you don't like my ways then you can either shape up or ship out, and I'm warning you don't you ever dare to speak to me again in that tone of voice. How dare you show me such disrespect!" No, that wasn't what he said. Instead he said, "My son, all that I have is yours." I realized this parable isn't about a Prodigal Son. No, it's about a Great Father who had two screw-up sons, and thus is a parable about God the Father's love for us. I was overwhelmed by the Father's love for the Elder Brother whom, by the way, actually had received twice what the Prodigal Son had received from the Father.

I received two revelations as I meditated upon this famous passage. One was that the enemy fights against intimacy between the Father and His children. He tries to get the children of God to rebel and leave. If there is repentance and they return to Him, Satan wants to trick them into forfeiting their status as sons and instead relate to the Father as "one of your hired men." This was the mindset the

40

Elder Brother was already working from as indicated in his statement, "All these years I have worked for you and never disobeyed your orders." He saw himself as a worker earning the love of the Father. I saw that God did not want his born-again children relating to him in the status of hired men, but as sons and daughters.

That sermon was the context of a statement I made that was later quoted by a critic of revival in which he tried to argue that the renewal lacked a focus on godly sorrow. I was talking about how in the renewal the Holy Spirit was giving Christians joy. In reference to the Prodigal Son's homecoming party, I said, "They [Christians] already feel so icky about themselves." The remark was never intended to dismiss the need for godly sorrow which produces repentance (2 Corinthians 7:10). My comment was directed to the lack of joy that comes from an emphasis upon doing rather than being. I was referring to the "bunkhouse thinking" of "I'm no longer worthy to be called your son, just make me one of your hired men." This is a mentality that has not understood grace; nor one's position in Christ; nor had faith to ask the Father in Jesus' name for appropriate, legitimate requests which would result in experiencing more of the kingdom of God on the earth and bring more glory to both the Father and the Son. (See John 14-17 for the biblical basis for such requests.) My reference to many Christians feeling "icky about themselves" was rooted in a realization that too many believers can't accept God's grace and so have locked themselves away from the intimate place with the Father. They have resigned themselves to be thankful to be forgiven just enough to be "like a hired-man" rather than a son or daughter.

The second revelation was the Father's heart for both sons, the magnitude of his grace towards both sons, and the gracious words to the Elder Brother, "My Son, all I have is yours." As I write this chapter I hope my writing is from the perspective of the Father's heart for the historical denominations, especially the primary denominations of the Reformation, the Lutherans, and the Calvinists. To these denominations, and the many other historical denominations the Father says, "My Son, all I have is yours." As I was meditating upon this statement I realized

41

that God was visiting His church with a season of refreshing, and I felt His heart was that all be invited. I pictured the Father going out to the rest of the church, inviting them to the party just as the Father invited the Elder Brother to the party.

I believed this outpouring, which has become known as the Toronto Blessing, was primarily a "time of refreshing" especially for tired, burned out leaders in ministry. I had only recently experienced such a refreshing in my own life. I felt like the church had been in a spiritual desert for several years that I had found water, and now my job was to tell others that water had been found! The first sermon I preached in Toronto, and then for several years the first sermon I would give in a new church, was based upon the words of Jesus in John 7:37ff, especially the words, "Jesus stood and cried out, saying, 'If anyone thirsts, let him come to Me and drink.'"

It wasn't too long after the outpouring in Toronto began that the voices of the critics began to be heard. This book is not written primarily to answer the critics. Rather, this book's purpose is to show revival's biblical basis and historical precedent, and to give knowledge of the contemporary fruit of revival. Hopefully, this will help remove the misperceptions, heal the hurts, and create a thirst for the "more" of God that is available to all.

My theology is not a theology of the spiritual haves and have-nots. Rather— in the language of Cardinal Joseph Suenens of Belgium, and Dr. Robert Culpepper, a former missionary professor of theology in Japan for the Southern Baptist Convention—it is not a matter of having, but of appropriating what has already been given to us through the work of Jesus Christ on our behalf. My theology of the Holy Spirit is not one based upon our work or merit that purchases for us some special gift or anointing. No, it is instead based on realizing what our Father has already given to us in Christ Jesus, and then appropriating that which is already ours. He has already made the gracious provision for us in the cross. I believe the powers of darkness have worked overtime to steal from the church the realization of what we have inherited with the Holy Spirit, especially in the area of

42

the "equipping of the saints for the work of ministry" through impartation of gifts or the filling of the Holy Spirit.

During the summer of 1994, John Arnott called me and told me about the "roaring like a lion" sounds heard in a meeting in Toronto. In the context of how they began I could understand how, even why, they were occurring, but I also sensed this could create problems. Later, other "prophetic" animal sounds began to occur, like the sounds of the "four living creatures" in Revelation 4. I was concerned that attention would be drawn to the bizarre nature of this new phenomenon and away from the good fruit.

It seems to me that the bizarre always gets the most attention. Novelty draws the most news. Perhaps that is why God will often add new or novel phenomena for new seasons of the outpouring of His Spirit. Really they're usually not new, just forgotten from earlier visitations in the nearly two-thousand-year history of the church. For example, laughing in the Spirit was called "jubilation" in the Roman Catholic Church of the Middle Ages and earlier. Falling was called "swooning" by the Methodists long before it was called "slain in the Spirit" by the Pentecostals. In the 1950s my family was Baptist. My parents and grandparents called uncontrollable laughter in church "getting happy." Before the "laughter" occurred in our little country Baptist church it had occurred in both the Holiness movements and the early Pentecostal movements. However, in faithfulness to the advice of Dr. Drummond, I was becoming uneasy with the focus of the renewal by August of 1994, especially with the focus on the "prophetic" sounds of the four living creatures and the roaring. I wanted to bring what I felt was a needed correction to the movement while honoring those in authority at Toronto.

I loved John and Carol Arnott and wanted to respect them. They had set their hearts to experience more of the God they read about in the Bible. For months prior to the outpouring in Toronto, they had set apart half of the day to worship and pray. When I consider the challenges faced by Pastor John Arnott, I am amazed at the wisdom he exercised. Crowds were coming from all over the world.

43

They would line up hours before the doors of the church opened. He had to relocate the church from its former location which accommodated 400 in the sanctuary and 300 more in the overflow room to its present location that initially seated about 5,000. He had to provide ministry teams and worship teams for six nights a week. Now, for a few weeks, that is not so hard, but how do you do it for eleven-and-one-half years? The press was frequently in the meetings or writing about the meetings. And, of course, the type of meetings and their press drew an abnormal percentage of wounded, burned out, desperate people and leaders. In this crowd were a few unstable people as well. John Arnott faced huge challenges in pastoring the renewal/revival in Toronto. (It started out a renewal, but I believe it grew into a revival. This book is a defense of the viewpoint that Toronto produced a revival in the world, just as Azusa Street did, and the primary reason was transference of the anointing—the amazing power to impart what we had received to others who then took it to their country or city or church.)

If there was one area where greater wisdom might have been exercised, it was in regard to the animal sounds. Yet, I understood John's position. A few years earlier, God had visited his church in a mighty way. That initial outpouring had been quenched by John's attempt to correct some abuses. Because of that, John had promised God that if He would come again, he would not try to correct too quickly and, in doing so, quench the Spirit again. I respected him for this position, and at the same time thought that, in this case, his enjoyment of the prophetic, and his perspective that these sounds were prophetic signs, was too much of a green light to the people in the meetings. Then once they happened, they took on a life of their own. The critics focused on this bizarre event with the result that many were persuaded to write off Toronto merely as a place of bizarre behavior where people made animal noises. Most of the real and wonderful work of God was ignored in the fuss over this distracting element.

Critics of revival and its accompanying phenomena have found it difficult to explain what they see in meetings. When you don't have a grid for God to move in power through the church, you are forced to try to explain the phenomena and demonstrations of power in another way. Unfortunately, what emerges is what I call the "Beelzebub Principle." It was obvious to the Pharisees that Jesus was moving in unusual power. They couldn't deny that power was present to heal and deliver, but because some of Jesus' actions and sayings didn't fit their theology, they said He was doing what He did by the power of a ruling demon, the Lord of the flies, Beelzebub (Matthew 12:24). They also considered Him a blasphemer, a glutton and a drunkard, as well as being mad. Rather than deal with His theology, they resorted to the *ad hominem* argument. That is, they tried to destroy His credibility through personal attacks rather than deal with what He had to say.

In like manner, John Wesley and George Whitefield, the key leaders of the Great Evangelical Revival of England of the eighteenth century, were accused of having a white powder up their sleeves that caused people to fall under their hands as they ministered. There was nothing up their sleeves, but they did carry anointing in themselves. They had received a powerful impartation from the Lord.

Critics of current revival claim that demonstrations of power are the result of psychological manipulation and suggestion. This accusation is often leveled at the "suggestive" practice of lining people up for prayer with "catchers" standing behind them. I think it might be helpful to explain that.

During the initial three to four years of the outpouring of the Spirit, I had such faith that God was going to knock people down that I would ask pastors who had invited me to come, "How many people will your church lay?" I told pastors to put tape on the floors because so many people would want to be prayed for and the power of God was always so strong that we needed lots of space. I had the tapelines about every seven feet apart as a way to maximize the use of floor space.

Was this mechanical, was this human manipulation, and was this psychological suggestion? No!!! You see, if you understand you are living in the moment of a divine visitation you have so much faith that these things are going to happen that it is not presumption; it is simply understanding that this is a *kairos*[7]

45

moment, a special season, a time of sovereign visitation. When you understand that you are living in a divine visitation, you expect God to touch the people; your responsibility is to be as prepared as possible. Your job is to try to bring as much order and decency to the meeting as possible, while at the same time accommodating what God is doing. (This mechanical charge was leveled against Charles Gradison Finney based upon his *Lectures on Revival*, but I believe the accusation is unfounded. One should read the *Autobiography of Charles Gradison Finney* before reading his *Lectures on Revival.* In doing so, you will understand that he too knew he was living in the time of a sovereign visitation from God.)

I found that order in the meetings facilitated the work of the Spirit. For example, before we put the lines on the floor, it was very chaotic. Using lines and people to catch those who were falling helped us bring order to the situation. The lines and catchers weren't to provide psychological suggestions. No, they were an attempt to apply the 1 Corinthians 14 passage about doing things decently and in order.

I wanted to keep the Renewal biblical in focus. Again, I wasn't talking about the phenomena, but about the messages. I felt like God gave me a corrective message as an internal friend to the current Outpouring of God. The title of the message was "Jesus." When I arrived in Toronto in August, an article in Time magazine had just been published regarding the Toronto Blessing. I was given a copy of the article and once I got to my room in the Arnotts' home I read the article. In doing so, I was consciously reading to see if it mentioned my name. It didn't, and I was saddened. It merely referenced me as a pastor from St. Louis. Not only was I sad that my name wasn't mentioned, I was even more grieved that I was sad in the first place. This fact made it clear to me how much more I needed to grow up and mature in Christ. It pointed out how I still needed emotional healing. Then I felt a nudge of the Holy Spirit. It seemed like He spoke in my thoughts, "Read it again and see if My Name is in it." I realized this was in reference to the name of Jesus. I discovered that not only was the name of Jesus not in the article, neither was it in about twenty other articles from newspapers and magazines that I had collected. I was shocked to find that His name only occurred about three times in twenty articles. I was so convicted that I began to weep. Then the Lord gave me the inspiration for the message. The primary text was Hebrews 12:2-3 "Let us fix our eyes on Jesus, the author and perfecter of our faith, who for the joy set before him endured the cross, scorning its shame, and sat down at the right hand of the throne of God. Consider him . . ." The sermon contained five points dealing with the necessity of keeping our focus on Jesus.

With the first point, "Jesus should be the focus of our mountaintop experiences," I was trying to address three abuses that I saw—an overemphasis upon experience, an overemphasis upon Bible study that doesn't result in greater intimacy with Jesus, and an overemphasis upon receiving prophetic words. I believe we are enriched by all three of these things in our Christian lives, but they can't become the focus. Proper biblical preaching should lead to greater experiences with Jesus and greater focus upon His majesty, expressing the words of the Greeks who addressed Philip, "Sir, we seek Jesus."

Later, when talking with John Wimber, he mentioned to me that this was his favorite message of the whole renewal. This meant a lot to me because, of all my teachers during my first eighteen years of ministry, I know of no one who had a greater commitment to the Bible than John Wimber. He lived his life by trying to be faithful to the Word of God. He entered the healing ministry because of his commitment to the integrity of the Word and its plain and clear calling to the ministry of healing. He tried to settle disputes and charges against pastors in as biblical a manner as possible. He wanted the main and the plain things of Scripture to be the main and the plain things of the preaching and teaching of the Vineyard.

I so deeply regret the decision of the Vineyard to dis-fellowship the church in Toronto. I believe had John not been so ill, and consumed not only with his own health problems, but with the deep emotional concern of realizing his oldest son was dying of cancer, he might not have made this decision. Until the decision to dis-fellowship occurred, often 30% of the pastors attending the special pastors' meetings we had around the world were evangelical. Afterwards, the percentage dropped to about 3%. As for the renewal's relationship to the evangelical community, the dis-fellowshipping of Toronto was a deadly shot in the head. I have one comfort in this; two people with whom John had met within a couple of weeks of his death came to me individually and told me John had spoken to them on many things, many personal issues, and that in the course of his sharing he told both of them that he had made a mistake in regard to the dis-fellowshipping of Toronto.

I cannot stop here about John Wimber; I must right some terrible wrongs that others have written. (I owe John this debt because he is the one who first made me aware of the importance of impartation, and through his teachings I rediscovered the importance of the Gospels to the church. Most of the church had reduced the canon of authority for today to the Epistles of Paul, neglecting the practical teaching of the Gospels for power ministry.)

I first read the work of a heresy hunter in 1986 which quoted John's words out of context making them seem to say almost the exact opposite of what they were intended to say in context. The author of the book quotes a New Age person and then quotes John using the same language the New Age leader had used. The intended effect was for the reader to conclude that John believed what the New Age person believed. But, nothing could be more false. Had I not owned the workbook from which the quote was made out of context, I would have been mislead by the author and undergone a seduction myself. But recognizing the quote, I looked it up in its context and was shocked by the gross misrepresentation. A high school English teacher would or should have flunked a student for such misrepresentation of facts.

Nearly a decade later, another heresy hunter would not only attack the "Revival" calling it "Counterfeit," but would try to destroy the credibility of John Wimber and James Ryle. This author purposefully quoted statements by John

Wimber, Todd Hunter, and James Ryle even though he knew each had changed their opinion and had publicly stated so, often years prior to the publication of the heresy hunter's book.

How sad it is that the Renewal came to be defined by its detractors, especially the heresy hunters and their radio programs, resulting in their seduction of the truth and having a counterfeit "scarecrow" erected in the church garden to scare away those who might have come and drank and had their spiritual lives renewed. Most evangelical leaders were convinced by John Wimber's dis-fellowshipping of Toronto and the heresy hunter's books and radio programs focusing on "animal noises" that the Renewal was not real or at best very mixed. How sad that something which played such a short and minor role in such a great move of God was used to scare people away.

The book, *'TORONTO' IN PERSPECTIVE: Papers On The New Charismatic Wave of the Mid 1990s*, edited by David Hilborn and sponsored by ACUTE (the Evangelical Alliance Commission on Unity and Truth among Evangelicals published in 2001) reveals how difficult it is to discern God in the initial days of outpourings of the Holy Spirit. This book reveals the tremendous struggle the Toronto Blessing brought to Great Britain. There were some who championed it as a move of God very courageously, and there were others who fought it as a work of Satan. It was the most divisive thing to hit England since the last revival. However, though I appreciate the attempt of the ACUTE group to steady the helm during the storm, it is sad to see that, at the time of the writing of the book, the consensus seemed to be that this move of God was at best a "renewal" and didn't become a "revival." Even one of the earlier supporters of the move in Great Britain is quoted as saying, "Toronto came in with a bang but, frankly, seems to have ended with a whimper."[8] It is sad the book leaves one wondering what happened to the hopeful beginnings of the move in Great Britain that sparked from the Toronto Blessing.

I don't know if I believe the Toronto Blessing ended in England with a whimper, or if I would interpret what really happened in the following way. I believe the Holy Spirit saw the rejection by so much of the church, and out of His concern to renew the church, created a metamorphous into the culturally more acceptable expression of renewal represented by Nicky Gumbel's Alpha Course.

The task of building a bridge from the side of the Pentecostal/Charismatic/Third-Wave Evangelical world over the great gap of misunderstanding and mutual skepticism to the world of the Cessationist Evangelical is not an easy task. In order to build this bridge of understanding between these two camps, it is necessary not only to look at the Scriptures, but also to look at historical theology. Historical theology not only considers what the Bible says, but looks for when an interpretation arose and asks if it has been the predominate viewpoint of the church.

What are the major issues related to the rejection of the idea of "impartation" or the "transference of the anointing," to the continuation of all the gifts of the Holy Spirit, to the continuation of all the offices of the church as listed in Ephesians 4:11-12, and to most renewal and revival movements including the Toronto Blessing? Here, I believe are some key ones:

1. A worldview that came into the church through Thomas Aquinas in the 1200s, three hundred years prior to the Reformation, that shifted the perception that truth and reality come from two sources—the spirit realm and reason—to the idea that they come from reason alone.

2. Rationalistic-Enlightenment thinking that developed in the 1700's and continues with us based upon a philosophical presupposition that nothing supernatural can happen.

3. An understanding of the end of time from a Dispensational viewpoint that developed around 1830. The Dispensational viewpoint has a defeatist attitude toward the end of time and views the last period of time to be a time where the church is lukewarm, not in revival. It also believes this

weak, desperate, lukewarm church will be raptured away prior to the end-time tribulation.

4. The Protestant Polemic against the charismata continuing after the Apostolic Age, which finds its most complete and developed doctrinal expression in the writings of B.B. Warfield.

I'd like to focus a bit more on B.B. Warfield, a famous professor at Princeton Theological Seminary, who is considered by many the most influential cessationist scholar of the last century. In 1918 he published the cessationist classic *Counterfeit Miracles*, which was believed to prove beyond doubt the case for cessationism—the doctrine that the revelatory and miraculous charismata (gifts of the Holy Spirit) ceased after the "Apostolic Age" and/or with the canonization of Scripture. He staunchly defended the fundamentals of the Christian faith against the onslaught of Liberal theology which denied everything supernatural in the Bible, including the miraculous gifts and events described in Scripture. Yet I was told during my seminary education that his book Counterfeit Miracles drove the final nail in the coffin of belief that miracles have continued throughout the history of the church. All subsequent voices for cessationism have drawn their arguments from Warfield. To dismantle Warfield's theology effectively undermines cessationism as a valid school of thought.

There are several key areas to understand in order to recognize the flawed theology that Warfield cites against the continuation of the charismata:

1. Instead of seeing the primary function of the charismata as a continued expression and demonstration of the kingdom of God, the cessationist understands the *primary* function of the miraculous to be evidential,[9] i.e., it validates the message of the gospel and its messengers, Jesus and the Apostles. Thus, the miraculous is no longer required today, as the message of the gospel has already been validated, and is now embodied and finds its full expression in the canon of Scripture. In his effort to defend the operation of the miraculous charismata in the ministry of Jesus

and the apostles on the one hand, and to deny their continuation afterwards, Warfield drew, for his concept of miracle, from the two intrinsically divergent concepts of biblical faith and Scottish common-sense philosophy—the former based in a faith-oriented, super-naturalistic, subjective, spiritually discerned worldview, and the latter based in a common-sense oriented, naturalistic, objective, scientifically-analyzed worldview. Thus his entire polemic is based on a flawed, self-contradictory foundation as expressed in his concept of miracle.

2. Warfield's historical methodology is inconsistent in its criteria for evaluating reports of the miraculous and the charismata in the biblical period vs. post-biblical periods. Warfield's evaluation of the veracity of the historical record required him to draw from his flawed, self-contradictory cessationist concept of miracle. Which worldview he drew from depended on his end goal, to affirm or deny the particular historical account of the miraculous in question:

   • For the biblical period there is a presumed, unquestioned acceptance of the miracle accounts; an idealistic, "Golden Age" evaluation of miracle events; an assumed inerrancy in the biblical testimonies of the miraculous, and a rejection of the use of historical-critical methods.

   • In contrast, for the post-biblical period there is a presumed skepticism of the miracle accounts; a naturalistic, rationalistic evaluation of miracle events; character attacks (*ad hominem* arguments) used to reject post-biblical testimonies of the miraculous as valid; and the same historical-critical methods rejected in evaluating biblical miracles are used to evaluate post-biblical accounts.

3. Warfield's own professed methodology of biblical interpretation (hermeneutics) is primarily sound. Yet when analyzing the validity of his

biblical arguments for cessationism against the backdrop of his own professed interpretive methodology, several things stand out:

- He applies his own rules of interpretation inconsistently, and only when they conveniently serve his evidential, cessationist position.

- He totally ignores the doctrines of the Holy Spirit, the Kingdom, and a large number of key and supporting passages dealing with the continuation and operation of the charismata. Warfield's book, *Counterfeit Miracles,* gives only a handful of pages out of hundreds to the exegesis of pertinent texts, and even then ignores many of the texts which contradict his position.

- Warfield's own principles of interpretation—minus his cessationist presuppositions—when honestly and consistently applied to Scripture, lead to the conclusion that the function of the charismata is primarily to express the gospel of the kingdom that Jesus preached in the power of the Holy Spirit.

If we are to close this divide, or to "bridge" this gap, then I believe it will need to be done by good biblical interpretation, a consistent historical method for the evaluation of miracles, and an honest reporting on the positive fruit and not just the most bizarre events connected to renewal and revival movements. For a thorough study which examines the flaws in the doctrine of cessationism from a philosophical, historical, and biblical perspective see Jon Ruthven's book, *On the Cessation of the Charismata: The Protestant Polemic on Postbiblical Miracles.*[10] It is the best book I have studied on the subject. It provides an exegesis of all the major passages related to the subject and a first rate analysis of the philosophical presuppositions of cessationism. Only on the basis of genuine evangelical, scholarly, radical exegesis of the text will we find a place to agree. Again, the reason this is so important is that cessationist beliefs automatically rule out the continued ministry of "impartation" which often involves the gift of prophecy, gifts of healings and/or words of knowledge, as well as a fresh filling or baptism in the Holy Spirit.

In the early years of revival, my children asked me if I had heard what the man on the radio was saying about me, and about Toronto. People asked me, "Aren't you going to respond?" I would say to them to the tune of the old rock and roll song, "Ti-i-i-i-i-i-i-i-i-i-i-i-i-i-ime is on my side, yes it is." For every terrible anecdotal story based upon someone's experience, I could give a great anecdotal story of someone else's experience which was very positive and healthy. You might say it was a battle of anecdotal stories. And since the critics controlled the microphones, I saw no way of winning that war. Besides, subjective anecdotal stories don't prove or disprove whether or not an experience or a movement is of God, the devil, or the flesh. I understood that only time would prove whether or not what was happening in Toronto was really of God or not.

As I mentioned in the last chapter, enough time has now passed for the real test—the lasting fruit. The stories you will read in this book are not limited to one person's experience. They are not even primarily the stories of personal experience but rather stories of the *fruit* that came out of those experiences—stories of victory, stories of harvest, of missions, of evangelism, of ministering to the poor, the widow and the orphans. These stories reveal objective, calculable, demonstrable fruit—actions of mercy and the salvation of millions. Two such stories are how one and one-half million have come to the Lord just through the ministries of Leif Hetland and Rolland and Heidi Baker.

Thousands of churches have been planted in the southern part of the African continent by those powerfully touched by the Toronto Blessing. One man touched by Toronto has planted about one thousand five hundred house fellowships in a Muslim country through his ministry. Scores of thousands of people in Muslim and non-Muslim countries have been converted by the ministry of one pastor and his church from the Ukraine who were touched through my ministry. A German apostolic leader, Walter Heidenreich, was powerfully touched by God in Toronto in 2000 and has been having a tremendous effect evangelistically among the people of Mongolia, the Philippines, and Germany.

It's significant to me that the initial outpouring in Toronto coincided with similar activity around the world. I consider it all one globally distributed, but single, work of the Spirit. When considering the fruit of this "revival," we must include what the apostolic leader, Dennis Balcombe, told me occurred in north China also in January of 1994—the same month the Toronto Blessing began. This powerful time of visitation resulted in the salvation of scores of thousands. Leaders and people were receiving powerful impartations of fresh anointing from the Holy Spirit. Laughter and spiritual drunkenness were very much a part of this outpouring. They had not heard of Toronto. In 1994 the American missionary to the Indians of southern Mexico, David Hogan, reported that a tribe had been confused by why people began to laugh and fall to the ground in the worship service. This was a stoic culture that devalued emotion; they neither cried at funerals nor laughed at weddings. These Indians were illiterate, had no radios, no electricity, and no outlet to the world. They had not heard of Toronto, or Brownsville, or Rodney Howard Browne, or me. Yet, they didn't miss the *kairos*[11] of God.

Evangelist Bill Prankard, a friend of John Arnott, introduced the gospel to the Inuit in northern Russia. He returned to find them experiencing the holy laughter of the Lord. When he asked who had told them about Toronto, they replied they had never heard of Toronto, but they had read the second chapter of Acts.

Sometimes I am asked why North America and Western Europe have not had the same kind of results that China, Mozambique, and Mongolia have experienced. I once said, with tongue in cheek, "Because China and Mozambique didn't have an established church to fight the move of God." Tragically, the more I meditate upon the question, the more I believe this is the truth, especially when you consider that opposition has not come from the secular media, but primarily from certain parts of the religious media.

What is the Spirit saying today? He is beckoning the church, the bride of Christ, to open its eyes, to see that the people of the world are ripe unto harvest. The harvest is upon us now! The Lord has heard the cries of His people and He has come down to deliver. He is saying to those who will take the time to come aside and see the "burning bush," "I am sending you!" And, if the world wants to know who has sent us we are to reply, "I Am has sent us." This is very important. We are not to proclaim a message about the "I Was" or a message about the "I Will Be." Our message must not be limited to a God who once empowered His saints for supernatural ministry, but can't be expected to continue doing what He did in the "golden age" of the early church. Neither is our message to be limited to what our God will do in the future when He comes again. No! Our message is to be about what our God is able to do in the present for those who are in need now. It is a message that explains what we see God doing now is a deposit, a sign, of what shall happen to all those who believe in Him when He does come. Each healing is a sign of every believer's healing when we receive our transformed bodies "in a moment, in the twinkling of an eye."[12]

Jesus said he would not return until the "gospel of the kingdom" has been preached "in the whole world as a testimony to all nations"[13] (meaning "ethnic groups" in its context). That time is coming closer.

All eyes are on the Middle East, one of the last strongholds of the enemy which still holds millions in bondage to the false religion of Islam. Armies are on the move to invade this last frontier of the kingdom of darkness. From the north, particularly the Ukraine, eyes are set on bringing the gospel with its accompanying signs and wonders to the Middle East. From the east, an army of 100,000 missionaries, Chinese, are willing to be martyred in order to bring the gospel through the Islamic countries on their way to Israel. From the south, Mozambique, Rolland and Heidi Baker, along with Surpresa Sithole are now looking to bringing the gospel which has powerfully impacted the Moslems of Mozambique to the Arab kingdoms and nations of Northern Africa, and finally to the Middle East.

From the southern part of the Western Hemisphere eyes are on this last battlefield in the spiritual war for the souls of men. The Brazilians believe God has called them to raise up the greatest army of missionaries of this new century, and many are looking towards the Middle East and to Africa. I ask, "What are we going to do who live in the United States?" We who led the world in the modern missionary movement of two centuries ago, and who led in the last two missionary expansions of the twentieth century, what are we going to do?

I believe the answer is in whether or not we embrace and experience the next visitation of God. From the last visitation in the mid 1990s, many have left their extended families, jobs, careers, and pastorates to go into the nations. I and/or others in my ministry have met them in Mozambique, China, Brazil, Ukraine, Qatar, Pakistan, and other nations throughout the world. Only heaven knows the true fruit from the 1990s outpouring of the Spirit around the world. But, so much more could have happened. What could have happened if the misrepresentation of the outpouring had not occurred? What more could have happened had the churches embraced the outpouring of God instead of generally rejecting it? My hope is that enough books will be written from the historical perspective of almost 11-13 years later, that we will have better discernment.

I have a hope for the next move not to be missed by the majority of the church. I am hoping that through the study of revivals of the past, knowledge will be gained that will help us to see that certain phenomena are normal for times of revival. Revivals are birthed out of someone receiving a fresh "impartation" of the Holy Spirit, someone who catches the fire of God and then goes to spread the "fire." Impartations often characterized by things like weeping, deep conviction of sin, clearer understanding of grace, more intimate experience of God as Father, shaking, falling, laughing, social concern, more salvations, holiness, and missionary expansion are signs of revival. Not every revival has all of these signs, but these are signs that have been part of many revivals of past times and past centuries. Studying church history—especially the kind that has not been

57

"cleansed" of the reports of phenomena—is important to discernment. We must learn to recognize the ways of God in His church. This is not the same thing as building a belief system on the "tradition" of the church in the sense of the reflections of men and the doctrines of men. No, this is looking at the historical accounts of the effects of the Holy Spirit upon the lives of men and women caught up in a time of visitation. This is a study of the history of the way God has worked in, upon, and through people who have been touched by His "empowering presence," people who have had "impartations" from God. It is a study of the connection between these phenomena and the fruit that came through the lives of the people who experienced them.

Another thing that brings me hope that the next visitation may be experienced and embraced by more of the church is a higher commitment on the part of the church to biblical study. Reformation theology helped to restore the doctrine of salvation by grace through faith. It helped the church recapture the more biblical understanding of the work of Christ upon the earth during His thirty-three years. But, it did not recapture the work of Christ on our behalf in heaven. Neither did it recapture the message of the kingdom, nor the fullness of the work of the third person of the Trinity, the Holy Spirit. Reformation theology in effect became a hindrance to discovering or returning to the more biblical understanding of the message of the kingdom and the work of the Holy Spirit. It limited the Holy Spirit primarily to His role in salvation without consideration of His role in executing the will of the Son in the life of the church today. Nor did it consider His relationship to the continued growth of the kingdom of God in the interim church age, in the "now-not yet" period which is characteristic of the time until the second coming of Christ. As this historically restricted understanding of the Holy Spirit's role is replaced with a more biblical understanding of the Holy Spirit, there will be a greater openness in the church to future moves of God.[14]

Let me summarize what my heart has tried to do in this chapter. I believe God loves the world and is trying to reach it through the church, His Body on earth. The Lord Jesus desires to continue to execute His will "on earth as it in heaven" because He "is the same yesterday and today and forever." This means that the purpose of the Father, revealed through the Son, is to be continued by the activity of the Holy Spirit from the time of Pentecost until the Second Coming of Jesus. Everything the Father has belongs to all the church, not just the Pentecostals or Charismatics. It belongs to all those who by faith appropriate what has been given through grace.

This means that those who move in grace-based gifts are not anymore holy or saved than those who don't. Neither are they more mature in the Lord. But, it does often mean they are seeing more fruit in the approaching end-time harvest. If what I have received has not been based upon my works but is a free gift, then how can I boast in what God has done through me?

I hope that as a result of reading this book, there will be a hunger for greater intimacy with God, an intimacy that leads us to the places where His heart has been drawn—to the widows, orphans, poor, unregenerate peoples of the world. I hope the spirit of the message of this book comes across as an echo of the Father saying, "All that I have is yours!" I hope many will become open and come to the party (Luke 15). Then, having experienced the Father's love and refreshing, and having sat close to Him in fellowship, arise from the banqueting table and go in new strength to carry out His will. Not as a "hired servant," but as a grateful son or daughter who rejoices in carrying out the will of the Father they love so dearly, because they have been so ravished by His love in an experiential, real, and living way.

The reason behind the more confrontational paragraphs of this chapter was to try and dismantle erroneous beliefs that rob the children of God of the hope of experiencing the "more" of God in this life. These beliefs have caused millions of believers to think they cannot expect the things written about in this book. Since they do not believe they are possible, they do not cry out or search out the possibilities they have in God and His provision at the Cross.

My desire is to see in the church at large what we are seeing on the short-term missionary teams we take to the nations. You don't know who the Pentecostals are from the Presbyterians, or the Methodists from the Mennonites, or the Catholics from the Church of God-Cleveland, or the Baptist from the Brethren. Instead we find ourselves loving each other with a quick bonding that is almost supernatural and having a joyous time casting out demons, healing the sick, and laying hands upon leaders for impartation of more grace-based gifts. All that matters is Jesus and seeing Him continue to build His church through the present day ministry of the Holy Spirit working through us.

We are amazed that we can identify with the words of the Apostle Paul, "To this end I labor, struggling with all *his* energy, which so powerfully works in me" (Colossians 1:29). We are working but the fruit of the labor comes from *His* energy working through us. When we see the blind eyes open, the deaf hear, the lame walk, diseases disappear, persistent pains driven away, the poor served, and the widows cared for, we know it was *His* power that made it possible. There is such joy in this type of Christian endeavor that I sometimes warn the people on the teams, "This is go great, so enlivening, that it is addictive." I want the blessed Trinity to be our addiction—the reality that we must receive or we go into withdrawal. I want the kingdom of God and its present-day emphasis upon doing what Jesus did (see John 14-16) to be a primary means of experiencing the presence of God.

Don't settle for living your life like one of the "hired men" living in the "bunkhouse" when the Father wants you by His side at the dinner table, enjoying your inheritance. He doesn't want you to just study about Him from a distance, learning what He did in days gone by. No, He wants you to experience His arms around you in loving embrace. He wants you to experience His grace, His power, and knowledge of His ways. He wants you to appropriate the things Jesus purchased for you at the cross. Our Father doesn't think it is a terrible thing to become so happy that we laugh in His presence. His joy can cause laughter just as

His godly sorrow can cause crying. As my friend Rolland Baker has been preaching, "Faith is not the absence of experience, but the expectation of it." Run into His arms. Appropriate His grace. Work with Him in His power! Listen to the cry of the Father, "My son/daughter, all I have is yours!"

The next chapter will clearly portray the continuation of the working of the Holy Spirit to heal, deliver, and even raise the dead beyond the apostolic era of the church. It includes powerful accounts of people who were mightily used to accomplish such things. In this discussion it will become apparent how the church began to lose this awesome power of the Holy Spirit and His gifts. Much will be said about revival as well—as impartations most often occur in a season of revival, and it is difficult to write about impartations apart from the reality of the environment of revival. Often revival is sparked with someone receiving a strong impartation, followed by other hungry souls coming for a transference of this anointing—an impartation for their lives.

CHAPTER 4: IMPARTATION AND VISITATION – THE HERITAGE OF THE SAINTS

Unfortunately, we live in a church culture that places little value on the rich heritage of the historical church. This is the day of "new" and "now," where changes and advancements in every area of our lives bombard us at such a pace, we are left hard-pressed to remember yesterday (rotary dial phones?), much less the last century. As a result, we tend to look at today's moves of the Holy Spirit through the tiny peephole of the present, instead of through the telescopic lens of history. Our history is a wonderful story of how God has moved among His people throughout the entire church age. It's our history that gives proper context and brings clearer understanding to what is going on around the world at this very moment. Instead of looking at the current renewal movement as something aberrant and strange, a departure from what is "normal" for God, we will see that God has *often* chosen to invade His people with the glory of His manifest presence. From the days of the early church fathers to the Dark Ages to the Age of Reason to the present, we see a timeline marked by the footprints of Jesus, Emmanuel, as He has walked among us, revealing Himself, refreshing the remnant, and restoring power and vitality to His Bride.

As we look back at our lineage of saints, I hope to show that the signs and wonders and other phenomena that many today consider to be outside the realm of orthodox Christianity have really always been a part of what God intended for His church. When Jesus promised the Holy Spirit, He never put a time limit on the fullness of the Spirit's presence. When Paul explained the gifts that the Spirit gives, he never said they were only temporary gifts. If all the gifts and resources of heaven were necessary to the first Christians, how are the last Christians supposed to bring in the final, great harvest without them? Why would we expect God to equip His people with "power from on high" at the start of the race, and then leave them to crawl, weak and empty, across the finish line? I do not believe Jesus is coming back for a lukewarm, impotent remnant that has just barely made it to the end, hoping to get raptured before faith is tested. Rather, I believe we are only just beginning to see the most powerful move of God yet. Jesus is coming back for a radiant, majestic Bride, clothed in works of righteousness done in the power and name of the One who does not change!

THE EARLY CHURCH FATHERS

Cessationist doctrine teaches that not all the gifts of the Holy Spirit are operative today - that the "manifestation" and "power" gifts died out with the last of the original Apostles and are no longer needed now that we have the complete canon of Scripture. The following excerpts are taken from the writings of the Ante-Nicene fathers, those who wrote before the Council of Nicea in 325 A.D. (I am indebted to the scholarship of Morton Kelsey, probably the leading researcher on the history of healing ministry in the church from whose work I have gleaned.)[15] These were the disciples of the first disciples; the first generation of leaders after the Apostles had died. Their ministries of healing and deliverance give testimony to the fact of the Spirit's miraculous working in that time. These gifts of God's manifest power were not "emotional esoteric experiences" as some charge against the signs and wonders we see today. They were core elements of the gospel they preached for they preached a gospel of salvation to the whole man. They preached a Jesus of compassion who cared about the sickness of a man's body as well as his soul. They preached a Jesus who cared about captivity to demonic beings as well as bondage to sin. In short, they preached Good News!

Justin Martyr (100-165, martyred in 165 A.D.)

Justin Martyr wrote in his "apology" addressed to the Roman emperor:

> For numberless demoniacs throughout the whole world, and in your city, many of our Christian men exorcizing them in the Name of Jesus Christ . . .have healed and do heal, rendering helpless and driving the possessing devils out of the men, though they could not

be cured by all the other exorcists, and those who used incantations and drugs.[16]

Writing about the charismata, the gifts God pours out upon believers, Justin Martyr calls attention in several places to the power to heal as one of the particular gifts that was being received and used.

Hermas (Died c.150 A.D.)

From the *Shepherd of Hermas* one can see the strong emphasis that was on the ministry of healing in the early Ante-Nicene church:

He therefore, that knows the calamity of such a man, and does not free him from it, commits a great sin, and is guilty of his blood.[17]

Of this, Morton Kelsey comments in his book *Healing and Christianity: A Classic Study*:

Indeed the healing of physical illness was seen in this period as telling evidence that the Spirit of Christ was actually present and at work among Christians. Since both bodily and mental illness were a sign of domination by some evil entity, the power to heal disease was prime evidence that the opposite spirit—the Spirit of God—was operating in the healer. Thus the healing of "demon possession" was often spoken of in conjunction with curing illness from other causes.[18]

Tertullian (160–225 A.D.)

According to Kelsey, "[Healing] was simply a fact of Christian experience which pagan officials could verify if they wished."[19] During persecutions in North Africa, Tertullian wrote in protest to the proconsul:[20]

The clerk of one of them [Roman officials], who was liable to be thrown upon the ground by an evil spirit, was set free from his affliction; as was also the relative of another, and the little boy of a third. And how many men of rank (to say nothing of common people) have been delivered from devils, and healed of diseases! Even Severus himself, the father of Antonine [the emperor], was graciously mindful of the Christians; for he sought out the Christian Proculus, surnamed Torpacion, the steward of Euhodias, and in gratitude for his having once cured him by anointing, he kept him in his palace till the day of his death."[21]

According to Kelsey, "Tertullian...explicitly identified persons who had been healed and testified to their great number and the wide range of physical and mental diseases represented. Elsewhere he also says that God could, and sometimes did, recall the souls of human beings to their bodies."[22]

Origen (185–254 A.D.)

Concerning Origen Kelsey writes:

Origen wrote his great treatise *Against Celsus* to take pagan thinking apart piece by piece, and here he spoke in several places of how Christians "expel evil spirits, and perform many cures"—many of which he had himself witnessed. Or again, "the name of Jesus can still remove distractions from the minds of men, and expel demons, and also take away diseases." Several such statements occur in this work, which was written especially for the intellectual leaders of the pagan community.

Cyprian (Bishop of Carthage c. 248)

Cyprian testified to the healing of serious illness during baptism. He wrote:

"This, finally, in very fact we also experience, that those who are baptized by urgent necessity in sickness, and obtain grace, are free from the unclean spirit wherewith they were previously moved, and live in the Church in praise and honour." [23]

Irenaeus (flourished c. 175–195 A.D.)

Of Irenaeus, Kelsey comments:

Perhaps the most interesting discussion of healing among the ante-Nicene fathers came from Irenaeus in Gaul, who undoubtedly wrote more freely as he was somewhat removed from the danger of persecution that faced most of these thinkers. In *Against Heresies,* one of his telling points was that heretics were not able to accomplish the miracles of healing that Christians could perform. They did not have access to the power of God and so could not heal.[24]

Unfortunately, Irenaeus's remarks later became the basis for the idea commonly taught today that unless one's doctrine is 100% correct, any miracles or manifestations of the Spirit cannot be of God, but are demonic at their source. This teaching ignores the fact that God is much more interested in whether or not we are *relationally* correct with Him, than in whether or not we have all our doctrinal ducks in a row. The first disciples were sent out to heal the sick and set the demonized free long before they understood even what we consider the most basic foundations of the Christian faith. For example, the Trinity would not be doctrinally agreed upon until the fourth century, and the orthodox understanding of Christology would not be worked out until the fifth century.

Summarizing the power encounters Irenaeus had witnessed, Kelsey continues:

> Irenaeus attested to almost the same range of healings as we find in the Gospels and Acts. All kinds of bodily infirmity as well as many different diseases had been cured. Damage from external accidents had been repaired. He had seen the exorcism of all sorts of demons. He even described the raising of the dead. His pagan readers were well aware of these miracles of healing, as he makes clear, since this was often the path to conversion for pagans, as well as the means of bringing bodily health to both Christians and non-Christians.
>
> There is **no indication** that Irenaeus **viewed any disease as incurable or any healing as against God's will**. Indeed, the whole attitude he voiced was that **healing is a natural activity of Christians as they express the creative power of God, given them as members of Christ by the Holy Spirit**.[25] (Emphasis added)

It's important to note that Irenaeus was writing primarily to refute the Gnostic heresies of his day. Why is this important? Many famous healers of the Pentecostal/Charismatic tradition in this century have been accused of being influenced by Gnosticism—the claim of having a special understanding or revelation of Scripture, esoteric insight into "hidden" knowledge. Yet the "secret knowledge" of Gnosticism taught a distinct separation of matter and spirit. Matter is evil; spirit is good. Therefore, what happens in the realm of the flesh, whether it be sickness or immorality, is of no importance. Because this teaching devalued the natural body, assuming God was not interested, there was no value placed on the ministry of healing and they simply did not believe in it. The ministry of Christ's compassion had no place in Gnosticism. How ironic that those accused of Gnostic influence today are actually ministering in direct contradiction to basic Gnostic assumptions!

Further historical testimony to the Spirit's on-going gifts can be found in the writings of Theophilus of Antioch (died c. 181), Arnobius and Lactantius from near the end of the Ante-Nicene period (300–325) and Quadratus, "one of the earliest apologists, who wrote in Rome that the works of the Savior had continued to his time and that the continued presence of people who had been healed left no question as to the reality of physical healing."[26]

Augustine (354-430 A.D.)

Augustine was the undisputed theologian in the West for 1,000 years. His influence is very important to the history of healing. In his early years of ministry he wrote critically of healing:

> These miracles are not allowed to continue into our time, lest the soul should always require things that can always be seen, and by becoming accustomed to them mankind should grow cold towards the very thing whose novelty had made men glow with fire.[27]

However, about 40 years later he corrected this view which seemed to be antagonistic towards the on-going ministry of healing in the church. He wrote in his last and greatest work, *The City of God*, completed in 426, a whole section that gave high value to the ongoing ministry of healing. In this section he noted that over seventy healings had been recorded in his own bishopric of Hippo Regius in two years. After the healing of a blind man in Milan, Augustine wrote, *". . . and so many other things of this kind have happened, even in this present time, that it is not possible for us either to know of all of them or to count up all of those that we have knowledge of."* [28] [Italics added]

Later, Augustine's writings would have a tremendous impact on the reformers Martin Luther and John Calvin. His strong views of predestination and God's sovereignty would change the view of the church from the historic

"Warfare Worldview" to a "Blueprint Worldview." Rather than looking at the consequences of sin's curse as the work of the enemy that the church has the authority and power to come against in continuing the work of Christ who came "to destroy the devil's work" (1 John 3:8), Christians began to see all things as foreordained and to passively accept what they believed to be God's will. Ultimately, this would have a very negative impact upon the theology of healing in the church. For the sake of historical accuracy, it's important to remember that before Augustine died, he became known for the healing anointing and authority to deliver flowing through his own life.

What happened?

Looking back over the more than 400 years of early church history, the fathers were collectively saying, "Miracles have not stopped, but still occur today!" Why, then, do we have such division within the church today on this issue? How did the church, which witnessed so much healing its first thousand years, become so closed and skeptical towards this vital ministry? I believe we have erred by focusing the redemption we have in Christ totally in the future, with only moral changes in this present life. I contend that this was not the understanding of the early church. It believed in a present power not only for moral change, but also for authority over demons, power over sickness and disease, and for experiencing the reality of the spiritual gifts in their lives— especially in the corporate life of gathered congregations.

Granted, this book is supposed to be about the doctrine of impartation and anointing, but before we can directly address that issue, we need to understand the validity of what that anointing is for! Does God still anoint people to move in signs and wonders? When we see ministries of miraculous healing, deliverance, even the raising of the dead, can we be sure this is truly of God? What about meetings where there is a tangible sense of the supernatural and we witness all manner of emotional and physical responses? Can this be the work of the Holy Spirit? Much of mainstream Christianity today would answer, "No."

Again, historical context is important to understanding how the church has been influenced in her interpretation of Scripture. (In this book, I can only give a very brief summary of our theological history since that topic would fill another entire book, but those who are interested in more detail should contact Global Awakening for more in-depth materials and referral to other excellent resources.)

REASON AND REFORMATION

Thomas Aquinas

Prior to the Reformation, in the 1200s, Thomas Aquinas had already begun to adopt an anti-supernatural theology. Western civilization had crumbled, decimated by corruption, anarchy and epidemic disease. Cities were empty. Education had collapsed. Death and despair permeated all of society. People lost hope for any good in this life and spiritual emphasis shifted from the concerns of this life to a focus on the next.

Aristotelian philosophy became the basis for rising Arab culture. In this context, Aquinas wrote most of his *Summa Theologica*, intended to be an apologetical work appropriate for the Arabs. In attempting to be relevant to their philosophical mindset, Aquinas' work became a synthesis of Christian and Aristotelian thought. It was a theology based on the senses and ability to reason, and left little room for the supernatural as it pertained to earthly life. His writing became the benchmark of church theology for the next several hundred years.

Interestingly, at the end of his life, Aquinas changed. On December 6, 1273, he had a supernatural encounter with God and wrote, *"I can write no more. All I have written seems so much straw compared with what I have seen and what has been revealed to me."*[29] [Italics added] Three months later he died on a mission trip for the Pope and others had to finish his book. We will never know what he might have written had he lived long enough to process his experience into his theology.

The Reformers

On October 30, 1517, Martin Luther nailed his *95 Theses* to the door of the Whittenburg Church in Germany and the Reformation "officially" began. Neither Luther nor Calvin ever challenged the Aquinas-Aristotle synthesis in their writing. (However, near the end of his life, Luther did pray for his friend and collaborator, Philip Melancthon, as Melancthon lay at death's door from a high fever and witnessed his miraculous recovery.) Both Calvin and Luther felt keenly compelled to challenge the authority of the Roman Catholic Church. I admit this is greatly over-simplified, but the reasoning went like this: "Since the Catholics are using healings to validate false traditions, the healings must either be false or the work of the devil." The reformers cried out for a return to the objective authority of Scripture and, in the process, became quite anti-supernatural. It's not hard to understand the animosity of the reformers and why they so vehemently threw out anything that might bolster what they considered a grossly illegitimate claim to spiritual authority. Simply remember the horrors of the day, done in the name of God. Protestants were being viciously persecuted, tortured and burned at the stake by a religious organism that had long lost touch with the Word of God.

In the same period, a group called the Anabaptists appeared on the scene. They were having subjective, revelatory experiences of prophecy. Calvin and Luther felt that this further threatened and undermined a return to the authority of Scripture, especially when those prophecies did not line up with the Word.

The Age of Reason

Coinciding with this perceived need to reject the supernatural came the influence of the Age of Reason. The Scientific Revolution in Europe of the 1700 and 1800s profoundly affected the church's interpretation of Scripture. Skepticism flourished towards anything that did not have a material, natural explanation that fell within the limits of human comprehension and logic. These two forces coupled to radically change the landscape of theology regarding present-day supernatural works of God. "Higher criticism," which explained away all the miracles of the

Bible in natural terms, first arose in German seminaries. Within fifty years, a rejection of the supernatural for today was taught in most U.S. seminaries. By the late 1800s, it was widely taught that even biblical "miracles" never happened. "Right reasoning" was on the throne, taking precedence over Divine revelation and experience. If it couldn't be explained, it didn't happen.

Fundamentalism and Liberalism

Fundamentalism came on the scene as a backlash to liberal theology, yet it only addressed the issue of biblical inerrancy and inspiration. Neither liberals nor fundamentalists had a theology of the miraculous, particularly healing. Fundamentalists viewed the miracles of the Bible as something that was needed only for that time to confirm and establish a new message. Once the gospel had been "kick-started" and codified in Scripture, miracles were no longer necessary.

It's interesting that today, in regard to the gifts of the Holy Spirit, Pentecostals have more in common with Roman Catholics than they do with other Protestants, for the Roman Catholics have never been cessationist in their doctrine. John Wimber once said that those who have the hardest time receiving healing are certain Protestants, while those who receive the easiest are Roman Catholics as they are more open to the miraculous.

THE ROAD BACK TO PENTECOST

From what's been covered so far, it might sound like the church went for centuries without any faith in or practice of the supernatural gifts of the Holy Spirit. That is far from the case. Long before the rise of Pentecostalism at the beginning of the 1900s, God was revealing Himself in supernatural power in the midst of the most conservative, mainline denominations. It's a little known fact that many of today's cessation-teaching churches were birthed in renewal movements marked by charismatic manifestations. It is only the widespread ignorance of history that has cut so many of us off from our spiritual roots.

The First Great Awakening

Jonathan Edwards

In 1735, revival broke out in the American colonies in what became known as the First Great Awakening through the ministry of Jonathan Edwards. Jonathan Edwards is the preeminent theologian on religious experience. To this day, no one has written a more thorough and reasoned discussion of the subject. I have read that he was one of the greatest thinkers of America. He was the best defender of the Great Awakening. His wife was so touched in the revival that she would be overcome for hours by the Spirit of God. On one occasion she was experiencing a powerful visitation that lasted the better part of four days. Listen to some of the accounts of this as quoted by Guy Chevreau in his book *Catch the Fire*:

> Wednesday night, the church in Northampton was hosting protracted revival meetings. Mrs Edwards was so filled with the grace of God that it "took away her bodily strength." She writes: "I *continued* to have clear views of the future world, of eternal happiness and misery . . ." She and some friends had to stay at the church about three hours after the meeting was dismissed, because most of the time, her "bodily strength was overcome . . ."[30]
>
> *[Chevreau notes: "The expressions 'took away my bodily strength', 'overbear the body", and 'fainting' seem to be eighteenth-century equivalents to falling, resting, and 'slain' (in the Spirit) experiences"[31]]*

The following morning Mrs. Edwards was again overcome by the presence of God:

> Two hours later she accidentally went into the room where Mr. Buell was talking with some people about the reviving work of the Spirit; her strength was "immediately taken away", and she sank down on the spot. They propped her up on a chair and continued with their conversations; again her strength failed her, and she dropped to the floor. They took her up to bed, where she lay "for a considerable time faint with joy, while contemplating the glories of the heavenly world". . .
>
> Mrs. Edwards does relay that during this time, she "felt a far greater love to the children of God, than ever before. I seemed to

73

love them as my own soul; and when I saw them, my heart went out towards them, with an inexpressible endearedness and sweetness . . . This was accompanied with a ravishing sense of the unspeakable joys of the upper world" (I.lxva)[32]. She was out from noon until four, "being too much exhausted by emotions of joy, to rise and sit up." Late that afternoon, she regained enough strength to head off to the meeting, and then returned to bed.[33]

Mrs. Edwards continued to have similar experiences of God's empowering and joyful presence throughout the revival. Mrs. Edwards records her experiences for seventeen days and there is no indication these types of experiences discontinued during the revival. She simply discontinued writing about them.

What was the fruit of these experiences for Sarah Edwards?

As to the fruit borne, (Mr.) Edwards marks a new and deeper spirit of worship, such that Sarah expressed "a longing to sit and sing this life away" (I.377b).[34] There were often vehement longings and faintings after more love to Christ, and greater conformity to Him; especially longing after these two things; "to be more perfect in humility and adoration." (I.378a) [35] A further note is sounded; one which, given its essential gospel mandate, silences any and all critics; there was a great sense "of the duty of charity to the poor, and how much the generality of Christians come short in the practice of it."

For all that was done in and through Mrs. Edwards, there was "no appearance of spiritual pride; but on the contrary, with a very great increase of meekness and humility, and a disposition in honour to prefer others, as well as a great aversion to judging others" (I.lxviiib)[36]. This as we shall see is a clear and distinguishing mark of a true work of God. Mr. Edwards brings these final words of assessment to bear:

Now if these things are enthusiasm, and the fruits of a distempered brain, let my brain be evermore possessed of that happy distemper! If this be distraction, I pray God that the world of mankind may be all seized with this benign, meek, beneficent, beautiful, glorious distraction!

[Authors note: The detractors and critics of revival accused those being affected as having "distemper of the brain" or "distraction.". Also, "enthusiasm" was a pejorative term used against the revival.]

And what notions have they of religion, that reject what has been described, as not true religion! What shall we find to answer those expressions in Scripture: the peace of God that passes all understanding; rejoicing with joy unspeakable and full of glory, in believing in and loving an unseen Saviour; all joy and peace in believing; God's shining in our hearts, to give the light of the knowledge of the glory of God, in the face of Jesus Christ; with open face, beholding as in a mirror the glory of the Lord, and being changed into the same image, from glory to glory, even as by the Spirit of the Lord; having the love of God shed abroad in our hearts, by the Holy Spirit given to us—I say, if these things which have been mentioned, do not answer these expressions, what else can we find out that does?

Those that do not think such things as these be the fruits of the true Spirit, would do well to consider what kind of fruit they are waiting and praying for, and what sort of fruits they expect He should produce when He comes. I suppose it will generally be allowed, that there is such a thing as a glorious outpouring of the Spirit of God to be expected, to introduce very joyful and glorious times upon religious accounts; times wherein holy love and joy will be raised to a great height in Christians; but, if those things be rejected, what is left that we can find wherewith to patch up such a notion, or form an idea, of the high, blessed, joyful religion of these times? What is there sweet, excellent, and joyful, of a religious nature, that is entirely of a different nature from these things?[37]

It makes it difficult to be a detractor of a move of the Spirit when your wife has been powerfully touched by that move of God. Edwards was asking his critics what better way to see the outworking of the above mentioned verses of Scripture than through the present manifestations that were accompanying the revival. However, he always judged whether the manifestations were from God or not, not by the degree of the manifestation, but rather from the fruit that followed. Edwards believed there was little power in religion that didn't affect the emotions and will. Religious affections were the driving power of Christianity. Only when the revelation of divine truth went deep enough to touch the affections did this divine truth then have power to affect the will and lifestyle of the believer. The Holy Spirit had to work through our affections, not just our understanding or our knowledge. Edwards noted the difference in character and fruit between the members of his church prior to the revival and those touched in the revival. Edwards was always looking for fruit. More than any other person in America, he carefully studied the relationship between bodily manifestations and fruit, between the internal working of the Spirit and the outward manifestations upon the physical body of these internal workings.

What did these manifestations look like? How were they described? The following quote is a sample of some of the terms used by Edwards to describe the phenomena. "'extraordinary affections', accompanied by physical manifestations of fear, sorrow, love, joy; of 'tears, trembling, groans, loud outcries, agonies of the body, and the failing of bodily strength', of 'fits, jerks and convulsions'."[38]

Why have I chosen to include these insights from the "Great Awakening" which was called the "Great Clamor" by its critics while it was occurring, especially since this book is on the subject of impartation? Because I believe revival itself has a characteristic of being spread through impartation. Sometimes the impartation is an impartation of a vision/understanding of what God is presently doing, that the season of refreshing has begun. Sometimes the impartation comes through reading an account of what God is doing in another area or hearing the testimony of others who have been touched in the fresh outpouring; other times by seeing it first hand; other times by being touched in the meetings; or by having hands laid upon you by the leader of the meeting or being prayed for by one of the leaders of the move of God. Edwards notes this during the Awakening he found himself was leading:

> There were **many instances** of persons who came from abroad on visits, or on business, who had not been long here before . . . they were savingly wrought upon; and partook of the shower of blessing which God rained down here, and went home rejoicing, **till at length the same work began evidently to prevail in several other towns in the country.**[39] (Emphasis added)

This impartation for carrying revival can be seen in the First and Second Great Awakenings, in the Holiness Revival of the nineteenth century, the Pentecostal Revival of the beginning of the twentieth century, the greatest revival in Baptist history in Shantung Province of northern China in the '30s, the Latter Rain Revival and the Healing Revival of the late '40s, and the Charismatic Renewal both of Protestantism and Catholicism, the Jesus Movement, and the Third Wave Movement—of the '60s, '70s, and '80s respectively; and the move of God connected to Claudio Freidzon, Rodney Howard Brown, myself, John Kilpatrick and Steve Hill, Steve Gray, and others of the '90s. It was Rodney Howard-Browne's prophetic insight that God had told him "he would lay his hands on 1,000 people who would help him take revival around the world" that encouraged me to go see him and receive prayer from him multiple times. I believed in the truth of impartation, and I had asked to be one of the 1,000.

Now let us return to our historical perspective moving from the Great Awakening in the colonies of America to the work of God in England. Just prior to this revival in North America, the Great Evangelical Revival had already broken out in England under the ministries of John Wesley and George Whitefield.

Wesley and Whitefield

Wesley, the founder of Methodism, witnessed demonic deliverance in his meetings as well a variety of physical responses to the overwhelming power of God, such as people being thrown to the ground—later called swooning, and later still, "slain in the Spirit."

Note this series of excerpts from Wesley's journal:

> In the midst of the dispute, one of the ladies present felt as if she were pierced by a sword. Before she could be brought to another house, where I was going, she could not avoid loudly crying out, even in the street. But no sooner had we made our request to God than He sent her peace from His holy place. . . .[40]

> The next Saturday at Weaver's Hall a young man was suddenly seized with a violent trembling. In a few minutes, the sorrows of his

heart increased and he sank down to the ground. We never ceased calling upon God till He raised him up full of peace and joy in the Holy Spirit. . . .[41]

Thursday while I was preaching at Newgate, I asked them to pray that if this [salvation for all men] was the will of God, He would bear witness to His word. Immediately one, then another, and another sank to the earth. They dropped on every side as if thunderstruck. One cried aloud. We besought God in her behalf and He turned her heaviness into joy. . . . In the evening I was again pressed in spirit to declare, Christ "gave himself a ransom for all" (1 Timothy 2:6). Almost before we called upon God to set to His seal, He answered. One was so wounded by the Spirit that you would have imagined she could not live a moment. But soon His abundant kindness was revealed to her, and she loudly sang of His righteousness. . . [42]

By the end of April, we understood that many were offended at the cries of those on whom the power of God came. One of these was a physician who was afraid these cases might be fraud. Today while I was preaching at Newgate, one whom the doctor had known for many years was the first who broke out into strong cries and tears. The physician could hardly believe his own eyes and ears. He went over and stood close to her, observing every symptom, till great drops of sweat ran down her face and her entire body shook. He did not know what to think, being clearly convinced it was not fraud nor any natural disorder. But when both her soul and body were healed in a moment, he acknowledged the work of God. . . [43]

By May many more than before were offended. At Baldwin Street my voice could scarcely be heard amid the groanings of some and the cries of others, calling aloud to Him who is able to save.

A Quaker who stood by was greatly displeased at the commotion and was biting his lips and scowling angrily. Suddenly he dropped down as if thunderstruck. The agony he was in was terrible to behold. We begged God not to charge him with his folly. God answered and the man soon lifted his head and cried aloud, "Now I know you are a prophet of the Lord! . . . ."[44]

At Newgate another mourner was comforted. I was asked to step into a house to read a letter written against me. The letter stated that I was a deceiver of the people because I taught that God wills all men to be saved. One person who had long asserted the contrary was there when a young woman came in. Just as we rose from giving thanks, she reeled four or five steps, then dropped down.[45]

These were the accounts of sinners and religious detractors who were knocked down to the ground, slain in the Spirit. Revivals are often accompanied by such phenomena. It is difficult for us to accept that God's Spirit would cause people to be thrown to the ground, but in Scripture when there is a theophany, (visible manifestation of God), most of the time the people become afraid, very often they fall, and other times they tremble.

The greatest evangelist of the Great Evangelical Revival was George Whitefield. He began leading this revival at the young age of twenty-one, in 1735. He was concerned about some of the phenomena he was hearing about in the reports of John Wesley's meetings. Wesley wrote concerning this:

On Saturday George Whitefield and I discussed outward signs which had so often accompanied the inward work of God. I found his objections were chiefly grounded on the gross misrepresentations he heard concerning these facts. The next day he had an opportunity of informing himself better, for no sooner had he begun to invite sinners to believe in Christ than four persons collapsed close to him. One of them lay without either sense or motion. A second trembled exceedingly. The third had strong convulsions over his entire body but made no noise other than groans. The fourth convulsed equally and called upon God with strong cries and tears. From this time, I trust we shall all allow God to carry on His work in the way that pleases Him.[46]

The amazing thing revealed in Whitefield's journals was the repeated statements about George being weak in body, often very ill, and God coming in power with the preaching of the Word. There were accounts of deliverances, but not accounts of George praying for divine healing with the laying on of hands. Healing in this phase of Protestant history was still a lost doctrine, only later to be rediscovered by the later Holiness Movement; then by the Faith Cure Movement which included Reformed, Baptist, Christian and Missionary Alliance, and other writers; and then by the Pentecostal people.

When reading the journals of Wesley and Whitefield, one can't help but think of how Jesus rebuked the Pharisees of His day for honoring the prophets when their actions towards Him indicated that, had they lived when the prophets lived, they would have stoned them rather than honored them. It is amazing how we honor today those who were ridiculed and maligned during their ministries. The lesson of history is that it's easy to be favorable towards renewal or revival from the safe distance of time, but hard to be open to participating in the "great clamor"—the label by which the Great Awakening was originally known.

Wesley and Whitefield would be considered "Counterfeit Revival Leaders" if they were conducting their ministry today. They would be guilty of participating in the false "slain in the Spirit movement." They would definitely be accused of emphasizing esoteric experiences and hyping their meetings. Recordings of some of their meetings would be played over the radio—especially the more bizarre would be featured: screaming, wailing, weeping, roaring, etc.—those things which often occurred in their meetings. Because their meetings were accompanied with enough power to cause the affections (emotions) to be moved upon by the Spirit of God, could it be possible that these very phenomena were what attracted the attention of the English and American people of that day?

What was the fruit of the Great Awakening in the colonies of America? Whitefield was drawn to America eleven times, and died in the colonies. Was it real revival or people just getting caught up in esoteric experiences? Decide for yourself. According to John Havlik and Lewis Drumond in *How Spiritual Awakenings Happen*:

> In one period of three years during the awakening, at least thirty thousand persons were converted in New England. And in the same period at least fifty thousand persons were converted in all the colonies. When one remembers that the total population of the colonies was about two million, these numbers are no less than amazing. A similar awakening today would have to result in more

than five million conversions to achieve the same percentage. [47]

The Second Great Awakening

The Second Great Awakening began to gain steam around 1792 when God began to visit colleges. By 1800, many churches in the United States were experiencing revival, with the most famous of those meetings being the Cane Ridge Revival in Kentucky.

The Scottish Presbyterian Revivals

The Cane Ridge Revival was birthed out of a Scottish Presbyterian tradition. The Presbyterians had a prolonged communion service which would culminate once a year and last for 3-5 days. There had been 5-6 such meetings in Scotland where the "fire fell" or where God would "light the fire again." The "wild meetings," as they were called, began in Ulster peaking around 1624. "It was in these Ulster communions that we first have reports of people fainting dead away and being carried outside in a trance."[48]

The greatest revival of Scottish Presbyterianism broke out in 1742 at Cambuslang, Scotland. Estimates of attendance ran as high as 30,000 persons. George Whitefield preached there, having just returned from one of his trips to America. He preached with great anointing and passion. Church historian, Morton Kelsey describes what occurred:

> Small groups of people, under deep conviction, talked all the night. Whitefield preached the thanksgiving sermon on Monday, after which people were reluctant to leave. No one could estimate the number of converted. Almost every conceivable physical exercise, including falling in a swoon, afflicted some participants. The ministers deplored disruptive behavior during the services, but in spite of their appeals many cried out, even during communion, and in later interviews swore they could not control themselves however much they tried. . . . But in these three or four waves of revival, the huge rural gatherings, with all the extreme physical exercises, dismayed or frightened possibly a majority of Presbyterian clergymen. . . . Cambuslang was the focus of much of the controversy. Within nine years at least fifty-eight books, plus endless

81

articles, either praised or condemned it.[49]

The local pastor, McCulloch, to defend the revival developed a questionnaire to assess its effects. "The effects on the local congregation were lasting, although the revival ebbed very quickly. Conversions continued until 1748, but with annual decreases. Crimes all but ceased in the immediate aftermath, but not for long. Approximately four out of five converts remained in the church for the next decade.[50] For those who question the fruit of such renewal experiences, we might compare this to today's retention rate of 6% from crusade evangelism after just one year. The Cambuslang renewal produced a retention rate of 80% after ten years!

The same controversy that swirled around Cambuslang resurfaced when the Cane Ridge Revival hit. What was this revival like? James B. Finley was a Methodist circuit rider who was among the thousands converted during this move of God. Finley wrote:

> The noise was like the roar of Niagara. The vast sea of human beings seemed to be agitated as if by a storm . . . The scene that then presented itself to my mind was indescribable. At one time I saw at least five hundred swept down in a moment, as if a battery of a thousand guns had been opened upon them and then immediately followed shrieks and shouts that rent the very heavens. [51]

Although Cane Ridge did not originate with the Baptists, it was part of what became known among Baptists as the Awakening of 1800. Dr. Lewis Drummond, co-author of *How Spiritual Awakenings Happen*[52] stated in his lectures on evangelism at the Southern Baptist Theological Seminary that because of this revival, the Presbyterians doubled, the Baptists tripled, and the Methodists quadrupled.[53] But, often when God pours out His Spirit division results. The Presbyterians would be split into two denominations due to the Cane Ridge Blessing. It was too much for some, and so it was rejected by them.

Peter Cartwright and Methodist Revivalism

One of the great Methodist leaders of the 1800s was Peter Cartwright. He had been touched in the Cane Ridge Revival, and was soon converted and called into the ministry. During the early days of Methodism in this country it is reported that many young Methodist circuit riders did not marry because they knew that about 50% of their number died before reaching the age of thirty. Peter Cartwright was one of the courageous early circuit riders; one of their most famous evangelists of that era. From his autobiography he speaks:

> Many nights, in early times, the itinerant had to camp out, without fire or food for man or beast. Our pocket Bible, Hymn Book, and Discipline constituted our library. It is true we could not, man of us, conjugate a verb or parse a sentence, and murdered the king's English almost every lick. But there was a Divine unction attended the word preached, and thousands fell under the mighty hand of God, and thus the Methodist Episcopal Church was planted firmly in this Western wilderness, and many glorious signs have followed, and will follow, to the end of time.[54]

What a powerful, honorable history of the Spirit the Methodists have!

Cartwright wrote concerning the Cumberland Revival that soon followed Cane Ridge:

> The Predestinarians of almost all sorts put forth a mighty effort to stop the work of God. . . . Just in the midst of our controversies on the subject of the powerful exercises among the people under preaching, a new exercise broke out among us, called the jerks, which was overwhelming in its effects upon the bodies and minds of the people. No matter whether they were saints or sinners, they would be taken under a warm song or sermon, and seized with a convulsive jerking all over, which they could not by any possibility avoid, and the more they resisted the more they jerked. If they would not strive against it and pray in good earnest, the jerking would usually abate. I have seen more than five hundred persons jerking at one time in my large congregations. Most usually persons taken with the jerks, to obtain relief, as they said, would rise up and dance. Some would run, but could not get away. Some would resist; on such the jerks were generally very severe.[55]

Cartwright's interpretation of these phenomena is worthy of noting:

> "I always looked upon the jerks as a judgment sent from God, first, to bring sinners to repentance; and, secondly, to show professors that God could work with or without means, and that he could work over and above means, and do whatsoever seemeth to him good, to the glory of his grace and the salvation of the world." [56]

Charles Finney Spreads the Fire

Charles Finney was the greatest revivalist of the 1800s in America. Some say he was the greatest American evangelist of all time. [57] His biography is filled with power encounters that he experienced and witnessed. Just hours after his conversion he experienced a mighty baptism with the Holy Spirit. This sovereign "impartation" from heaven would radically change his life. He describes his experience:

> Without any expectation of it, without ever having the thought in my mind that there was any such thing for me, without any recollection that I had ever heard the thing mentioned by any person in the world, the Holy Spirit descended upon me in a manner that seemed to go through me, body and soul. I could feel the impression, like a wave of electricity, going through and through me. Indeed it seemed to come in waves and waves of liquid love for I could not express it in any other way. It seemed like the very breath of God. I can recollect distinctly that it seemed to fan me, like immense wings.
>
> No words can express the wonderful love that was shed abroad in my heart. I wept aloud with joy and love; and I do not know but I should say, I literally bellowed out the *unutterable* gushings of my heart. These waves came over me, and over me, and over me, one after the other, until I recollect I cried out, "I shall die if these waves continue to pass over me." I said, "Lord, I cannot bear nay more;" yet I had no fear of death. [58]

After this experience, the first person Finney spoke to went to get an elder. The elder came to help Finney because Finney had been so wiped out by the power of the experience. This elder of the church was a serious and grave man but, as Finney was telling him how he felt, the elder fell into a "most spasmodic laughter. It seemed as if it was impossible for him to keep from laughing from the very bottom of his heart."

Finney received a second impartation from heaven, which he called the baptism in the Spirit, within twenty-four hours of the first and then began to preach the day after his conversion. He would have many baptisms in the Spirit. His controversial ministry would see thousands falling under the power of the Holy Spirit, healings, deliverances, shakings, groanings, and weeping. Some who fell under the power would not be able to get up for long periods of time. In an era of sparse population and no media, Finney would be used to bring half a million people into the kingdom of God!

Phenomena have been very much a sign of the power of God in revivals. Often, these phenomena also produce controversy and division within the churches. It is sad that when these things are written up later, our church historians often sanitize the accounts of the meetings, removing the supernatural dimension.

When several Southern Baptist seminary professors of evangelism were asked by phone, "What was the greatest revival in Baptist history?" The response was unanimously, "The Shantung Revival in China." Healing, falling, electricity, laughing in the Spirit, even the raising of the dead is recorded in "The Shantung Revival," a book by Mary Crawford, one of the Southern Baptist missionaries who experienced this revival first-hand in the early 1930's. In it are accounts of almost everything that has been characteristic of the Toronto Revival and the Pensacola Outpouring. Unfortunately, most Southern Baptists are not aware of what happened during their greatest revival. Several years ago, the book was reprinted with almost all of the phenomena of the Holy Spirit edited out. Global Awakening has republished this book with its entire original content.

The Development of Pentecostal Revival

Revival ushered in the 1900's just as it had the 1800's. The Frontier Revival, or Second Great Awakening, was followed by the even more powerful Pentecostal Revival, which dates back to 1901. Again, we would see people falling, shaking,

85

rolling, weeping, wailing, dancing, laughing in the Spirit, and speaking in tongues. The uniqueness would be that, for the first time, tongues were tied to the baptism of the Holy Spirit as the initial evidence.

Azusa Street would occur in 1906. The first name for the Azusa Street Revival was the "Los Angeles Blessing." Hungry people would travel from every inhabited continent to find more of the manifest presence of God and then return to spread the Pentecostal revival in their country. Participants believed in impartation, the transference of anointing, and were empowered to carry the revival back to other places. Like the Latter Rain Revival of the 1940's, this revival emphasized the return of all the spiritual gifts of 1 Corinthians 12, including the "sign gifts" of tongues, interpretation of tongues, prophecy, working miracles and gifts of healings.

It is disappointing to me how much prejudice there still is in the church towards Pentecostals. When I was taking a course on evangelism in seminary we studied every revival in North American church history except two, the Pentecostal Revival and the Latter Rain Revival, which was a Pentecostal revival in its origin. It is shameful that these revivals are not even mentioned in our evangelical seminaries and colleges. It is not healthy to allow our prejudice to blind us to the facts of how powerfully God has used Pentecostals. In their early days, when they had no institutions, buildings, money, or programs, they were used to reach more lost than any other part of the church—more than the Reformed, the Lutheran, the Anglican, the Baptist, the Methodist, and the Roman Catholics. These denominations, with all their history, buildings, finances, organization and programs, were surpassed in evangelism by the Pentecostals. Why? The Pentecostals embraced the outpouring of the Holy Spirit's power, and the restoration of the power ministries of the Holy Spirit as still for today. *Sōzō*, the Greek verb meaning "to save" and its noun derivative, *sōtēr*, meaning "salvation" are used in the Bible to refer to not only the saving of the soul, but deliverance from demonized situations, and physical and emotional healing. It was this understanding of the fullness of our salvation, embraced by the Pentecostals, which gave such spiritual power to their message.

Pentecostalism was preceded by leaders like Charles Spurgeon (1834–1892) who were looking for the restoration of a fully empowered, apostolic church as seen in the days of the first Pentecost. Spurgeon was a Calvinist, yet he had a healing ministry and moved in words of knowledge during his services. He prophesied a great move of the Holy Spirit in the next fifty years.

It was in those next fifty years that we saw the birth of the Holiness Movement, spear-headed by some of this century's giants of the faith, A.J. Gordon, A.B. Simpson, and Andrew Murray. This renewal movement emerged from within several existing denominations, as there was no "Holiness" church in existence at the time.

The holiness movement emphasized a second work of grace following initial regeneration. The purpose of this second experience was a "filling" with the power of the Holy Spirit which enabled the believer to experience sanctification— practical victory in his daily experience, not just positional victory in the spiritual realm and the life to come. It was a return to the doctrine of "Christ is Victor," which was the prevailing understanding of the Cross of Christ during the first 600 years of church history. In short, it means we understand that the Cross didn't just secure our ultimate salvation, but that all of Satan's power was met head-on and defeated, breaking the dominion of the curse. The death of Jesus was certainly a "substitutionary atonement," but the scope of what He did goes far beyond that. By His death and resurrection, Jesus conquered all the powers of hell. Because of His victory, Christians may walk in authority and power over death in all its forms—spiritual, emotional and physical.

Out of this return to historic "Christus Victor" theology, came the Faith Cure Movement. This movement would be eclipsed in about twenty-five years by the birth of the Pentecostal Movement. With the great disdain of evangelical Protestants for the Pentecostal Movement, which embraced healing, there was a reaction by Evangelicals away from the Faith Cure Movement into an even stronger cessationist position.

I often hear the phrase, "I'm not concerned with phenomena; what I'm concerned about is evangelism." Can there be any question that the mightiest moves of the Spirit—that have resulted in the greatest numbers of people coming to God—have been those times of revival characterized by powerful outpourings of spiritual gifts and manifestations of God's very presence? It is also clear from church history that most of these leaders first received their own impartation of the Spirit prior to accomplishing such powerful things in Jesus' name. Men and women like Maria Woodworth Etter, John G. Lake, Smith Wigglesworth, Charles Price, F.F. Bosworth, Aimee Semple McPherson, Tommy Hicks, Lester Sumrall, T. L. Osborne, Oral Roberts, Kathryn Kuhlmann, Reinhard Bonnke, Benny Hinn, Bill Johnson, myself, and a host of others all received a powerful "impartation" from God before they were so powerfully used of God. Other men like, A. J. Gordon, Andrew Murray, A. B. Simpson, E. W. Kenyon, A. T. Pierson, D.L. Moody, and R. A. Torrey, also testified to having received the "baptism in the Holy Spirit. These men were less connected to entering the healing movement through an impartation. Like the late John Wimber, they saw healing in the Bible and wanted to be faithful to the Bible, and in doing so began teaching on healing. Their impartation was more for evangelism, and their approach to healing was based upon the promises of Scripture.

WHAT ABOUT TODAY?

We began Part I of this book asking the question, "What's the fruit?" When we see men and women who claim an anointing of God to move in signs and wonders, healings and deliverance, and when we see ministries accompanied by all manner of phenomena, can we know it is of God? We've certainly seen the historical impact of men and women used in the past and the fruit of earlier outpourings of the Spirit. What about more recent times?

Like many streams flowing into one great River of God, the 1940's brought the revival ministry of William Branham in 1946, the Sharon Orphanage Revival of 1947, the Healing Revival of 1948, and the evangelistic ministry of Billy Graham in 1949. Although diverse in nature, I do not believe these were separate moves of God, put one great outpouring that manifested in a variety of ways. Since then, I believe we have been accelerating towards the greatest revival of all, the last harvest before the return of Jesus Christ for His Bride.

I see the great River of God of the 1990's revival in a similar manner: Claudio Freidzon in 1992, Rodney Howard Browne in 1993, John Arnott and myself in 1994, John Kilpatrick and Steve Hill in 1995, and Steve Gray in 1996. There are many others who were used in these periods of revival both in the 40's and the 90's, but space and time do not allow us to mention them all.

In this last decade evangelists like Benny Hinn and Reinhard Bonnke have preached to millions at one place. I was in India at the same time Benny Hinn was ministering to millions. My crowds were from 25,000-100,000 per night. What drew the people were the miracles of God.

What about Evangelist Billy Graham? Because he doesn't move in miracles, does his success invalidate my arguments? I think not. About twenty-five years ago, I was studying about people being filled with the Holy Spirit. I read where Billy Graham was up in the mountains of California near a lake where he had an experience with God. This experience resulted in a more complete surrender to the purposes and power of God for his life. This happened shortly before his famous 1949 Los Angeles meetings where he gained national notoriety.

There are so many more men and women who have been powerfully anointed by God to bring about revival through the various giftings of the Spirit. I can only name a few here. Later in this book, I will share many more stories with you of people who are being used *right now* to change the world. But before we consider them we must consider how the Lord of the Church brought it from the brink of almost losing the understanding of the importance of impartation and the gifts of the Spirit to a full blown massive recovery effort orchestrated by the Holy Spirit. This will be so important to God for His church that he will cause both Protestant and Roman Catholic to pray for a new "Pentecost." This is one of the most amazing stories in the history of the church. Once you see what God purposed to do and then effected in His church it gives you a much bigger picture of how important this new "Pentecost" was to the heart of God.

CHAPTER 5: WINDS OF CHANGE – THE SPIRIT'S WORK OF PREPARATION FOR RESTORATION

RISING EXPECTATION IN EUROPE

During the time of Finney's ministry in America, God was also working in the hearts of many evangelicals in England. There was great expectancy building during the 1800s regarding the fulfillment of end-time prophecies. Prior to the outbreak of the Civil War in the United States, the prevailing end-time view was post-millenialism which taught that Jesus would return after the church had been successful in establishing the kingdom of God upon the earth and taking the gospel of the kingdom to all nations. There was a popular view that, as His appearing came closer, the church should expect a great end-time revival where the earlier "sign gifts" of 1 Corinthians 12 would be restored to the church.

After the Civil War, a dispensational pre-tribulation rapture theory became the most popular view of the end times in the United States. This view was predisposed to deny an end-time revival or the restoration of the "sign gifts." This view was popular in the United States, but had only a small impact upon the Christians in Europe. For hundreds of years the church, both Catholic and Protestant, had not expected the average person to be able to move in the gifts of healing, working of miracles, prophecy, tongues and interpretation of tongues. Other gifts, like words of knowledge and words of wisdom were redefined to remove their supernatural aspect. Sometimes prophecy was also treated in this manner and was considered the equivalency of preaching. This was the classical Calvinist interpretation and almost as strongly held to by the Lutherans. But, by the last half of the 1800s, this view was changing to expectancy for the restoration of the gifts and offices of apostolic Christianity.

Daniel 7 and Revelation 13 were key prophetic passages and they were believed to be in the process of being fulfilled during the late 1700s. Vinson

Synan, Dean of Regent Divinity School and the most famous church historian of the twentieth century, wrote, "As the French Revolution unfolded, biblical scholars were certain that these passages were literally being fulfilled. The introduction of a new 'revolutionary' calendar and the installation of a prostitute in Notre Dame Cathedral as a newly crowned 'Goddess of Reason' seemed to underscore the apocalyptic event of 1798 when French troops under General Berthier marched on Rome, set up a new republic, and sent the Pope into exile. This was seen as the 'deadly wound' marking the end of papal hegemony in the world."[59]

A student of biblical prophecy interpreted the 1260 years mentioned in Revelation and the "times, times, and half time" in Daniel to be from the year 538, the end of the Goths rule in Rome, to 1798 as the fulfillment of the prophecy. Synan continues, "To Protestant scholars this interpretation meant they were living in the very last days. The second coming of Christ was near; the millennium was shortly to begin; the Holy Spirit would soon be poured out upon all flesh as a further sign that the end was near. The long night of waiting was almost over. **At any time the charismata would again be manifested in the earth as on the day of Pentecost**."[60] (Emphasis added)

Evangelicals in England and on the Continent continued to expect an end time outpouring of the gifts of the Spirit. In 1857, Charles H. Spurgeon preached a prophetic sermon, "The Power of the Holy Spirit." He said:

> Another great work of the Holy Spirit, which is not accomplished is the *bringing on of the latter-day glory.* [Italics Synan's] In a few more years—I know not when, I know not how—the Holy Spirit will be poured out in far different style from the present. There are diversities of operations; and during the last few years it has been the case that the diversified operations have consisted of very little pouring out of the Spirit. Ministers have gone on in dull routine, continually preaching—preaching—preaching, and little good has been done. I do hope that a fresh era has dawned upon us, and that there is a better pouring out of the Spirit even now. For the hour is coming, and it may be even now, when the Holy Ghost will be poured out again in such a wonderful manner, that many will run to

and from and knowledge shall be increased—the knowledge of the Lord shall cover the earth as the waters cover the surface of the great deep; when His Kingdom shall come, and His will shall be done on earth as it is in heaven . . . .My eyes flash with the thought that very likely I shall live to see the out-pouring of the Spirit; when "the sons and the daughters of God shall prophesy, and the young men shall see visions, and the old men shall dream dreams."[61]

A GROWING HUNGER IN THE UNITED STATES

In the United States the emphasis upon the restoration of the gifts of the Holy Spirit, and upon receiving an experience of the Holy Spirit subsequent to conversion, was moving from the fringes of the church to its center. This was becoming more visible especially during the last twenty-five years of the nineteenth century. The emphasis within the Holiness Movement had been primarily the Methodist viewpoint that power for sanctification or holiness was a "second definite blessing." This was now becoming a dual message where the "second blessing" included the Holy Spirit's gifts of power. The Keswick Movement was a more Calvinistic movement and was represented by such men as Baptist A. J. Gordon and Presbyterian A. B. Simpson. But one of the strongest leaders in this new emphasis upon a subsequent experience of power was D.L. Moody, founder of the Moody Bible Institute, and R.A. Torrey, Moody's successor and President of Moody Bible Institute. Moody's Northfield Conferences became a major impetus to the teaching of a "baptism in the Holy Spirit" for power.

Moody would die in 1899, just before the outbreak of the expected and much sought after and prayed for "New Pentecost." These Northfield Conferences in Massachusetts were the meetings where E. W. Kenyon was tremendously influenced in the formation of much of his theological views. His greatest source of quotes is from the Baptist A. J. Gordon. Kenyon would later influence the man who brought the "finished work" teaching to the Assemblies of God denomination in its formative years. This "finished work" teaching influenced Holiness teacher Phoebe Palmer who emphasized confessing what the Word of God taught concerning your sanctification until you possessed it.[62] Phoebe wrote and ministered earlier than both Gordon—who influenced Kenyon so much—and Kenyon. I do not mean Phoebe had the fullness of understanding regarding the finished work that Gordon and Kenyon had, nor did she apply it in the same manner. She applied it for sanctification and Kenyon for healing.

Simpson, Gordon, Andrew Murray, and Kenyon would all apply this same approach to physical healing. Confess the truth of God's word based upon the "finished work of Christ" until the possession of the reality is yours. This was the message of the "Faith Cure" movement of the last quarter of the nineteenth century. It was picked up by the new Pentecostal denominations, and later healing evangelists like T. L. Osborn would express their indebtedness to E.W. Kenyon who was representative of this teaching. F. F. Bosworth's book, *Christ the Healer* would be a summation of the conclusions of the "Faith Cure Movement."

Some were also expecting the restoring of the offices of the prophet and the apostle to the church, not just the gifts of healing, miracles, tongues, and interpretation of tongues. In the 1830's a man by the name of Edward Irving, a famous Presbyterian pastor in London, who saw people in his church experience tongues, prophecies, and other gifts, believed God had restored the gifts of apostles and prophets. He was excommunicated by the Presbytery as a heretic for such a belief. Some time later he died a broken man in disgrace.

One of the saddest notes associated with the answer to the century of prayer for the Pentecostal outpouring with its restoration of the gifts was its rejection by some of the very groups that had cried out for just such a visitation. Perhaps it was because of the way it came at Azusa Street. In the day of Jim Crow laws and the segregation of the races, the idea that God would choose a one-eyed black man with little formal education as the instrument of the revival, and to locate it in a former livery stable on the wrong side of the tracks, was more than many could handle. God just seems to like showing up in stables.

Phineas Bresee, the head of the newly formed Pentecostal Church of the Nazarene denomination, had himself received a powerful impartation at the occasion of his sanctification. ("Sanctification" here is the Holiness Movement expression that refers to a powerful work of grace in the life of the individual that frees one from the power of sin. This was a powerful, emotional experience; it was definite, and it followed their conversion experience.) Yet, Bresee rejected the Pentecostal message and removed the Pentecostal name from the denomination. However, Bresee did receive an extremely powerful impartation from God. He writes:

> I sat alone in the parsonage, in the cool of evening, in the front parlor near the door. The door being opened, I looked up into the azure in earnest prayer, while the shades of evening gathered about. As I waited and waited, and continued in prayer, looking up, it seemed to me as if from the azure there came a meteor, an indescribable ball of condensed light, descending rapidly toward me. As I gazed upon it, it was soon within a few score feet, when I seemed distinctly to hear a voice saying, as my face was upturned towards it: "Swallow it; swallow it," and in an instant it fell upon my lips and face. I attempted to obey the injunction. It seemed to me, however, that I swallowed only a little of it, although it felt like fire on my lips, and the burning sensation did not leave them for several days. While all of this of itself would be nothing, there came with it into my heart and being, a transformed condition of life and blessing and unction and glory, which I had never known before. I felt like my need was supplied. I was always very reticent in reference to my own personal experience. I have never gotten over it, and I have said very little relative to this; but there came into my ministry a new element of spiritual life and power. People began to come into the blessing of full salvation; there were more persons converted; and the last year of my ministry in that church was more consecutively successful, being crowned by an almost constant revival. When the third year came to a close, the church had been nearly doubled in membership, and in every way built up.[63]

Jesus said, "I will build my church, and the gates of Hades will not overcome it." (Matthew 16:18b). Jesus does not belong to the Vineyard movement, nor any other new apostolic network. Neither is He a Roman Catholic, Baptist, Assembly of God, or Nazarene. He is the pioneer of our faith, the original "Christian," the "anointed one." It has been said that God does nothing without first setting His church to pray, then He responds to the prayers. God definitely did this in preparation for the greatest release to His church in 1,700 years or more, or maybe even since the first Pentecost. I have addressed already this restoration within Protestantism, now I want to share what the Holy Spirit was doing within the Roman Catholic Church.

STIRRINGS WITHIN THE ROMAN CATHOLIC CHURCH

This is an amazing story of grace within the Roman Catholic Church and its part in preparing the way for a new Pentecost. I am drawing entirely on the material from Monsignor Vincent M. Walsh's book, *What is Going On: Understanding the Powerful Evangelism of Pentecostal Churches.* In this book he relates how God was moving within the Catholic Church to cause it to pray for a new Pentecost. He definitely believes the Catholic Church contributed to the Pentecostal Revival through its prayers which were joined to the prayers going up by many Protestants as well. Here is the account:

> Blessed Elena Guerra (1835-1914) the first person beatified by Pope John XXIII, founded a religious congregation of women (The Oblate Sisters of the Holy Spirit) dedicated to spreading devotion to the Holy Spirit. Sister Elena formed prayer groups which she called "Pentecost Cenacles," hoping that "Come Holy Spirit" might become as popular a prayer as the Hail Mary. Sister Elena wanted the Church united in constant prayer as were Mary and the apostles, and advocated 24-hour prayer cenacles.
>
> In 1885, she felt called to write to the Pope but resisted this grace until many years later when the Lord revealed to a devout woman in her kitchen what He wanted Elena to do.
>
> Between 1895 and 1903 she wrote twelve confidential letters to the Pope calling for renewed preaching on the Holy Spirit.
>
> Pope Leo (papacy years 1878-1903) responded to Elena's letters by publishing Provida Matris Caritate (The Provident Charity of a Mother) asking for a solemn novena between the Ascension and Pentecost throughout the Church. This was not enough; Sister Elena prodded the Pope through her spiritual guide. Pope Leo wrote his famous encyclical on the Holy Spirit, Divinum Illud Manus ("That

Divine Gift"). The encyclical was excellent but the response from the Church was poor.

Possibly even more important, at the insistence of Blessed Elena, he dedicated the 20th Century to the Holy Spirit, invoking on January 1, 1901[64], the "Veni Creator Spiritas" ("Come Holy Spirit") upon the whole world . . .[Parentheses author's]

Mrs. Anna Mariea Schmitt is a surviving member of a small village in Czechoslovakia that was wiped out by the Nazis in 1938.

In the eleventh century, when her village was faced with starvation because severe cold had ruined their crops, a beautiful lady appeared on the mountain. She never identified herself but taught the villagers to invoke the Holy Spirit. By following her teaching, they were filled with the Holy Spirit manifesting all of the Pentecostal gifts, including healing, prophecy and tongues.

They avoided starvation that winter because the bread that they had baked was multiplied and their supply lasted miraculously until the next harvest.

Each successive generation manifested these same charisms. The power of prayer and God's presence were so strong, the village needed neither jails, nor hospitals. When someone was sick, the whole village united in prayer, expecting God to heal. There was no divorce and families welcomed all the children sent by God. The Bible was read in the home and the children were taught how to live in the power of the Spirit. Each Sunday, their celebration of Mass was joyful and they shared a fellowship meal afterward.

In the 1930s they were told, through the prophetic word, that a severe testing would come upon the village and empty it. This prophecy was fulfilled in 1938, when the Nazis killed almost everyone. During these executions, the Holy Spirit gave them perseverance and no one renounced their faith due to the threats. Anna Mariea herself survived both Nazi and Russian concentration camps.

The story shows a remarkable parish, totally immersed in the Holy Spirit for nine centuries. However, one more part makes the story almost too good to be true.

This totally charismatic village was visited many times by Bishop Angelo Roncalli, later Pope John XXIII. Anna Mariea delighted to sit at his feet and listen to his teachings about Jesus. He was totally at home amidst the openly charismatic manifestations of this Pentecostal village.

When Angelo Roncalli became the Pope [in 1958] and called the Second Vatican Council, he asked the whole Church to say a special prayer which began, "Renew your wonders in this our day, as by a

New Pentecost." [Pope John XXIII died in 1963.] In 1967 as a total surprise of the Spirit, the Catholic Pentecostal Renewal began.

In those early days, we constantly thanked Pope John, knowing that this new Pentecostal Movement would never have been accepted without his Council. We often would say, "If only Pope John knew what would happen because of his prayer for a New Pentecost."

Now we realize what Pope John knew all along. Before any of us experienced Catholic Pentecostalism, he had witnessed a little village where a beautiful lady taught the people to invoke the Spirit and to use charismatic gifts.

Anna Mariea was asked if she thought that Pope John's prayer for a new Pentecost was inspired by this village. She thinks that his desire for a new Pentecost was born in his heart long before visiting their village. He seemed to know all along what was possible when people invoked the Holy Spirit.

The stories of the little village and of his choosing Blessed Elena as his first beatification, show the true dream of Pope John XXIII for Church Renewal "as by a new Pentecost in our day."

Two important 20th Century Popes, Leo XIII and John XXIII, openly sought the fire of the Holy Spirit on the Catholic Church. In 1901, the fire seemingly fell upon a group that lived out the prayer cenacle dream of Sister Elena. Pope John's dream of God renewing His wonders in our day "as by a New Pentecost" is indeed happening on an unbelievable scale.

However, for the most part, these signs and wonders are happening outside of the Catholic Church and, in some countries, are attracting thousands away from Catholicism.

The Council (Vatican II) was inspired by Pope John's dream. During those years (1963-1966) the Church spoke of "signs and wonders" and of regaining early Church poverty and enthusiasm.

No one hears those words now. In all honesty, Pope John seems to have been pushed into the background, as if his Pentecostal dream was too naïve. If we don't awaken soon, we will discover that the Pope's Pentecostal dream was all too true, but we were not open to the fire of the Spirit.[65]

ARE WE READY?

Just as the Roman Catholic Church petitioned God for another Pentecost at the turn of the century and then again in the 1960s, but still couldn't embrace the Spirit when He came, so was the response of the majority of the Protestant church. The Roman Catholic Church relegated the new presence of the Spirit to special groups outside the regular worship service. In like manner, many traditional Protestant denominations allowed their "closet charismatic" fellowships of pastors and leaders. But they, too, did not dare bring the new dynamic of the Spirit into the normal worship service. They, too, relegated the Spirit to special events and groups, but not the regular Sunday worship service. The result was that those who wanted to experience the fullness of the Spirit in corporate gatherings, not just some small group hidden from the rest of the congregation, left to join or start new charismatic churches where this freedom was permitted.

For many, there is a need for the graces and gifts of the Spirit to be ordered by the formal rituals of the church. Prophecy has been reduced to ritualistic charges given at ordination. The laying on of hands too has become a ritual to set people into their place of service. The call of laborers is no longer from the Lord through the prophets of the church, but the wisdom of the nominating committee and the vote of the congregation. For too many, the local church is no longer functioning as a theocracy where God is in control, but either a pure democracy where the majority vote wins the decision or a republican form of government where representatives from the congregation lead it through the session, leadership team, or whatever term is used.

The problem with this form of church life is that it has lost the sense of the Presence of God leading, guiding, sustaining, calling, supplying and visiting. Little wonder or mystery is left in the church meetings. I'm afraid the pastor of the largest Baptist church in South Africa was right when he said to me, "We pray for the Holy Spirit to come, but when He does, the first thing we tell Him is, 'Now sit down on the back seat and behave Yourself.'" Impartations are wonderful, but they are also messy. They can be loud and disruptive to the ritual when they occur.

When God comes to visit His church in revival or renewal, He will behave in a manner true to Who He is; He *does* think He is the Head of the church. When He comes, He comes to take over, not to sit in the back seat and conduct Himself to the pleasing of people. This same pastor, who had been reluctant to allow the Holy

Spirit free reign in his church, also said to his congregation, "I don't aim to be disrespectful, but when we were praying for God to come, our prayers were like, 'Here kitty, kitty, kitty, and ROOAAAAARRRRR, the Lion of Judah showed up.' He was so much stronger and fiercer than the tamed, controllable 'kitty' we were expecting." To quote C. S. Lewis concerning the lion Aslan, "He is good, but he is not safe."

I am afraid this last move of God that came to the church in the 90's and quickly spread around the world, was rejected largely because of the tension between man and God for control of the liturgy or order of the service. It seems to me that every major revival of the twentieth century involved God attempting to restore His control over the church in an experiential way, not just in a theological or doctrinal understanding of this reality. Almost every one of these moves emphasized the restoration of the gifts of the Holy Spirit, a return to the use of the word "Apostolic and/or Pentecostal," experienced a new order of men and women who were sent forth (the basic meaning of the word apostolic) as missionaries or as new preachers of the gospel, and experienced a new vibrancy in worship. This was true for the initial Pentecostal Outpouring with Parham in Topeka, Kansas 1901; the Welsh Revival of 1904; the Pentecostal Revival of Azusa Street in 1906; the Revivals in the 20s and 30s under Smith Wigglesworth and a host of other Pentecostal Healing Evangelists; the 1947 Latter Rain Revival; the 1948 Healing Revival; the Charismatic Renewal of 1960s; the Jesus Movement of the late 1960s and early 1970s; the Third Wave Movement of the 1980s, and the "Laughing Revival" of the 1990s.

Perhaps one of the reasons "impartation" became the most forgotten and most neglected "elementary teaching" of the New Testament church is because, through prophecy and the laying on of hands, God is in the "driver's seat" of the local church and the church. He appoints, He calls, He empowers, He sends to the nations, and He truly is leading His church. Church is no longer a safe place to visit. You can no longer set your clock by the liturgy when God runs things by His Spirit.

Impartation has been a powerful tool of the Holy Spirit in the spreading of each of these mentioned moves of God around the world. I know that the Toronto Blessing was only a part of the "Laughing Revival" as some have called it, but through Toronto alone, over 55,000 churches were touched by the Spirit in just the first year. Millions of people came to what began in a little storefront church at the end of an airport. The most amazing thing about the Toronto Blessing was how *transferable* it was. One newspaper article in London likened it to the Beijing flu. How was it transferred? It was transferred primarily through the laying on of hands, often accompanied with prophecy. Now, after nearly twelve years, it is still being transferred around the world. But, it is only being received and still being transferred in those places where people are willing to allow God to take control and lead His church.

In this new millennium, we Christians no longer find ourselves in a predominantly Christian culture. We now find ourselves in a pagan culture in much of the world. We are more similar to the first two centuries after the Crucifixion and Resurrection of Jesus than at any other time. If the church is to be the leaven that leavens the whole lump, if we are to see the kingdom of God ever expanding, then we will not be able to trust in our might or power, but must rely on the Spirit of God (Zechariah 4:6). We need to recapture all the "elementary teachings" of Hebrews 6:1-2, including the one most lost in the history of the church—the laying on of hands.

I agree with Pope John Paul II who in his major encyclical, *The Splendor of Truth,* reaffirmed the importance, even necessity of the working of the Holy Spirit unbound from the rationalistic approaches of our day, free to do His work in the "new evangelism":

> At the heart of the new evangelization and of the new moral life which it proposes and awakens by its fruits of holiness and missionary zeal, there is *the Spirit of Christ,* the principle and

strength of Holy Mother Church. As Pope Paul VI reminded us: "Evangelization will never be possible without the action of the Holy Spirit." . . . As Novatian once pointed out—here expressing the authentic faith of the Church—it is the Holy Spirit "who confirmed the hearts and minds of the disciples, who revealed the mysteries of the Gospel, who shed upon them the light of things divine. Strengthened by his gift, they did not fear either prisons or chains for the name of the Lord; indeed they even trampled upon the powers and torments of the world, armed and strengthened by him, having in themselves the gifts which this same Spirit bestows and directs like jewels to the Church, the Bride of Christ. It is in fact he who raised up prophets in the Church, instructs teachers, guides tongues, works wonders and healings, accomplishes miracles, grants the discernment of spirits, assigns governance, inspires counsels, distributes and harmonizes every other charismatic gift. In this way he completes and perfects the Lord's Church everywhere and in all things.[66]

Ralph Martin—addressing contemporary Roman Catholicism in his book *The Catholic Church at the End of an Age: What is the Spirit Saying?*—has insightful analysis that has parallels for Protestants:

I remember when the contemporary manifestations of the charismatic renewal first broke out in the Catholic Church in 1967 some theologians opined that the charismatic gifts of the Spirit were really not necessary in the twentieth century since they were given to the early Church because she lived in the hostile environment of a pagan society and needed such manifestations of the Holy Spirit to confirm the preaching of the gospel.

I hope it is clear from the previous chapters and the witness of our own experience that we are no longer living in a Christian society and that we need all the 'power from on high' that we can get. How rapidly Christendom is dissolving before our eyes! How rapidly one age of Church history is ending and another is beginning! How much has changed in the last twenty-five to thirty years! How quickly we are again coming to the situation the early Church was in as she lived her life and preached the gospel in the midst of a pagan society. How desperately we need a new Pentecost![67]

I might add that this restoration of the gifts of the Spirit must also include a restoration of all the dimensions of the lost doctrine of the New Testament church—the laying on of hands. It must include the one "elementary teaching" most stolen from the church by the devil—the doctrine of "laying on of hands"—which included the understanding of "impartation" of both gifts and the Holy Spirit Himself. Why has this doctrine been so fought by the devil? Because of its power to bless the church. For this reason, the devil will fight by using misunderstanding and division within the church to stop the restoration of the ministry of impartation. Until this doctrine is fully restored to the church, she will not be able to claim that all grace is at work in her."

We have considered the reality of "impartation" from Scripture, my personal story, and from the testimony of history. Beginning with the story of Rolland and Heidi Baker—how they received powerful impartations and the resulting events now taking place in Mozambique—in the next section of this book I want to share with you powerful stories illustrating the immense fruit which can follow impartation. These are stories of people from around the world, with different backgrounds, and involved in different ministries. The commonality is a shared experience with the power of God—some having even received an impartation to see into the spiritual realm—that radically transformed not only their personal walk with Jesus, but their ministry. You will see how they have been pushed into the harvest field because of their experiences, and what the lasting fruit has been.

PART II: INTO THE HARVEST FIELD – FRUIT

THAT WILL LAST

"YOU DID NOT CHOOSE ME, BUT I
CHOSE YOU AND APPOINTED YOU TO GO
AND BEAR FRUIT – FRUIT THAT WILL
LAST."

JOHN 15:16

"ASK THE LORD OF THE HARVEST,
THEREFORE, TO SEND OUT WORKERS
INTO HIS HARVEST FIELD."

LUKE 10:2B

CHAPTER 6: EXTREME PASSION – A NEW MODEL IN MOZAMBIQUE

I would like to introduce you to a move of God that is perhaps seeing the most phenomenal harvest of souls of the present day. My dear friends in this ministry are reliving every word and page of the Book of Acts, proving that Jesus Christ is indeed the same—yesterday, today and forever! (Hebrews 13:8)

Rolland and Heidi Baker are long-term missionaries in Mozambique, Africa. Their saga is so remarkable; the stories of miracles, divine appointments, provision, heroism and heart-rending experiences could fill several volumes. They've written their own book, entitled *Always Enough* published by Chosen Books/Baker Book House in the United States and published outside the United States by Sovereign World under the title *There is Always Enough*. I highly recommend it! My attempt in this chapter is to tell of the connection God made between my ministry and theirs, specifically as it relates to impartation. The Bakers are my heroes; all I am is their cheerleader. For whatever reason, God did choose to use me to be a blessing to them.

THEIR BEGINNINGS

Just so you can appreciate the greatness of God and the faithfulness of God, let me begin with a little background. Rolland Baker is the grandson of H.A. Baker, an early Pentecostal missionary to China. Rolland grew up listening to his grandfather telling him stories of the miraculous work God led him to do among the Chinese. He listened to stories of children being taken up to heaven in visions, quoting passages from the Bible that they had never read, and more.[68]

Rolland's Story

Most of all, Rolland was impacted by stories of great sacrifice that his grandfather and grandmother made in order to take the gospel to the poorest of the poor, the orphans and street children of a remote region in China. H.A. Baker chose to serve those nobody else was interested in. In the hills of Yunnan Province, children were being forced to work in the tin mines. The owners would work them to death and then throw them away. Some of these children had escaped and made it to the streets of Kunming. There, Rolland's grandparents reached out to these nearly dead children, taking them into their orphanage. These children clothed in rags would become heaven's princes and princesses.

H. A. Baker never sent out appeals for money or tried to raise money through normal fundraising means. Instead, like George Mueller, who also ran an orphanage dependent upon God to answer his needs through prayer, he prayed for his needs to be met. And, they were! Other missionaries told him "You are wasting your time among these poor orphans," but they were wrong. God's strategy led to supernatural manifestations of His power in that region of China, which produced lasting results. Many of these boys grew up into mighty men of God. They poured out their lives, continuing to take the gospel to those who had not heard the name of Jesus, until they were either martyred or until natural death came to their worn out bodies which had been dedicated to the kingdom of God.

Rolland's father, James Eugene Baker, (H.A. and Josephine Bakers' only surviving child) was an Assemblies of God missionary who started three Bible Schools in Asia. He went home to be with the Lord in January of 2003 at eighty-nine years of age, survived by his wonderful wife of fifty-six years and co-laborer in the Lord, Marjorie. James was a powerful teacher, anointed and gifted to teach by the Holy Spirit.

Rolland has patterned his work in Mozambique upon the model he saw in his grandfather. The revival that God brought to this corner of China under H.A. Baker has sparked another revival on the continent of Africa two generations later. If the powerful prophetic vision and word received by his wife, Heidi, is really from God, what they have begun in Africa will touch the world.

Rolland is a cool headed, analytical man with the IQ of a genius. He turned down a full scholarship to Caltech in California, choosing instead to prepare for ministry. Rolland is also a man of great faith with a passion for people and for God. I remember when he told me the story about a twelve-year-old boy who died because there wasn't a tetanus shot in the whole nation of Mozambique. Rolland had driven to South Africa to get the medicine, but by the time he returned the boy had died. Though this had happened about a year earlier, his heart was still so moved with compassion and sadness for this boy, and the many others who have basic medical, physical, and spiritual needs, that tears filled his eyes as he shared this story. Rolland is God's oak tree, planted by the waters, which shall not be moved.

Heidi's Story

Heidi, on the other hand, is God's babbling brook. She is the most passionate woman for God's presence and face that I have ever met. She is the Protestant "Mother Teresa." And she married "George Mueller" (Rolland). What a couple. She is effervescent, joyous, child-like in her faith, a mystical person who practices the immediacy of God. God is her best friend and she is madly in love with Jesus. Rolland said this about Heidi, "When I met Heidi she was like a twelve-year-old child in her faith in trusting God. When she was touched at the Toronto Airport Christian Fellowship she became like a six-year-old in her simple trust in her Heavenly Father."

Heidi did not grow up on the mission field like Rolland. Instead, she grew up in an affluent area of southern California, part of an upper middle class family. I share a little more about her that the reader might better appreciate the supernatural call upon her life.

Her parents, James and Glenetta Farrell, adopted a boy, Zachary, whom they lost at an early age to congenital heart disease. Later, they faced the prospect of losing Heidi as well. During that time, Heidi's mother cried out to God, "Lord, let her live and I will give her back to you." I believe God accepted Glenetta's prayer because Heidi seems to have always been strongly drawn to the spiritual dimension of life. She grew up desperate to know God, often crying out as a young girl, "God, where are you?"

One of Heidi's most important school experiences happened when she was in the 6th grade. She had a teacher who had been a missionary, who had just returned from the mission field. This missionary would show pictures and tell about the refugee children where she had ministered. Heidi would hear these stories and weep. God was putting in her a heart for the nations even before she was "born again."

In high school Heidi went to work with the Choctaw Native Americans in Mississippi as part of a Peace Corps mission. During this time she went to hear a Native American preacher on the reservation. When the invitation was given, Heidi ran to the altar to give her life to Jesus. She was weeping and wailing so loudly they tried to calm her down, telling her everything was okay, that she hadn't been such a bad sinner. She just cried out, "No, it's not all right! I am a sinner!" She was 16 years old at the time.

Heidi began to attend a Pentecostal Holiness Church where it would not be abnormal to experience very expressive worship accompanied by tambourines, people jumping with joy and excitement, tongues, prophecies, long dresses, bee hive hair-dos, no make-up, prohibition on women wearing slacks and other blended expressions of both Holy Ghost power and a legalistic religion. She was touched in a church that was confusing legalism with holiness—nonetheless, a church open to the presence of the Holy Spirit.

One night, Heidi went to the altar seeking more of God. Everything went to a brilliant white light and she heard the audible voice of God. Among other things, Jesus told her she would be a missionary to Asia, England and Africa. This amazed her as she did not think women could be preachers. Because this communication did not come from her, she went out from that point with great boldness. She has lived her life with extreme focus since the age of sixteen, without doubting or looking back.

In California, the Holy Spirit told Heidi not to marry the man she was engaged to—he was not the right one for her. Her marriage would be an "arranged marriage," not by her parents, but by God. During Christmas 1979, on a mission trip to Mexico City, she again heard an audible voice from Jesus that said, "You are going to marry Rolland Baker." Rolland was a friend from the small church where they both attended. Occasionally, they had met for fellowship and prayer, but had never "dated." Jesus even told Heidi the day Rolland would ask her to marry him. Rolland proposed just as the word of the Lord had told her. When Heidi met his parents prior to their wedding, Heidi was shocked to find out that Rolland's mother was her sixth grade teacher, the missionary that God had used to build such a heart for missions in her life.

THEIR JOURNEYS BEGIN

Asia

Their lives were lived by faith from the beginning of their marriage. They left the wedding to go to the mission field of Indonesia with only $30.00 and their airplane tickets. They did not have any support but they had complete confidence that God would provide for their needs. Mel Tari met them on the island of Bali, and then had to leave them on their own after just one day. For the next five years, they spent several intervals of time in Indonesia until the government's policy against missionary visas forced them to leave in 1985.

For seven years, Rolland and Heidi led teams in several Asian countries, presenting the gospel through dramatic dance and song, as well as teaching. Released from the legalism of her early Christian experience, Heidi put her ballet training to good use. Rolland was gifted in photography and media production. Finally, they believed it was no longer the will of God for them to continue this method of going from one place to another with 3-4 day events. God was giving them His heart for the desperately poor. He was leading them to give themselves to the poor, to come alongside them with all they had and disciple those they led to the Lord.

They went to Hong Kong where they often worked with Jackie Pullinger, known for her ministry among the drug addicts of Hong Kong's poorest and most violent slum area, the "walled city."[69]

Once the police came to where they were living in a Hong Kong slum area, assuming these Westerners had been kidnapped. They couldn't believe anyone would voluntarily live in such circumstances. Heidi began sitting with the little grannies that lived in cage-like dwellings in subway tunnels, under bridges— anywhere they could find shelter. She showered them with love and they, in turn, taught her Cantonese. As God touched these homeless grannies, many of them were healed. Many brought Heidi their Buddhist idols so she could help destroy them. Soon a "granny" church developed.

At this time, Rolland began to notice a similarity between their ministry and his grandfather's. He preferred to start at the bottom rung of humanity, reaching out to the outcasts and "riff-raff" rather than following the strategy of many missions organizations that advise you to reach the "influential" people first. Although Rolland is an excellent teacher, his method of ministry isn't based upon teaching, but upon modeling. His philosophy of ministry is, "Don't tell people what you're going to do, just go do it. Don't tell people what to do, just do it, and ask others if they want to help."

By now, Rolland and Heidi had been blessed with two children, their son Elisha and their daughter Crystalyn. Both have grown up knowing little of what most Americans consider "normal." Their lives have been immersed in the miraculous and supernatural. Both are currently young adults in ministry school and plan to spend their lives on the mission field as well, continuing in this family's wonderful spiritual heritage.

London

After four years in the slums, Heidi became seriously ill. While convalescing in Fairbanks, Alaska, God spoke to Heidi about going to London to earn a doctorate degree. The idea seemed ludicrous to her. She was too sick to move, read, or even see. As she recalls, "God was teaching me about trust. There is always enough of everything we need, if we trust in Him alone." Turning the Hong Kong church over to their dear friend, Lesley-Anne Leighton, an anointed missionary co-worker from New Zealand, Rolland and Heidi left to study at King's College, University of London. Both were accepted into Ph.D. programs in Systematic Theology. In London, the couple studied the deep issues of Christian doctrine with some of the keenest minds in the church, then tried to figure out what all that theology was supposed to look like in practical life by ministering to the homeless in the parks at night.

Mozambique

In 1995, Rolland and Heidi heard the unmistakable call to go to what was then ranked the poorest nation in the world, Mozambique. A church had grown out of their London street ministry so, once again, they went through tearful good-byes as they turned over their precious flock to the care of others.

The horrors and trials that awaited them in Mozambique, a nation ravaged by seventeen years of civil war, deep poverty, corruption, and AIDS, defy description. Yet, God went with them.

They started with 80 children that no one wanted—children who were living like animals in a bombed out shell of a building with no power, water, windows, or plumbing. A backed up septic system had turned the grounds into an open sewer. The children scavenged for food in the bush and ate with bare hands. Corrupt caretakers, assigned by the government, beat the children and stole whatever meager rations the government sent for them. They owned just the rags on their backs and slept on hard concrete floors. Any furniture had long since been burned for fuel. The law of the jungle prevailed as these children only knew violence and theft as means of survival. Many had witnessed the brutal murder of a parent; many had been intentionally maimed, raped, and discarded...and the stories continue on. Satan, who comes to kill, steal and destroy, had certainly done his worst here. This was the battlefield—Chihango—where love would be put to the ultimate test. Could such evil be overcome with the goodness of God? You will just have to read their book to find out how God answered with a resounding, "Yes!"

TOUCHED BY GOD

Let me jump to 1997, where our stories meet. After fifteen years of serving in the slums of Indonesia, Hong Kong, and London, and a one and one-half years among the broken children of Mozambique, Rolland and Heidi were in desperate need of a fresh touch from God. I believe that just as God set up a divine appointment for Cornelius who also served God's people (Acts 10), God was setting up a divine appointment for Rolland and Heidi. God set up an appointment with Himself and the Bakers' in Toronto, Canada.

Toronto

Rolland had gone to Toronto before Heidi ever did. He made his first trip to attend the second Catch the Fire Conference held in October 1995. He stepped into a revival atmosphere, an atmosphere permeated by the presence of God Himself, in the midst of His people. Rolland was profoundly touched. He said that he would just weep and sob for hours as he walked up and down the aisles at the church during ministry time.

When Rolland called Heidi in Mozambique, Heidi said that he sounded like another man. When she heard his voice, it was soft and repentant. He told her how much he loved her, how much he appreciated her, and asked her to forgive him for not telling her enough. He was full of new joy and renewed by the Presence of Jesus.

114

When Rolland returned to Mozambique, he insisted that Heidi also go to Toronto. He knew that she was exhausted physically, emotionally, and spiritually. The past seventeen years had taken its toll on her whole person. Heidi knew all this was true and wanted to go where God had touched her husband so profoundly. What God did to Rolland in Toronto made him a credible witness to her that this was truly a real move of God.

On the plane to Toronto Heidi cried out to God to touch her. She said, "God, if you don't touch me, I am so tired I would like to just take a job at K-Mart. I don't think I can continue in ministry without you touching me afresh." Though I know that Heidi would not have left the ministry, this expression did represent her sense of desperation.

Heidi made her first trip to Toronto Airport Christian Fellowship (TACF) in July 1996 for the Healing Conference. She was very sick at the time. When she first went to Toronto the doctor was afraid for her life. He was very uncomfortable with her making such a long difficult trip. She had severe blood poisoning, chronic fatigue syndrome, and pneumonia. Sharon Wright prayed for her at the conference and she was healed!

Rolland and Heidi both went to "The Party is Here" conference in the fall of 1996. Heidi wasn't too impressed, but when Rolland joined the speaker in a celebration call, Heidi began to laugh, fell to the floor, and had to be carried out of the meeting.

Heidi made her third trip to TACF in January of 1997. This was the third-year anniversary meeting and I was there as one of the guest speakers. During the first day there, Pastor John Arnott told me about Rolland and Heidi. He explained that God had touched Rolland, and now his wife, Heidi, had come to visit. All he told me, and all I knew about the Bakers at that time, was that they had been missionaries for seventeen years and for the past one-and-a-half years had been in Mozambique.

During those meetings I preached the message that I have preached many times. It is called "Pressing In." This is the sermon that I have seen God use to build faith for an impartation of fresh anointing of the Holy Spirit all over the world. Its bottom line message is that God is looking for people who are desperate to be used by Him—people who are not content to be average, but want to be mightily used of God. While I was preaching this message, about three-quarters of the way through, Heidi left her seat and came to the altar where she began to pray for God to touch her. Whenever one person makes this move in the meeting, the sermon is essentially over. Hundreds then immediately follow the lead of the first person and come to the altar to pray and to have hands laid upon them for prayer from myself and/or others on the ministry team for an impartation of the Holy Spirit and/or gifts of the Holy Spirit.

The Prophetic Word

I remember seeing Heidi praying at the altar. She looked up at me with tears streaming down her face. Immediately I was aware of a strong impression to speak the following prophetic word to Heidi. "Heidi, God wants to know, do you want the nation of Mozambique?" I didn't try to figure the word out; I just gave it. Heidi answered with a strong voice, "Yes!" Then I said, "God is going to give you the nation of Mozambique! You are going to see the dumb speak, the lame walk, the blind see, and the dead be raised!"

Immediately God backed up this prophetic word with His mighty power and presence. Heidi said that it felt like God immediately placed her in an oven, or put heaters around her because she had became extremely hot. I remember seeing her perspiring till her hair was wet from the sweat. I had seen this a few times before and knew it was from God, though I still don't understand what God is doing when this happens. I have just seen the fruit of these experiences of God's presence enough times to know it is God.

Heidi continued to feel so much power in her body that she was becoming afraid of the intensity. Finally the power of God was so strong that she said, "God,

I'm going to die!" Immediately, she heard the audible voice of God say to her, "Good, I want you dead."

The Promise of Revival

After this she heard God speak again in an internal voice, "Hundreds of churches and thousands of people." Upon hearing this Heidi began to laugh. This was the laughter of amazement and wonder at a word from God that was hard to believe could be possible. Then Heidi asked the Lord, "How? How can this be? Rolland and I have started four churches in seventeen years and it has nearly killed us!"

After a while Heidi lost all ability to move from her neck down. She was like a quadriplegic. She cried out, "God, this is getting too weird, even for me." Again she heard the Lord say, "What I am asking you to do is impossible for you to do by yourself. You are going to need the whole church to help you. I want you to know that I don't see things the way you do. I am going to send someone to help you, and the person I send is just as important to me as anyone who stands on the platform and speaks to thousands of people." Heidi remained helpless for extended periods of time while at the Toronto Airport Christian Fellowship. A friend would have to come and lift her head to help her drink.

This was the most powerful experience of the Spirit that Heidi had ever had in her life. It was the most intense, the longest in duration, lasting seven days and nights, and it produced the greatest fruit. Sometimes, when people saw Heidi in her state of helplessness and often drunkenness in the Holy Spirit, they would laugh at her thinking it was funny. Heidi told me, "No, it wasn't funny; it was actually very scary for me to be so utterly undone by the Spirit of God."

Since then, Heidi has experienced this phenomena many times. She has asked God, "Why do I get so touched by the Holy Spirit in North America that I appear to be drunk and often almost incapable of functioning, but in Africa these things don't happen to me?" God has showed her, "Human control is not an issue in Africa, but in North America control is a big issue. I want people to see

117

someone who is willing to be totally yielded to Me." Heidi has accepted that she is to be God's model of someone who is not embarrassed to be totally yielded, regardless of how weird it might look to others.

STANDING ON THE PROMISES OF THE PROPHETIC WORD

It's important to be aware that receiving a prophetic word doesn't mean suddenly everything is going to become easy. More often, the prophetic word is what God uses to strengthen us during those difficult times that are soon to follow. I have noticed that there is often a relationship between the intensity of an experience with God and the degree of difficulty the person will be facing in fulfilling the call of God on their lives. The prophetic word, with its powerful experience in Toronto, would soon be tried. Initially, it certainly did not look as if the prophetic word from me was true in the natural. Instead, just the opposite seemed to be happening.

Tribulation

During the next eighteen months the Bakers would face great obstacles, suffer great loss, and experience many personal trials and tribulations. Heidi was soon diagnosed with multiple sclerosis. Her doctor told her that if she went back to Mozambique she would certainly die. She had gone to the doctor because she was having problems with falling and losing strength in her body. The doctor strongly advised her not to return to Mozambique. Her response was, "I have a prophetic word from God that He is going to give me the nation of Mozambique. If I have to preach from a wheelchair until God raises me up then that is what I will do, but I must go back to Mozambique."

The enemy seemed to be throwing all he could against the Baker family after this prophecy. Not only did Heidi come down with MS, but also Rolland ended up in the hospital with cerebral malaria. This can be a life threatening disease, especially in Mozambique, which has the worst health care of any country in the world. Their daughter, Crystalyn, was stricken with malaria three times during the next year. Elisha, their son and eldest child, also went through a very difficult emotional time following the prophetic word I gave Heidi.

The good news is that God brought them all through. Heidi believes she was healed of her MS through the prayers of the young orphanage children. She told me, "Whenever I would fall down the children would run to me and pray for me and say, 'It is okay, Mama Aida. Jesus is going to heal.' I rapidly got stronger until there were no more symptoms." Rolland recovered from his cerebral malaria and Crystalyn survived the three bouts of malaria in a short period of time. God was also faithful to bring Elisha through his emotional battle.

The enemy didn't just attack their health; he came against their finances, their support for their mission work. A high percentage of their support came from one church in the United States that believed what was happening in Toronto was deception and from the devil. Rolland and Heidi were admonished to distance themselves from Toronto, or lose their support.

This was one of the most difficult things the Bakers would face following the prophecy I gave Heidi in Toronto. This church had been their most loyal and staunch supporter. The pastor of the church was led to help them by the strong leading of the Holy Spirit some years earlier. This rejection was most difficult to bear. But, again, they stood their ground. They could not deny that what had happened to them in Toronto was of God. They were convinced it was. Their experience in Toronto cost them almost all of their pledged support.

Again, God was faithful. God spoke to the pastor of this church and instructed him to continue to support them from his personal finances, though the church remained firm in its earlier position. In addition, God began to give the Bakers favor with many churches around the world. During all this time it remained the position of the Bakers to not send out appeal letters, newsletters soliciting support, or even to tell others about their needs. God is and always will be the Rock upon which they stand. He is the Faithful One.

During this first year after receiving the prophetic word, the enemy expanded his attack to the orphanage itself. This was no ordinary orphanage. Heidi had rescued all these children from the streets and dumps where they had been discarded. God would give Heidi visions or dreams in which she would be made aware of where a child had been abandoned. She would then go to where God showed her and find the child. So powerful was this foundation of love that secular psychologists from European countries came to study the children. They could not figure out how the children could be so well adjusted when they had been through so many terrible things prior to coming to the orphanage. The answer was the love of God which they personally experienced through the Holy Spirit during times of worship, and which was demonstrated by the staff of missionaries and nationals who worked together for the glory of God to rescue these throw-away children. The Bakers and their staff had spent two years of time, labor, and money fixing up Chihango for these children, only to lose it all, when to everyone's shock government officials summoned Heidi one day to serve a forty-eight-hour eviction notice! Actually, it was a document demanding that the Bakers either comply with a long list of conditions or turn over the keys. They were to sign a paper saying they would no longer read the Bible, speak about Jesus, pray with the children, sing Christian songs, rescue any more street children, dispense medicine, etc. Of course, they could not make any such promises. As Heidi sobbed for her children in the Chihango office, a scornful official laughed and taunted her as he took the keys, saying, "You will never even talk to these children again!" Soon after, Heidi discovered a contract had been put out on her life as well.

What were Rolland and Heidi to do with the orphans? By now they had nearly 350 of them! And none of them wanted to stay behind under government staff. More important than the certainty of food and a roof over their heads, they wanted love—the love of Jesus that was being manifested through His people. Carrying everything they could on their heads, they followed "Mama Aida" and "Papa Rolland" and marched during the night, in pouring rain, out of Chihango.

The Bakers were out of money; they had no place for them to stay, no beds, no buildings, nothing. All they had was their little flat in Maputo. About one hundred of the children went with them to the flat, overflowing every room, the garage and driveway, even the bathtub. The other two hundred were placed with friends or returned to the streets. They continued to meet together for church in open fields.

Miracles

During those first few days God worked a miracle; a Baptist lady who heard of their plight took a pot of beans and chili over to the Bakers saying, "Heidi, this is for your immediate family." Heidi went to the back door, opened it, pointed to the orphans and said, "I have a large family." God multiplied the beans and chili as Heidi shared her food with not only her immediate family, but also the staff, and the one hundred orphans. Miracles happen in times of the greatest need.

Considering all the hardships, opposition, and apparent "failures," I'm not sure how many of us would have continued to believe the prophetic word I gave Heidi. Many have received a prophetic word or other direction from the Lord, yet lacked the faith to step out on it. Because Heidi believed the promises spoken to her, she began to pray for the deaf, the lame, and the blind. However, even though she prayed for every blind person she met, an entire year went by without seeing one blind person healed. She persisted because of the word that was given to her. Suddenly, in three provinces, Heidi and her staff prayed for three completely blind women and all were healed. The interesting thing is that all three women were named "Aida," the Portuguese translation of "Heidi." When Heidi told me this, I told her it was a sign that God wanted to open her spiritual eyes to see in the spiritual realm.

What happened after the eviction from Chihango? God continued to be their provider. Within two weeks, the Christian president of a nearby town, Machava, gave them a piece of property and a local church loaned them the use of a building for ninety days. Soon all 200 scattered children were reunited.

Needing a large tent for shelter and meetings, Heidi called a company in South Africa and told them she needed a circus tent immediately that would hold 1,000 people. They told her it would take six months to have one made. Heidi persisted and asked them to check again as she was sure God had directed her to their company. They called back in about twenty minutes to tell her that, sure enough, someone had ordered a tent several months before but had failed to pick it up! It would cost $10,000. Heidi responded, "We'll take it!" She didn't say Iris Ministries had no money. That very day, someone in California made a $10,000 donation to their ministry. But how were they going to set this huge tent up? The U.S. Embassy called. It was extremely rare for a U.S. Navy ship to be in Maputo harbor, but one was there. The men were restless and had called the embassy asking if there was something helpful they could do. Iris soon had the needed set-up crew!

Yet the greatest miracle was not one of healing or provision, but the birthing of a miraculous church-planting movement that now encompasses over 6,000 churches in ten nations. That is the subject of another chapter!

Let us take a look at others who have been touched by the current revival. Many will tell their own stories and share about the impact that impartations have had on them, as well as the lasting fruit that has been a part of their lives since these impartations. You will see how suddenly their lives were changed after their experiences with the presence and power of God.

CHAPTER 7: THE FRUIT OF CURRENT REVIVAL

The current renewal movement known as the "Toronto Blessing" has its full share of critics. Books and radio sound bites have made much of the rarest and bizarre physical phenomena, but say nothing of the profound changes God has worked in the hearts and spirits of countless thousands of worshippers. John Wesley once prayed, "Lord, send us revival without defects, but if this is not possible, send revival defects and all." He then said, "Careful people will assess the fruit of manifestations. Wise people will rejoice in what can be rejoiced in but will be slow to put all phenomena down to God. It seems we are going to have to live in the tension of rejoicing with caution!"

How sad it would be if the critics were correct in their charge that the manifestations of falling, shaking, laughing, electricity, etc. are the end in themselves? What good would that be? This renewal is so much deeper and bigger than that—so much bigger and deeper than any of us ever imagined in the beginning. Eleven-and-a-half years into this movement, one of the consistent themes and powerful works of the Holy Spirit is still to reveal the heart of the Father to restore and refresh His children. But there is another major theme. I feel it's important to discuss this since it addresses one of the chief concerns of those who remain skeptical. **Is this movement bearing lasting fruit for the kingdom? The answer is the great, untold story of this renewal.**

In one of the early renewal meetings in Toronto, David Ruis was leading worship and sang, "Let Your Glory Fall." The song asked for God's glory to fall in that place and then go forth to the nations. The first time I heard the song I said, "That will be the theme of this revival." This theme rang in my ears. I knew from history that missionary expansion always follows a period of revival in the church. As people are touched by the Holy Spirit, their love for Jesus is reignited so they respond to His call to the nations. They are conformed to the character of Christ and infused with His compassion for the lost. They are equipped with power to change the world.

Since this book is about impartation, I would like to share just a few stories of those who have been powerfully impacted by the renewal, in particular after I had the privilege of laying hands on them and praying for an increase of God's anointing in their lives and ministries. Just as men like Blaine Cooke and John Wimber imparted into my life, I have tried to be obedient to the command of Jesus, "Freely you have received; freely give" (Matthew 10:9). No one has been more surprised than me at how God has used this simple act of obedience to ignite the fires of revival around the globe!

After hearing that I was working on this book, many people sent me their testimonies as to how the impartation of gifts and anointing has impacted their lives. These stories will help you understand how quickly an impartation can change a person's life. To follow are summaries and excerpts from what they sent to me. As much as possible, in view of space constraints, I would like you to hear their stories in their own words.

ANIBAL MINDYK, ARGENTINA

I received the baptism of the Holy Spirit as I was praying one day on my own. During that time, I received the call to minister. In 1991, I began a church under the ministry of Omar Cabrerra. When Randy Clark came to Argentina in 1996 and was visiting our "Vision of the Future" churches, I received a word from the Lord through him. A friend wrote the prophecy down for me that day and I still carry it with me. What my friend remembers and wrote is, "God has given you a unique or specific anointing that will have great impact. He will send you to the U.S. and many countries as well as Canada with signs and wonders. You will be a prophet of fire."

That was the beginning of a twenty-day visitation from the Lord. An angel came with a torch of fire in his hand and put it in my hand. Then the angel made me swallow the torch. It burnt my mouth and throat. When it reached my stomach, it caused an explosion in which I screamed and screamed. Then I could not walk for twenty-two days without being slain in the Spirit when I tried to get up. Every little sin was magnified 1000 times. I would go nights crying in God's presence. People would have to hold me up to preach. Then everyone in the church would fall out or fall out and laugh and laugh. In the first meeting a woman with bone cancer had her arm in a cast, eaten away with cancer, and she was totally healed. Many miracles and signs and wonders have continued happening since.

JIM MANDEL, PHILADELPHIA, PENNSYLVANIA

In 1999, Jim was a businessman making about $500,000 a year, but he was an alcoholic and smoked a lot of marijuana. When he was thirty-four he experienced the Lord in a powerful way when Evangelist Bob Shattles prayed for him. He remembers that when Bob laid hands on him, "I shot back six feet like somebody hit me with a bolt of lightning" where he laid for about two hours shaking uncontrollably. His wife helped him home where he laid on the couch for three days while being taken up into heaven.

He received another powerful impartation while attending the Voice of the Apostles conference hosted by Global Awakening in 2003 in Harrisburg. Mandel says, "[When] Randy began to speak about a call to the nations with signs and wonders…I began to weep and could not stop crying." During the altar call Jim went up to the front to receive prayer. Then he describes his experience in his own words, "I started to feel my body tremble and shake like I was cold, but I was hot. Then Randy laid his hands on my head and it felt like a jolt of electricity shaking my body with force and I fell to the ground" and continued to shake. "When I was done, I got up and felt very dizzy and weak like my body lost muscle control. This lasted for about two hours. . . " Then he went home with joy because he knew that he received the impartation he was looking for.

Since these two powerful impartations, many miracles have taken place in Jim's life and ministry. In 2003, right after this impartation, he went to India and saw a crippled man being totally healed and made straight; many blind eyes and deaf ears opened; cancer, diabetes, paralysis and AIDS were all healed. In the United States he saw a girl who was in a coma with eight days to live totally healed and released from the hospital after prayer. In Mexico, the power of God fell on Jim as he held a small child handed to him by the mother. When he set the child down, everyone began shouting for joy. The formerly crippled and mute child was now running and crying out "Mama!" In a Mayan village, the power of God fell on the chief priest who suffered from severe chest pains. After the priest's healing, approximately 160 villagers received the baptism of the Holy Spirit and were healed of many sicknesses. Jim attributes these miracles and the increase of power to receiving an impartation.

MIKE KAYLOR, FORT LAUDERDALE, FLORIDA

To say that I was disillusioned with my life and ministry would be an understatement. Thirty years in ministry and five "movements" later I found myself asking the same question I had asked when I was a teenager in a Baptist church. "Is this all there is?" I was so desperate for the reality of the present day presence of God that I found myself consuming books of past revivals and their evangelists. I was tired of meeting with God's people but not meeting with God. "If God doesn't show up, I don't want to go on with pretense anymore," was the statement I found myself continually repeating.

For many years I had known about Randy Clark and had crossed paths with him on occasion. After all, it was at a meeting in Toronto with Randy that my wife had been healed of a debilitating pain in the upper part of her back and shoulders which no doctor could explain. I had heard of the tremendous outpouring of power and impartation happening in Randy's ministry trips and I knew that if my hunger was to be addressed, I needed to go where Heaven seemed to be opened. So, I made the arrangements and found myself on my first ministry trip with Randy, headed to Brazil.

One of the wonderful blessings of being on the trip was the fact that there was a special time set aside to pray for impartation for the team. As I stood waiting for "my time" to be prayed for, my mind raced with excitement and wonder as I saw people respond to the prayer with a myriad of reactions. I thought to myself, "What if I am the only one in the room that nothing happens to?" Before I could finish the thought Randy was standing in front of me and began to pray as he laid his hand on my forehead.

I suddenly found myself on my knees with uncontrollable shaking and my arms flailing all over the place. "What is going on?" I thought to myself. Then I realized I was in a place where I could either go with it or try to stop it. Who in their right mind would try and stop the very answer to years of prayer for more of the reality of

God. So I said, "Lord, let it come."

What happened next was not what I expected although to be honest I had no idea what to expect. A heat started on the inside of me until it consumed my whole body from head to toe. I felt like I was on fire! As this impartation continued I heard the Lord say, "You wanted it, you've got it!" I felt a strange tingling sensation going into my forehead. It was as if an angel placed something in my forehead, which happened three times. I began to receive an understanding about the realm of the angelic and the angels that had been assigned to me. The impartation continued into the next night with me having to be carried out of the meeting because I was unable to stand, much less walk.

The next day, as I began to process what had happened to me, I began to notice a difference during ministry time. As I prayed for a young girl, I felt a gust of wind come over me in a room that was totally enclosed. I asked my translator if she had felt it and she said that she hadn't. Then when it happened again she said, "No, but the Lord was making you sensitive to the angelic." I then was reminded of what the Lord had shown me concerning the angelic.

The following night I ministered at a Baptist church in Joinville, Brazil. When ministry time came, I laid my hand on the forehead of one of the young men. To my surprise, he literally flew back in the air eight feet. I looked at my hand and thought, "Something is really different!" The next person I prayed for was in need of healing. As I began to pray for her, she said that the area she needed healing in was becoming hot. She received her healing and I moved on to the next person and they told me the same exact thing. Heat was surrounding the area that needed healing!

I knew then that something wonderful had been imparted to me. These things had never happened before. One of the exciting things is that as I prayed for impartation for others, many of them seemed to receive the same consuming fire of God. As John Wimber said, "Whatever you receive, go and give it away." I felt like it was Christmas and I was going around giving away free gifts to anyone who would take them.

I fully believe that the impartation or download from heaven was given not because of anything that could be done to attain it. It came in response to a deep hunger that brought me to a place where I could receive.

PASTOR SILVIO, SAO PAULO, BRAZIL

We received the impartation through few ministries. There was a radical change in our lives. We went through a great renewal. We were traditional Baptists and we had a lot of resistance for this type of movement. It was in the year 2000 that we start to leave the traditionalism. In the year 2001, we had in our church Pastor Randy who contributed to this renewal. Through Pastor Randy, I could feel a big heat that came through the Holy Ghost. It was a glorious state. After this happened to me, my ministerial and personal life were transformed. Today I have the intense presence of God's Glory in my life and through His grace I have imparted this same anointing to other people.

In the beginning there was a great resistance from my family and church. When God started to move among us, the things got out of control. Some people thought that all that was emotional or that we were exaggerating. Others thought that all of that was just momentary. After a while, people started to see our transformation and soon they saw that it was not emotion but something that came from God.

After the revival in our church there was a need to change some things in our doctrine. Note: Pastor Randy Clark was with us three times. The first time in 2001, our church was traditional and we had around 350 people. When Randy came for the second time we already had moved and we had around 1200 people in our church. The third time we already had 3000 people. I know that this anointing came to bring another anointing, like the anointing to conquer the city, multitudes and the growth of the churches.

The anointing has a price. We lost dear friends who are pastors because they believed that I was not acting according to the Word of God and even today, they say I am in a very delicate situation. However, although all this happened, today we still have much more anointing and we know that this is better than everything.

FATHER BOB JEPSON (ANGLICAN), OCEANSIDE, CALIFORNIA (IN A LETTER TO RANDY)

I was ordained a priest in 1972. About that time I heard and read about the charismatic renewal. I experienced a deep desire for this experience of greater intimacy with God and to be filled with the Spirit and receive the supernatural gifts.

Also, I began conducting a weekly healing service in the parish where I served and witnessed a number of marvelous miracles. The first was the healing of bladder cancer in a woman I prayed for. The doctor confirmed all trace of cancer was gone one week after I prayed with her. In 1994 the Holy Spirit put it on my heart to pray for revival, for the nation and for the church. I heard about Rodney Howard-Browne and went to his meetings at the Abiding Place and received an impartation (1998, I believe).

When you [Randy] spoke at the Abiding Place, I obtained a copy of your book *Lighting Fires* which gave me tremendous encouragement. As a pastor, I related to almost everything in your journey. I grew up very insecure, extremely shy. By the grace of God, I've overcome depression, deep shame, self-hatred, and the fear of failure. My heart and passion has since been for a healing ministry, to see people come to Christ and be transformed by the love and power of God—the Father's love.

Now I've caught the mission virus, in great part thanks to you and my participating in the Brazil trip. I was blown away at those meetings in Curitiba and Recife. As I prayed for hundreds, I witnessed the healings, the signs and the wonders. God used me to transfer the anointing to many, including a woman psychiatrist who sought the anointing in order to bring emotional healing to her clients, and a woman pediatrician who told me God was calling her to preach Jesus in poor churches! Almost everyone I touched reported back that all their pain left their bodies. One night in Recife, when you prayed over the team, I went down and while lying on the floor of the cathedral I believe God spoke to me and said I was to take teams to South America wherever He opened doors. In July 2003, my wife, our son Peter and I spent three weeks in Arequippa, Peru. I taught and trained nine seminary students and the pastor of the Anglican church to pray for healing. We planned a healing service and fifty people attended. Several were healed physically. We had similar experiences at a youth conference and a women's prison.

I could tell many more stories of miracles. Let me add that in two mission trips to Uganda, both in 2001, I witnessed the same revival manifestations. In Kisoro, I taught thirty Anglican pastors on the healing ministry and for five days I was part of a team of sixteen Anglican and Pentecostal prayer warriors. This was my introduction to deliverance, big time. One Muslim man came to me for prayer saying that there was a "power in his head and this power tried to cast him in the fire." My response (what the Holy Spirit told me) was, "It is a demon that is trying to cast you into the fire and only Jesus can get rid of the demon." His reply, "I want to accept Jesus." Perhaps the greatest miracle I saw was deafness healed when I prayed for an older woman. She explained to me that "something popped in my ears and now they are fine!"

One final, exciting item. After you interviewed me and prayed for me in Redding, a woman came up to me and handed to me a vision of Bolivia, given to her during a forty-eight-hour intercessory preparation for the school there. *[Author's note: Father Jepsen has since led two ministry teams to Bolivia.]*

Randy, God used you to set this very ordinary, very broken, Anglican priest on fire for missions. Like you, I'm so excited to live to see this day of revival and be a part of this move of God shaking the nations (Isaiah 64).

TERESA SEPUTIS, CALIFORNIA

I had been a Christian for many years, having accepted Jesus as my Savior at age fourteen. But no one told me that Jesus had to be Lord (e.g. boss) of my life. So my Christian experience had not been very successful or powerful and I had never developed a deep and intimate relationship with God. That is why I ended up backsliding in my late 20s for about four or five years.

Shortly after I was married, I started feeling hungry for God, but I was afraid He would not want me back. I was afraid that God might strike me dead when I entered the sanctuary—but He did not. I began to read my Bible again and I noticed that what I saw at church and what I read in the book of Acts did not resemble each other. In the Bible, people were healed and set free from demonic oppression and God even spoke to them. But I wasn't seeing any of that at my own church or in my own life. And I began to wonder why.

That prompted me to seek God. I had never fasted before but decided to do a ten day fast and God spoke to me during that time. He told me that if I wanted to come back to Him, it had to be on His terms this time. He had to be the Lord and Master of every area of my life. I told God, "Lord, I have no idea how to do that. But if you will teach me, I am willing to give it a try."

That was the turning point. I started seeing God's victory in many areas of my life and I started hearing His voice clearly. My devotions and prayer time came alive. I began to get a real hunger for God and wanted to somehow serve Him. I enrolled at Fuller Theological Seminary. Although I dreamed of being in full-time ministry, I never thought it would really happen.

I began to have prophetic knowledge of people's needs, but I had never heard of the prophetic gift and didn't know what was happening. The pastor came to me and told me to stop prophesying or leave the church. But he would not tell me what prophecy was and I had no idea what behavior he wanted me to stop doing, so I did not know how to change my behavior to please him. I joined a Pentecostal inner-city church, but the Pentecostal practices pushed my comfort zone. I felt very frustrated because I did not seem to fit into any church culture. I was too Pentecostal for my old church and

I was not Pentecostal enough for the new one. So I began crying out to God, figuring that there had to be more to the Christian walk than what I was experiencing.

I got an email about some amazing meetings in San Francisco where God was showing up in unusual ways. That was in early April, 1994. I went to the meeting. A few people give testimonies about how God had changed their lives when He touched them at these meetings. When I got prayed for, I had this incredibly powerful encounter with God where my body began to shake. This lasted three hours, and during that time God kept telling me to trust Him. I got off the floor and walked over to a friend of mine. She was laughing and I figured I had just missed a good joke. She touched my arm and suddenly I was hit by the joy of the Lord. I started laughing and could not stop. I felt such a love for the people around me, even the ones who I did not know. That lasted from about midnight until about two in the morning. To my surprise, I still found that I had a lot of joy and my spirit felt happy when I woke up the next morning.

Those meetings went on daily for three weeks and I attended every one of them. I would go to work from 7:00 a.m. until about 6:00 p.m., then rush over to that church and stay there until about midnight or 1:00 a.m. And God met me powerfully each time I came. He began doing some inner healing in me and I began to feel loved and also to be able to love others with the Love of Christ.

I had a lot of "comp time" acquired at work and money was not an issue for me, so I kept taking time off work and flying to Toronto. I was even on the ministry team for a while. Randy did come and minister at several of the meetings when I was in Toronto. He laid hands on me and prayed for me multiple times. Every time he prayed for me, a passion for missions would burn in my soul.

There was another aspect of Randy's ministry that captivated me. He prayed for physical healings and people were getting healed. Randy seemed to expect healing to happen on a regular basis! One day, I was praying for people in the same general area as Randy was, and many of the people I prayed for were healed! I was a bit off in my thinking at the time, because I attributed the anointing to Randy instead of to the indwelling Holy Spirit, Who lived inside of me just like He lived inside of Randy. Fortunately, God is very patient in teaching us.

Randy came to minister in my home church in August of 1994. Late in the meeting I stopped praying for people and got in line to receive prayer from Randy. The song "Let Your Glory Fall" started playing. The chorus says, "Let Your glory fall in this room, let it go forth from here to the nations. . ." The power of God came on me and I ended up on the ground, surrounded by God's tangible presence. That song became a theme song over my life that I sang to the Lord all the time. I did not realize it then, but that song was a prayer and God would answer it.

In 1995, I joined a very small team that went with Randy to Moscow. Each night, after the conference, Randy would meet with us in the hotel to take testimonies and debrief with us. At the end of the debriefing session, Randy laid hands on some of the team members and prayed for them. Just after Randy prayed for me, the Lord began to speak to me and remind me how Randy had said, "I was not anyone special, but God can use little 'ole me." I found my spirit responding to God by welling up and saying, "God, Randy was a 'little 'ole me' and you used him. I am definitely a 'little 'ole me'—can You use me as well?" I saw God do all sorts of powerful things in Moscow at that conference. It became real to me that when I prayed for people, God would show up.

The second trip to Moscow in May of 1997 had more of an emphasis on prayer for physical healing, and I saw God do some amazing miracles when I prayed for people. I saw some deaf ears open and I saw some semi-crippled people walk, as well as several other smaller healings. The one that stands out most in my memory was when God grew back some missing body parts. There was a lady who had been in a fire and her kneecaps were burned off. When I prayed for her, God gave her new kneecaps! The thing that I took back from the second trip was that God really *will* heal the sick through me!"

[Author's Note: After returning from Russia, Teresa's ministry began to grow from very humble beginnings into an interactive, internet training school for intercession and prophecy called GodSpeak International. Thousands of students have participated, with many being launched into their own powerful ministries]

In June of 2001, we also started a healing school, where people learned to pray for the sick and see people really get healed. I sent out lessons and the students started sending back all sorts of powerful testimonies of how God healed the people they prayed for in response to the lessons. That convinced me that God really does want everyone in the body of Christ able to pray for and heal the sick. Recently that has become an important focus of my ministry.

In 2002, five days before leaving on a trip to Brazil, I was laid off from my software engineering job. I was shocked at losing that job and began to seek God for direction. Significant things happened to me on that trip with Randy. I had this incredible night where I saw the power and anointing of God in healing as never before. It seemed like everyone I would pray for was instantly healed. Each time I would start to pray for someone, almost as soon as I touched them, they would go flying backwards and fall to the ground shaking. When they got up, they were healed. I think I saw somewhere in the neighborhood of 50 or 60 healings that night. I felt that was a foretaste of what to expect from God in terms of healing ministry.

I had never seen this level of dramatic miracles before. I knew that this was happening under the strong anointing that was on Randy's ministry. Something inside of me kept telling me that God wanted to do that in my own ministry. When I got home from Belem, I knew that God was taking me out of secular employment to live by faith and work only full time for Him.

I have seen God open deaf ears and I have seen God open blind eyes, and I have seen crippled people walk. I feel that I am still growing up in the calling God has given me, but I am already seeing Him do the same sorts of things in my ministry that I saw Him do in Randy's. I can't help thinking of him as a spiritual father since God used him to impart into me, and to launch me into ministry. He also helped me gain enough boldness and confidence in the Lord to be able to conduct healing meetings in many different countries around the world.

DAYOUNG KIMN, CHINA

I first heard about "Toronto Blessing" from the late Jack Winter. It was 1995 when I first met Randy Clark at a meeting in Langley, British Columbia, Canada. At the end of the meeting, he invited people to receive prayer. At that time, my ministry was in the beginning stage in China. I visited the underground churches and trained them.

As I approached the front stage, Randy came down and I ran into him and asked for prayer. He prayed a very interesting prayer and this is how I remembered it. ". . . I pray for this man who is ministering to churches in China. Holy Spirit, fill him up! . . . I pray and impart all of my spiritual inheritance through the prayer I have received from Benny Hinn, John Wimber, . . ."

I did not remember the names of all those people but I felt very good and blessed. Following week I was on my way to China. As I was leading one of the meetings, I told the leaders that I was going to pray for all of them to do more of what Jesus promised we all could do. So, I invited Holy Spirit to touch them. I did not lay hands on anybody but the Holy Spirit moved among these leaders. I was told that many felt something and they were feeling heat in their bodies. One of the elderly ladies in her 70s who served the Chinese Red Army later told me that she was healed from severe arthritis. She could not sleep for forty years, she said. After the meeting, she got up to help her daughter work. After that, she went out ministering to the neighbors and brought them to the Lord. Someone told me that she brought about seventy people to the Lord. I also found out that many leaders whom I prayed with are pioneering more churches than ever and winning many souls to the Lord.

This made me think about what "impartation" was all about. Because of my experiences, I seriously meditated on the word, "impartation." In the year 2000, I began the ministry called Impartation Ministries International."

DR. DENISE MEISBURG, JACKSONVILLE, FLORIDA

About five years ago, I was attending a conference with my friend, Cheryl Schang. Cheryl had seriously damaged knees that no surgery or therapy could help. The medical professionals predicted her mobility would be severely impaired for the rest of her life. She believed in healing, and had been prayed for many times before, but was still waiting. Anyway, our conference was over and we noticed that some other meeting was going on in the facility next door so we went to check it out. As we walked in, Randy Clark was just finishing a message and leaving the stage to walk around and pray for people. As Cheryl came through the door, Randy suddenly said, "Somebody is getting their knee healed." Randy's ministry team prayed for Cheryl, and received accurate words of knowledge about other medical conditions that she had, but they were not praying for her knees. She had a heart condition, and it was healed, but not the knees! Randy was still asking, "Who's got the knee problem?" We cut through the crowd and got close enough for Cheryl to tell him, "It's me." Randy never touched her. Instead, he got on his knees and prayed very simply as he was bowed before her, "Jesus, I'm just the colt of the donkey you ride on." As Randy prayed that prayer, I felt a tangible wind blow across us. Cheryl was instantly healed. She started jumping and screaming, rejoicing and praising Jesus. In the midst of that, Randy turned to me and said, "And you, you will be involved in Jewish evangelism in Russia and the Ukraine regions." Randy had never met me and did not know I was Jewish. There were a few other things he didn't know.

As a little girl, probably first grade, I knew the reality of Jehovah. I still remember the vivid dreams I had at that time, dreams where I was flying around the world and somehow involved in "rescuing" people. In my early 20s, I came to know Jesus as my Messiah. I was led to be a part of the charismatic movement in the Catholic Church and became a cloistered nun under the ministry of Mother Angelica. After one year, I was sent out of the cloister with the counsel to become a medical missionary to the nations. I went to college and became an RN, but ended up getting married. My "missionary calling" was soon put on the shelf as I committed myself to ministering to my husband and our six children. Between family, a time-consuming nursing job, and home schooling our kids, how could I possibly be a missionary? But Randy's word was like God saying, "I haven't forgotten your call to the nations."

I decided, if God was going to use me, I'd better be prepared. I received my Bachelor degree in Biblical Studies at Berean University and a Masters degree in Religious Arts. I was ordained as a minister of the gospel by my pastor, Bishop Paul Zink, as a part of New Life International. Up to this point, I had not been involved in any kind of ministry except as an intercessor and as a leader of intercession at conferences. Over the next three years, I went at the invitation of Jewish Voice Ministries to Siberia, Ukraine and Belaruse, serving on teams that put on cultural festivals of Jewish music and dance. I was in charge of church relations, intercession and humanitarian aid. I would go in and meet with local churches, find the local intercessors, and start praying a month ahead of time for our four-day festival. At these festivals, interspersed between the music and dance, Jonathon Burnis would always share his testimony as a "completed Jew" and give an opportunity for the audience to receive the same experience with Jesus that he had. In every nation, at every event, we always experienced the awesome, profound, powerful, loving and mighty presence of the Lord God, wooing His people to receive the gift of salvation through Jesus Christ. We saw tens of thousands saved, and mighty acts of His miraculous wonderful healings.

I remember a young man in Berdansk; he was with his mother in a crowd of thousands. He had *never* spoken in his life and had the typical Down's-syndrome appearance. I received words of knowledge from the Holy Spirit and, applying these, prayed with the mother for his deliverance. We prayed for her son's healing in the mighty name of Jesus Christ. As I watched, the Down's-syndrome appearance seemed to "peel" off his face like a mask. Then he began to speak for the first time, saying, "Da, da" ("yes, yes"), as I asked if he knew how much God loved him. It was incredible!

In Krasnayarsk, Siberia, I met a group of twenty or so women who had been meeting faithfully, deep in the woods, to pray for revival for ten years! When they came into the prayer room I had set up, I could feel the intense presence of God. In a vision, I saw the arms of God reaching across Russia, as if to draw the nation into His heart. I heard God say that all of Russia would hear the gospel of Jesus Christ. Our meetings there were filled with God's manifest visitation and many miraculous healings. God healed a woman's blind eyes and one of her ears that was totally deaf. There were about eight thousand decisions for salvation in Jesus' name during the festival. Later I learned from Ian Ross that Hudson Taylor, the famous missionary to China, had once prophesied that a revival would break out in Russia, beginning in the heart of Russia. Krasnayarsk is in the dead center of Russia!

In Minsk, we met with five underground churches in spite of the totalitarian government's severe restrictions and penalties against unauthorized religious activity. We gave an altar call for those in the crowded hall to receive Jesus Christ as their Lord and Savior, and we ministered the loving healing of Jesus to His people. You can go to prison there for even talking about Jesus. Still, the people came and God worked many miracles there.

Randy's prophetic word was a pivotal event in my life. It changed my self-perception in regards to my calling beyond that of a wife, mother and nurse. It encouraged me to become equipped and ready. The prophetic word makes room for what God wants to do, if you'll believe it and act on it. I believe God has led me to be diligent and responsible to that word.

In 2003, I finished a doctorate degree in counseling so that I could get out into the secular marketplace. Through a grant, I have been able to set up a counseling practice that is offered, free of charge, to high-risk teens. Many have come to know Jesus and experienced His powerful, healing touch. I am also involved in marriage, family, abuse, addiction, and PTSD counseling.

In 2004, my husband and I went to the Catch the Fire conference in Toronto. We specifically went there from Jacksonville, Florida in order to thank Randy for his impact on my life five years previous. As I shared my testimony, he prophesied over me again, this time saying I was to be involved in national Jewish evangelism.

Randy didn't know that my husband and I were already just getting started with teaching the 'HaYesod' program, which is basically a Jewish roots class for Gentiles. Because of Randy's second word, I have reformatted the course to a curriculum to reach Jews, patterned after the Alpha course. God is now helping me finish this curriculum as I meet with other Messianic Jews for their input and ideas and pray for the plan of God on this issue. He is already opening doors to getting it published. I'm now teaching in Florida where there are over one million Jews. I hope this will be a pilot program for all of the U.S. as a strategic and reproducible course.

Three of our six children are now actively involved in missions. I know our ten-year old twin daughters, the youngest ones, have a calling on their lives as well. Jubalee was born dead; she had been dead for nearly twenty minutes. I remember shouting across the delivery room, "Jubalee, in the name of Jesus Christ, the same Spirit that raised Jesus from the dead quickens your mortal body and you will live and not die!" God restored her back to life and within an hour she had pulled out every tube that the doctors had inserted into her body! The girls have prophetically significant names given to me by God that proclaim the return of our King!

Randy's prophecy had a tremendous impact in helping me to take hold of God's calling, to exercise the faith to walk in it, and to have the motivation to prepare myself for its outworking. I have been privileged to see what I believe is only the beginning of a great, last days outpouring of God's glory in the world. But ministering in His power is not just about getting a prophesy or impartation. It's about knowing His heart. You can't use His power unless you know His heart! And that takes time. No prophecy or impartation can take the place of time with Jesus. Do you want to see His glory? Take the time to get to know Him!

The above testimonies from pastors, missionaries, and laypersons are glorious examples of how an impartation can radically change a person's life and ministry. Little wonder Jesus told His disciples to "wait" until they were clothed with power from heaven. These modern-day experiences certainly help us understand how that first small group of believers managed to change the world after Pentecost. What is the lasting fruit of impartation? Changed lives that have power to change the world! There are so many more stories of people who received impartations in our meetings that we couldn't begin to include them all in this book.[70]

In the next chapter I want to highlight an important kind of impartation—an impartation to "see." This kind of impartation is a key to greater miracles and more healings in one's life or ministry.

CHAPTER 8: IMPARTATION TO SEE

The Bible records several people *seeing* into the spiritual realm. Numbers 22:31 records Balaam's eyes being opened to see. "Then the Lord opened the eyes of Balaam, and he saw the angel of the Lord standing in the way with his drawn sword in his hand; and he bowed all the way to the ground." David also had his eyes opened to see the angelic in 2 Samuel 24:17. "Then David spoke to the Lord when he saw the angel who was striking down the people." In 2 Kings 2:9ff Elijah asks Elisha what he wants when he is taken up? Elisha responds that he wants a double portion of the Spirit that was upon Elijah. On the occasion of receiving this double portion anointing, Elisha saw what I believe were some of the heavenly host, some of the angels of God taking Elijah to heaven. In 2 Kings 6:17, Elisha prays for the eyes of Gehazi to be opened. "'O Lord, I pray, open his eyes that he may see.' And the Lord opened the servants eyes and he saw; and behold the mountain was full of horses and chariots of fire all around Elisha."

The New Testament also records events where people's eyes were opened to see into the spiritual realm and to see the angelic. Zacharias, the father of John the Baptist, saw the angel who appeared to him (Luke 1:11-12). Mary saw an angel who explained God's will for her (Luke 1:26-38). Mary Magdalene saw two angels near the tomb of Jesus (John 20:11-12). Peter is delivered from prison by an angel whom he saw (Acts 12:4-11). An angel appeared to Paul during the terrible storm at sea to encourage him (Acts 27:23-24). John, on the Isle of Patmos, received the Revelation of Jesus which was interpreted to him through an angel. Near the end of the book he sees the angel and falls down to worship it, but is told by the angel to worship God alone (Revelation 19:10).

In his book, *Jesus and the Spirit: A Study of the Religious and Charismatic Experience of Jesus and the First Christians as Reflected in the New Testament*, New Testament Professor James D. G. Dunn notes that visions and angelic visitations were one of three primary sources for authority in the lives of the earliest Christian communities. With the canon of Scripture, we have the benefit of an objective guide to the discernment of any experience. Nevertheless, it is important to note how God has continued, throughout history, to communicate with His people through means of supernatural visitation.

The prophecy I received on January 19, 1994, the night before I went to Toronto for the first time, changed my life. It gave me faith to expect a mighty outpouring of God, more than I had ever seen before in my life. However, months later I realized I had not appropriated nor recognized all that had been given to me through this prophecy. I had missed the "seeing" part of the prophecy. The prophetic word was, "Test me now, test me now, test me now! Do not be afraid, I will back you up. **I want your eyes to be opened to see My resources for you in the heavenlies, just as Elijah prayed that Gehazi's eyes would be opened.** And do not become anxious because when you become anxious you can't hear Me." (Emphasis added)

I realized many months later that I had been powerfully impacted by all of this prophecy, except the part about my eyes being opened to see His resources in heaven. Then, for about two years, I began to get other significant prophecies that had the same theme, "God wants you to see!" The most significant word I received came to me through the powerful, anointed servant of God, Ruth Heflin. I did not know who Ruth Ward Heflin was at the time, but she came to Philadelphia where I was ministering for 30 days to give me a word from the Lord she had received for me in Jerusalem.

Portion of the prophetic word given to Randy Clark at Deliverance Evangelistic Church, Philadelphia, PA. on Tuesday October 15, 1996:

For again and again thou shalt stand upon this platform and thou shalt begin to see in new realms of the Spirit; **for I remove every scale from thine eye and thou shalt see those things that thou hast longed to see;** thou shalt see that which is afar and that which is near. Thou shalt see that which is hidden and that which is revealed.

Thou shalt see in measures beyond any that thou hast experienced until this time. For it shall be the anointing of the seer that shall come greatly upon thee and **thou shalt see and describe that which thou seest and even as thou proclaimest it, so shall the miracles come forth, saith the Lord.**

For the seeing shall cause a new faith to be brought forth; a greater measure of faith than that which thou hast known; a greater measure of faith than that which thou hast walked in; a greater measure of faith than that which thou hast witnessed; **thou shalt see it in the heavenlies and thou shall speak it forth and so shall it be.**

This is the day, the day of the Lord. This is the day, the day of the Lord. This is the hour, the hour of visitation. This is the time, the time of manifestation; the manifestation of My Spirit, the manifestation of My power, the manifestation of My glory, the manifestation yea, of My mighty arm made bare with signs and wonders and miracles, signs and wonders—miracles—healings, yea a healing stream that shall flow to the north, the south, the east and west, and shall encompass all nations, a mighty healing stream, yea a mighty healing stream . . . (Emphasis added)

Because I had good friends who had prophetic gifts and open visions, my view of what it meant to "see" was somewhat skewed. The prophet Bob Jones told me by telephone that I did see, but my seeing was a "knowing," a "knowing" so strong that I would be moved to declare things in meetings and then see them happen. Though I would like to "see" open visions or even strong mental pictures, I am glad for this sense of seeing.

Faith is built up by "seeing." It is this built-up faith that then causes us to have the courage to speak out what we believe God is about to do in a meeting. A strategic passage for my understanding of moving in the power of the Spirit and seeing miracles is 2 Corinthians 4:13, "It is written: 'I believed; therefore I have spoken.' With that same spirit of faith we also believe and therefore speak."

I believe the "spirit of faith" Paul is speaking of, is related to understanding what God is doing in the moment. This risk-taking faith comes from a sense of knowing through some revelational gift of God or experience from God. The greater the faith, the more powerful the anointing will be on the meeting for healing, deliverance and miracles.

One of my very good friends, Gary Oates, who has been in the ministry for about thirty years, was with me on a trip to Brazil. He was so hungry for a touch of God, an impartation from God. Later he was just as hungry for an impartation to see as Jesus sees. For those who want to do what the Father is doing, the gift of "seeing" is a gift to be earnestly desired. Gary wanted his eyes to be opened to see into the spiritual realm. I will let him tell his own story:

GARY OATES

The biblical concept of impartation was not a doctrine I had any working knowledge of—and certainly it wasn't anything I taught or preached as a minister of the gospel. But all of that changed with one brief trip to Brazil in September 2000.

I had been hearing from friends who had traveled there with Randy Clark about the mighty revival breaking out in that nation. God was pouring out His Spirit and miraculous events, including supernatural healings, were taking place. I was really curious and hungry for more of God in my own life. I wanted to see first-hand if what my friends were telling me was actually true. At the same time I was hoping that I could bring back a deposit of the supernatural to our struggling church in Tallahassee.

The night of the first meeting, Randy spoke briefly about the value of impartation. He explained how he had been both the recipient of an important impartation and had also been used for important impartations to others who were affecting nations through the gifts they received. Then he lined up all the pastors (including me) and came down the line praying for impartation for each person individually. When he stood in front of me, I was focused intently on whatever he was going to pray in case there was a prophetic word. Yet as he touched my forehead, the power of God hit me and I went down like a sack of potatoes. I don't know how long I lay on the floor but I was out cold. When I finally got up, I was dazed and about half-drunk in the Spirit which was a relatively new experience for me.

At the meeting later that night, Randy called up the pastors on the team to pray over the Brazilian pastors. I hadn't done anything like that before but I obediently went up to offer my prayers. A Brazilian pastor and his wife came and stood in front of me. When I reached over to pray for them, the power of God hit them and they went flying backwards as if they had been shot out of a cannon. In fact, they literally skidded across the floor. I was shocked!

"What in the world happened?" I asked myself. I hadn't seen anything like that before when I prayed for anybody. "Maybe something *did* happen with the prayer of impartation Randy prayed," I thought.

The next person I prayed for was an older man standing in line with his hand on his heart. I didn't have an interpreter working with me so I thought the man had a heart problem. After much effort (and some sign language), I was able to understand his problem wasn't his heart. It was his stiff legs. He seemed to have no flexibility or mobility in his legs and could barely walk. He could only move his feet an inch or so with each step.

When I realized his problem, I prayed for his legs and the power of God came down upon him and he was totally healed. He started laughing and moving his legs up and down. He was so excited about what God had done, he was jumping up and down almost like the lame man healed in Acts 3.

Later I prayed for another man in the latter stages of emphysema and also with a hearing problem. God immediately healed the man's lungs and he no longer needed a hearing aid.

In 2001 I went on another Global Awakening trip with Randy to Brazil. Randy prayed for impartation again, and I saw an even greater increase in anointing for healing, creative miracles and a sense of the Presence of God.

When a third Global trip came about for June 2002, I was finally able to talk my wife Kathi into going. Our church appeared as if it was coming apart at the seams. After years of struggle and labor— the kind of draining effort only a pastor might possibly understand— people were now heading for the exits. I was desperate; I had to have a touch from God myself. I went from telling the Lord how I felt to making a request. "Lord, I pray that You will open my eyes on this trip so that I can see what You're doing. I want to see things from Your perspective." Looking back, I know God was directing those prayers. "Lord, I want to see beyond the natural...I want to see angels...I want to see into the realm of the Spirit," I prayed.

That 2002 trip to Brazil changed my life. My eyes were opened to see beyond the natural realm into the realm of the Spirit including the ministry of angels.

I received a second impartation through Davi Silva, a worship leader with the prophetic ministry/worship team of Casa de Davi. Davi had been healed of Down's syndrome when he was six years old and had been caught up before God's throne on eight different occasions. He has experienced angelic visitations on a regular basis. While traveling in a bus one day, I listened as Randy Clark was asking all kinds of questions about Davi's experiences. I was glued to their words! When his conversation with Randy ended, I tapped Davi on the shoulder and said, "That's what I want."

Davi doesn't speak English but he seemed to grasp what I was saying. He reached over and placed his left hand on my right hand. When he did, my hand started having an unusual tingling sensation. He left his hand there for the longest time, never really saying a word. I wasn't sure what was happening although I felt an impartation taking place that I didn't fully understand. When our bus arrived at its destination, I stood up to leave. Davi was standing there so I gave him a big hug. When I did, the Spirit of God came over me and my knees began to buckle. Tears began flowing down my cheeks.

Later that night, we gathered for the church service in a huge tent that seated some three thousand. It was during the worship service that I felt myself going upwards, leaving the floor and leaving my physical body behind. I was not aware of my physical body or any physical limitations. It was as if my physical body was non-existent. I had a dramatic encounter with the Lord—being caught up into His Presence where I saw the Lord Jesus while out of my body.

[Editor's note: This experience may have been similar to what the Apostle Paul describes in 2 Corinthians 12:2, "Whether it was in the body or out of the body I do not know—God knows."]

When He took my left hand, it was a strong grip. My left hand began to burn in a little spot that got bigger and bigger until the whole palm of my hand was on fire. I didn't know if I could take it any more with the power and Presence of God working within me. At that moment, He released me back into my body.

Having been in the Presence of the Lord, I virtually exploded when I came back into my natural physical body. The shock catapulted me backwards as if I had done a backward swan dive. I hit three rows of chairs and then the concrete floor. It was if I had landed on a bed of feathers. For about an hour, I lay mute on the floor. I couldn't move, not even a muscle. I had no understanding of what had just happened to me. I could hardly speak. If I had, it probably wouldn't have made sense to anyone. I felt physically drained and emotionally depleted.

The next night before the meeting began, I took a seat on the front row. Shortly afterwards, Davi Silva walked up and sat down one seat over. He smiled at me and then placed his hand on my left shoulder. The power of God suddenly surged through me and I fell like a dead man on the chair between Davi and myself, trapping my arm between my chest and the chair. Several guys saw my predicament and laid me down on the floor.

Again, I couldn't move. It seemed as if my body weighed ten tons. I felt like I was being pressed against the floor. All the while I was crying out, "God, I want more of You . . . I want more of You . . . I want more of You."

Instantly I was transported into a heavenly setting where Jesus was standing on the right side of a throne with a scepter in his hand. Standing no more than fifty feet away from the Lord in the midst of His light, I felt like I was going to die. I honestly felt this was the end. There was no way I could survive this. In fact, I thought maybe I had died and gone to heaven. It was that real. I saw the glory of God like I had never seen it before, and I found myself crying out, "God, forgive me . . . forgive me." I lost all sense of time and was later told I had been on the floor for two hours.

I couldn't walk, so several team members took me outside for some fresh air. They later brought me back into the sanctuary where Randy was preaching about a time his mother was taken up before the Lord. As he shared, the Presence of the Lord flowed over me like bolts of electricity going through my body. I was shaking and trembling so much I could hardly sit in the chair.

Randy later called me to the platform saying I would explain what had happened to me. I was still trembling and vibrating as the team members carried me onto the platform. Since I was unable to speak, Kathi took the microphone and explained a little of what had happened. As she did, the Spirit of God fell in that place. People began crying out; others were falling on their face in repentance. God was doing a spontaneous, yet miraculous work in that church.

Randy instructed the team members to lift my hands and lay them on each pastor's head. As soon as my hands touched the pastor's head, he went out in the Spirit. In hindsight I realized it was not about me; it was about the Lord. I was merely a contact point, a conduit of what God was doing.

Later when I was finally able to stand up I began praying for people and a long line formed. Almost everybody I prayed for indicated they were healed. All kinds of healings were taking place without any effort on my part. I knew it was truly a ministry of the Holy Spirit.

On that same trip to Brazil—though she had gone reluctantly—Kathi had a vision of being taken before God's throne in heaven. Within days, she was launched into a new realm of prophetic utterances and seeing angels as well. Randy later commented how unusual it was for both husband and wife to have such parallel experiences. But we did!

Our lives would never be the same again. It would not be the same for me, or Kathi, or those whose lives we would be able to touch across the nations of the earth.

In summary, there is little doubt that impartation played a key role in the experiences Kathi and I have had. From the initial impartation I received in 2000 from Randy Clark to the second impartation in 2002 from Davi Silva, our lives and ministry have been radically transformed.

Greater works in the miraculous realm are Jesus' words and expectation for His people. *". . . he who believes in Me, the works that I do, he will do also; and greater works than these he will do . . ."* (John 14:12, NASB). These works are happening in places large and small all over the world. I have seen them with my own eyes.

Yet, these miraculous events seldom happen outside the realm of impartation from an anointed vessel of the Lord. There are other keys, of course, such as a holy desperation for God, intimacy with Him, and living a separated and yielded life to the Holy Spirit. But impartation is central to fulfilling one's destiny—and in doing the works of Jesus![71]

Just as I was finishing the final draft of this book, I was told another pastor received a powerful impartation in a morning meeting, led by Gary and which I did not attend. This meeting took place in the city of Annapolis, Brazil in September of 2005.

Lucas Sheridan, a pastor from Texas, was out for about two hours on the floor during which time he received a powerful vision following the impartation. He was undone by the mighty presence of God touching him physically. I just had Lucas come to my room to tell me what happened to him at about 9:30 this morning. Almost nine hours later Lucas was barely able to walk; his eyes were still burning from the heat and his feet were still feeling very hot from the fire that came upon them. He was having difficulty talking and was struggling to keep coherent. He was very much aware of the continued presence of God on his life.

My experience in Annapolis, Brazil – September 6, 2005:
Gary began to speak about seeing in the supernatural. Sometime during Gary's opening remarks, it seemed like something fell from my eyes and I could see what appeared at first like "shadows of light" becoming clearer.

While this was happening, the Lord told me to have Kathi Oates pray for me. Much of what transpired—I simply cannot find words to explain it all. Even what is about to be explained sounds pretty weak compared to the actual experience.

I saw the angel of the Lord come to me with a sword in his hands. He was beautiful and bright with wings. He was clothed in white with something like gold chain link armor. The sword was a very large bright sword that glistened in the light. He took the sword and thrust it into my heart until the handle was all the way in my heart. The pain was intense. It made me double over in pain. The angel then began taking it around the circumference of my heart over and over again. I could literally feel it in the natural and the pain remained after this encounter was over. It felt as if I died. Kathi later felt as if the angel was "circumcising" my heart. I would agree. It felt like years of my "stuff" just began falling off of me. Hurts and strongholds were gone. I felt pain but I also felt weight being lifted off.

Then he stood back and began to blow fire on my feet. As my feet caught on fire in the vision, my feet in the natural also got very uncomfortably hot and for many hours my feet remained on fire. He said he was lighting my feet "to run to the nations." I felt so amazingly unworthy but I wanted to receive all that he was saying. He also said that "gone are the days when 'just doing the best you know how to do' will suffice." He said that I would know exactly what steps I was to take. He also told me that I would need to obey immediately.

He then asked if I wanted to see the King. With all my heart I said, "Yes. It's been my prayer for years." I was surprised at the hesitance I felt that was mixed with excitement. He then showed me the Lord. I cannot describe how beautiful, how terrible, how amazing Jesus looked. This part is immensely frustrating to describe. He had jet black hair and very dramatic features. His eyes were what most amazed me. I cannot accurately describe with words, but they were piercing and gentle at the same time. They were filled with passion. They were intense but meek. You could tell that there was absolutely no compromise in those eyes. He was the most good and gracious

Man I'd ever met. He wasn't smiling but He wasn't frowning. He face was beautiful yet terrible. It's frustrating trying to write about Him because I can still see Him but can't accurately describe the beauty.

But what affected me the most is that when I saw Him, I didn't recognize Him as the Lord. He wasn't a "familiar face" to me. He didn't look like I was expecting Him to look. That undid me. The conviction that came with that realization will most likely stay with me. I wept and am still weeping. While there was great conviction over this—there was an even greater, deep stirring of hunger to get to know Him. My life has been about Psalm 27:4 which contains a phrase that I want "to behold His beauty." I've wanted to know Him and thought I would surely know the Lord if I ever saw Him. And yet His face was strange to me. Kathi comforted me with the thought that the disciples didn't recognize Jesus on the road to Emmaus nor did Mary recognize Jesus in the garden tomb. But it created a hunger in me to know Him as He really is and not as I have created Him to be.

Then the angel said, "Do you want to see what the Lord is doing in this city?"

I said "Yes." He showed me this city (Annapolis) and right above it was a giant ball of fire. It was the Lord's fire of revival and a giant move of His Spirit. It was being held above the city by a giant net. The fireball was bulging, just waiting to break. Every once in a while some fire would fall through the net and touch people. Some times bigger pieces of fire would fall and the people of God would be encouraged. But the big sphere was still suspended over the city and was prohibited from falling.

The angel asked, "Do you want to see what the net is that is stopping the ball of fire from falling?" I did. So he brought me close to the ball of fire and I looked closely at the net. The crisscross rope that made the net had two different phrases upon it— UNFORGIVENESS and BROKEN RELATIONSHIPS. If these two things were not present, there would be a release of the Spirit's fire in Annapolis that would be known around the world.

Through the multiple examples I have listed from Scripture, and from testimonies like the two I have just shared from Pastors Gary Oates and Lucas Sheridan, it is clear that God gives revelatory gifts that may allow someone to literally "see" into the spiritual realm. However, there is a sense in Scripture where "seeing" is understood as "perceiving." Repeatedly Jesus accuses his detracting observers as "having eyes to see they see not." Obviously from the context, the "seeing" referred to here is an understanding of the significance of what God was doing in the works of Jesus. It refers to an awareness of the purposes of God in the moment or situation. These "understandings" are often received through "revelation gifts" such as prophecy, words of knowledge, words of wisdom, or discerning of spirits.

In Jesus' upper room discourse, there is a clear connection between "revelation" given by the Holy Spirit and doing supernatural works of God. In John 14:11-14, Jesus tells the disciples the Father is in Him and He is in the Father. He tells them the Father is living in Him and it is the Father doing the works and giving Jesus the very words to say. Then Jesus tells the disciples that "anyone" who has faith in Him will do what He has been doing. This is *because* Jesus was going to the Father. This is an obvious reference to His crucifixion, resurrection, ascension to His Father in heaven. This was necessary for the outpouring of the Holy Spirit (cf. John 7:37ff). It will be this new role of the Holy Spirit, under the New Covenant, which will make the "greater things than these shall you do" possible.

The reason Jesus gives for doing "whatever you ask in my name" was so that "the Son may bring glory to the Father." That is the reason we could ask Him "for anything in my name, and I will do it."

If you ask how one begins to do these "greater things," the answer starts in John 14:15 where it is rooted in love for Jesus. This love manifests in obedience to His commands. Upon this condition Jesus asks the Father to send us the "Paraclete," or another Counselor. The disciples were told that this other Counselor, the Holy Spirit, was already dwelling with them but would be in them. In John 14:18, Jesus connects the Holy Spirit's unity with Himself to be like that of Jesus' unity with the Father. It is so much so that to receive the Holy Spirit is to receive Jesus. Jesus literally says, "I will come to you" (v. 18b).

149

Jesus gives a key to receiving "revelation." I believe "seeing" comes from receiving the "all seeing One" on a continual basis. Revelation comes out of intimacy with the Godhead. Intimacy is connected to love manifesting itself through obedience. Jesus indicates that the one who obeys in love will be loved and will receive a revelation of Jesus:

> Whoever has my commands and obeys them, he is the one who loves me. He who loves me, will be loved by my Father, and I too will love him **and show myself to him.** (John 14:21, emphasis added)

Out of intimacy that comes from obeying and remaining in Jesus the vine, we the branches will bear "**much fruit.**" It is out of this abiding relationship that we, not just the twelve disciples, are enabled to bear much fruit:

> I am the vine; you are the branches. If a man remains in me and I in him, **he will bear much fruit**; apart from me you can do nothing. . . . **If you remain in me and my words remain in you, ask whatever you wish, and it will be given you.** (John 15:5, 7, emphasis added)

Again the result of our fruitfulness is the "Father's glory." In bearing much fruit we are "showing" ourselves to be the disciples of Jesus. I believe as we receive revelations from Jesus, these revelations produce belief that is so strong that we have courage to speak. Our speaking in faith produces the "much fruit" that reveals we are disciples of Jesus. This is how the words of Paul in 2 Corinthians 4:13, "**With that same spirit of faith we also believe and therefore speak** [emphasis added]" and Jesus' words in John 14-16 particularly fit together.

This understanding is made clearer in John 15:14-16:

> I no longer call you servants, because a servant does not know his master's business. Instead, I have called you friends, for everything that I have learned from my Father I have made known to you. You did not choose me, but I chose you and appointed you to go and bear fruit—fruit that will last. (Emphasis added)

Revelation produces fruit because it produces faith. Revelation is referred to here in the phrase, "everything that I have learned from my Father I have made known to you." This revelation comes out of the relationship of sonship and love revealed through knowledge of His Word and obedience to it.

Jesus says more about the promise of revelation in John 16:12-15:

> I have much more to say to you, more than you can now bear. But when he, the Spirit of truth, comes, he will guide you into all truth. He will not speak on his own; he will speak only what he hears, and he **will tell you what is yet to come. He will bring glory to me by taking from what is mine and making it known to you.** All that belongs to the Father is mine. That is why I said the Spirit will take from what is mine **and make it known to you.** (Emphasis added)

If "seeing" in the sense of "perceiving" is key to producing much fruit, then it behooves all of us to desire to "see" better into the spiritual realm and into spiritual truths. I have now been in ministry over thirty-five years and have discussed this with others who likewise have been in ministry over thirty years. They report that when they were able to "know" by "seeing," their faith exploded. If there are some who literally begin to "see" through a spiritual grace or gift, then would it not be the better part of wisdom to desire this literal "seeing" while at the same time grateful for any of the various ways God allows us to "see" by "perceiving"?

In trying to make this section more clear, let me say that I now "see/perceive" the desire of God during a meeting by "feeling" in my body the conditions He wants to heal—this is how the gift of word of knowledge most often works in me. I also "know" the direction of God for a situation through impressions in my mind. However, I know that greater certainty produces even greater faith, and the greater the clarity of the revelation, the greater the certainty.

I invite you to hunger and thirst with me for greater intimacy and humility to cry out for greater revelation. I can no longer be satisfied by learning more about Jesus. I now know it is possible to hear His voice audibly, to be taken into Isaiah 6 experiences today, to see Him in His exalted state as John did in the beginning of the book of Revelation. Though this is my greatest desire, I likewise desire to see into "the kingdom of God"—to see things from His point of view, to see heavenly beings interacting with us on our behalf. I believe impartations for this ability, this grace, are being transferred today, and I hope to receive myself.

In concluding this section I want to focus us on Jonathan Edwards, who in my opinion is the greatest theologian of revival, impartations, and manifestations. He taught us that the truth of a movement, whether or not it was of God, would be known by its fruit and not by its manifestations or phenomena. Now, eleven and one-half years after the initial visitation of January 20, 1994, I am writing this book to answer the question, "Where's the fruit?" I am responding to the critics because there has been time for those who were so powerfully touched to bring to the Master the sheaves of their harvest. They are coming with great joy, "bringing in the sheaves, bringing in the sheaves," as the old gospel song says. The fruit of Toronto has been impossible to ignore, and it is heaven's fruit!

In the next section we shall not just note the numerical fruit in the numbers of churches planted, numbers of churches renewed, and number of people brought into the kingdom, but also the fruit in the individuals who received the impartations. What did the impartation do to them? In the next section we shall begin by pointing out the primary reason for "impartations" and their resultant effects—an increase in "signs and wonders" or "evangelistic fruit"—where the ultimate purpose is that God be glorified.

PART III: EVANGELISM AND MISSIONS – THE POWER FACTOR

"BUT YOU WILL RECEIVE POWER WHEN
THE HOLY SPIRIT COMES ON YOU; AND
YOU WILL BE MY WITNESSES IN
JERUSALEM, AND IN ALL JUDEA AND
SAMARIA, AND TO THE ENDS OF THE
EARTH."

ACTS 1:8

"MY MESSAGE AND MY PREACHING
WERE NOT WITH WISE AND PERSUASIVE
WORDS, BUT WITH A DEMONSTRATION
OF THE SPIRIT'S POWER, SO THAT YOUR
FAITH MIGHT NOT REST ON MEN'S
WISDOM, BUT ON GOD'S POWER."

1 CORINTHIANS 2:4-5

CHAPTER 9: WHY IMPARTATION FOR SIGNS AND WONDERS?

GLORY REVEALED THROUGH MIRACLES

True Christianity hinges on a theology of Presence. The Christian life is based on a personal relationship with the living God whose ultimate desire is to be known by us as we are known by Him (1 Corinthians 13:12). He reveals His heart, His thoughts, His purposes to those who walk in friendship with Him. Though He is invisible, He can be felt, heard, and seen—sometimes by manifest visitation, sometimes by effect—just as we see the effects of the wind if not the wind itself. If you take away the elements of experience and revelation, you are left with religion—perhaps an admirable system of ethics and rules, but not much of a relationship. All through the Bible (the ultimate authority on revelation) we see the various means by which God chooses to reveal Himself. These include the working of miracles, healing, dreams and visions, the prophetic word, and other manifestation gifts of the Spirit. Sadly, those who dismiss these vehicles of God's self-revelation as having ceased are dismissing much of what is most precious and dynamic about a relationship with God.

Our God has an incredible desire to reveal Himself. Romans 1:20 tells us that all of creation serves to reveal His power and divine nature to mankind. Isaiah 65:1 tells us He reveals Himself even to those who are neither asking nor seeking for Him. 1 Corinthians 2:9-12 tell us that the Holy Spirit is sent to believers to reveal the very plans and thoughts of God. David, writing by inspiration of the Holy Spirit, prayed often for the glory of God to be revealed among the nations. Throughout Scripture, God promises to "show" or "reveal" His glory. Jesus came that we might see God's glory (John 1:14) as "a light for revelation to the Gentiles and for glory to your people Israel" (Luke 2:32). The Body of Christ is intended to further the revelation of God in this world (1 John 4:17). It should not surprise us, then, to see revival accompanied by demonstrations of the power and glory of

God. Even the gifts and manifestations of the Holy Spirit pale in comparison to when God chooses to "rend the heavens and come down" in His glory. His glory produces much more healings and powerful impartations than any of His gifts.

This is entirely consistent with God's expressed desire to reveal Himself! Those who think God has quieted down over the years or retreated behind the clouds until the return of Jesus really do not understand the passion God has for drawing people to Himself through the revelation of His glory.

What exactly do we mean by "God's glory"? Moses petitioned God, "Now show me your glory." Perhaps Moses expected God to shatter the heavens with lightening and thunder, or perhaps embellish upon the burning bush by setting the mountain on fire. Instead, God responded to Moses:

> I will cause **all my goodness** to pass in front of you, and I will proclaim my name, the LORD, in your presence. (Exodus 33:19, emphasis added)

Here God Himself defines His glory—it is His character, His nature as expressed in His names—that constitute His glory. As He passed by Moses, He proclaimed His compassion, His grace, His abounding love, His willingness to forgive and His perfect justness.

How does God reveal His glory in the world? The Bible contains eighteen categories of instances where the glory of God is mentioned. By far, the largest category is miracles and healings where God's glory is connected thirty times to a demonstration of His power through the working of signs, wonders and miracles. Based upon this fact, we could say that the *main way* God reveals His glory is through signs, wonders and miracles.

This puts a new perspective on what we are asking God to do when we sing "Glorify Thy Name, glorify Thy Name, glorify Thy Name in all the earth." We are actually asking God to work His mighty power in our midst. We are asking Him to reveal His nature as expressed in His covenantal name, Jehovah-Rafa, the Lord our Healer. We are asking for a revelation of God's *goodness*! This is so important in a world where so many think of God as distant, uncaring, unfair, angry, or just not there at all!

This also puts a new perspective on the phrase, "Don't touch His glory." Are we not in some way robbing God of His glory when we hold to a cessationist view of God's continued activity in this world?

The connection between God's glory and demonstrations of His power first occurred to me as I was reading the Gospel of John. The connection is first made in John 2:11:

> This, the first of his miraculous signs, Jesus performed at Cana in Galilee. He thus **revealed his glory**, and his disciples put their faith in him. (Emphasis added)

In John 11:4, Jesus understood the miracle of Lazarus' resurrection to be for His glory:

> When he heard this, Jesus said, "This sickness will not end in death. No, **it is for God's glory** so **that God's Son may be glorified through it**." (Emphasis added)

This passage teaches us that both the Father and the Son were glorified by this miracle. Jesus believed that in the witnessing of the resurrection of Lazarus the disciples and the others who were present were actually seeing the glory of God:

> Then Jesus said, "Did I not tell you that if you believed, you would see the **glory of God**?" (John 11:40, emphasis added)

John noted in his Gospel that though the Pharisees and Scribes had witnessed the miracles of Jesus they still did not believe. In this context, his Gospel states, "Isaiah said this because **he saw Jesus' glory and spoke about him**." (John 12:4, emphasis added)

This theme of the Father or the Son being glorified or Their glory being revealed through signs and wonders is most clear in the Upper Room discourse of Jesus recorded in John 14-16 and in the High Priestly prayer of Jesus in John 17. Jesus teaches that He will answer our prayers in His name so that by answering our prayers the **Father will be glorified**. When the following texts are read in their context, it is beyond a doubt that the reference is pertaining to doing acts of power, signs, wonders, healing and miracles. The "greater things than these shall you do because I go to the Father" in John 14:12 is clearly not a reference to moral ethics, but to charismatic acts done through charismatic gifts made possible by the future ministry of the Holy Spirit. John 14:13-14 continues:

> And I will do whatever you ask in my name, so that the Son may bring **glory to the Father**. You may ask me for anything in my name, and I will do it. (Emphasis added)

Jesus sees the Father's glory as in some way connected to our fruitfulness. In North America, there is much emphasis on the "fruit of the Spirit" but Jesus also spoke of fruit in the context of the powerful work of the Holy Spirit done through His disciples. "Fruit" is not limited to the "fruit of the Spirit" mentioned in Galatians 5, but must be understood to include healings, deliverances and miracles. This is the nature of the fruit in John 15:8, "This is to my Father's glory, that you bear much fruit, showing yourselves to be my disciples."

The New Testament and Jewish concept of discipleship in Jesus' time was for the disciple to become like the master, not only in His teaching, but in His life and living. Jesus continues to build His church and advance His kingdom through His disciples, and their disciples after them, by answering their prayers and enabling them to truly be His disciples.[72]

When we consider how important the power to work miracles, healing, and deliverances was to Jesus' understanding to how both He and the Father were glorified; and when we consider Jesus' commissioning of the Twelve, the seventy-two, and—through the Apostles—those who were to believe on their message, we cannot underestimate the priority Jesus placed upon the ministry of the expansion of the kingdom through the words and works that He modeled for His disciples. The modeling was for them to understand the nature of the kingdom of God. The kingdom was not to consist in talk only, but also in power (1 Corinthians 4:20).

Let me back up this statement by quoting from the *Implications and Conclusions* section of Ruthven's book on the cessation of the charismata. It is a long quote but I'm going to include it all because it does such a great job of capturing what I feel is the Father's heart for the church, especially as expressed by the Father to the Elder Brother in Jesus' parable when the Father says, "Son, all I have is yours." Ruthven observes:

> The frequent failure to respond to God's commands to manifest the kingdom of God in power is fully shared by most believers, "charismatics" and non-charismatics alike. Both groups shape their theology and consequent practice on the bias of their own experience—or lack of it—rather than on a fresh and radical (in its original sense) view of Scripture. The presence or absence of certain charismata in one's experience proves nothing at all about one's spiritual status or destiny (Mt. 7.21-22). Neither group (charismatics or non-charismatics) is more or less "saved" than the other; both are at once sinful, but justified by grace alone. Nevertheless the NT offers patterns as to how the gospel is to be presented, received and lived out. We must not attempt to reframe our failures into virtues, that is, by allowing what the NT describes as "unbelief" in and for the gifts of God, to be construed as having chosen "the better way" of a "stronger faith" without them. The rabbis' intellectualized biblical knowledge that led to their cessationism prompted Jesus to affirm that they knew "neither the Scriptures nor the power of God" (Mt. 22.29 // Mk. 12.24).
>
> Much divisiveness over the gifts of the Spirit today derives from a premise common to both sides of the debate: evidentialism. If spiritual gifts are adduced as proofs of spiritual status or attainment, rather than used as tools for humble service for others, then conflict naturally follows. The core temptation to the first and Last Adam (Christ), and by extension to all of us, was to use spiritual knowledge and power to accredit one's independent and exalted religious status, instead of through them rendering glory, obedience and service to God. Spiritual gifts are powerful weapons against the kingdom of darkness; but misapplied in evidentialist polemics they can wound and destroy the people of God.
>
> ***The charismata, then, reflect the very nature of God,*** who does not share his glory with another. Similarly, God is a Spirit of power, "who changeth not". If the church has "begun in the Spirit", let us not attempt to change God's methods to complete our course in the weakness of human flesh. Since it is the Father's pleasure to "give

good gifts to them who ask him," it must be our pleasure to receive them humbly.[73] (Emphasis added)

In the days of Jesus and the first disciples, the power for signs, wonders, healings, miracles, and deliverance wasn't just to authenticate the message; this power was the *expression of the message.* Signs and wonders were not just performed to validate the Good News; they were a vital element *of* the Good News! To put it another way, miracles don't primarily prove doctrine about God so much as they reveal the nature of God. God has not changed. Neither has the gospel message. God moves in power, in signs and wonders—healing the sick, in deliverances, multiplying food for the hungry, and raising the dead—primarily for this reason; He is good! And it is His desire to reveal His *goodness*—His glory— in all the earth.

One of the most exciting developments of this renewal movement and the ensuing wave of missions is seeing God invade earth with a fresh and powerful revelation of His glory among the nations. God is making Himself seen, heard and felt in all the ways that many once just read about in the Bible. Jesus Christ, Who is the same yesterday, today and forever, is reminding us that every page of God's Word is still valid and true for today because Jesus, the Living Word, has not changed.

Personally, I believe we are living in the grace of this outpouring of power because we are moving towards the *last* days, the days of the final harvest. There are two ministries in particular that I believe embody what God is doing in these last days throughout the earth. I have already written much about Iris Ministries, under Rolland and Heidi Baker. Let me introduce you to Global Missions Awareness and its founder, Leif Hetland.

"The day I ran away, I decided I wanted everything the devil had to offer."

A fourth generation Christian growing up in Stavanger, Norway, Leif rebelled at the age of 13, cynical and disillusioned with his faith. The dissonance between what was preached in the pulpit and what was lived out in the culture of "churchianity" drove him to seek the comfort and acceptance of a more tolerant group—the drug addicts and drifters of the streets. "I was looking for Jesus but didn't know it; I certainly couldn't see Him in the church. At church, no matter how much you did, it was never *enough*. You could never be good *enough*." Four years later—emaciated by alcoholism and drug addiction—the seventeen-year-old made his way home simply to escape the ruthless cold and hunger of the gutters.

All of Leif's fears about coming home were melted by the warmth of his father's embrace. But, in spite of the glorious welcome, the heart issues that had driven Leif away in the first place were still unresolved. Referring to the parable of Jesus, Leif explains, "I went from being the prodigal son to being the elder brother." Leif found himself falling back into the trap of feeling he needed to perform in order to win his Heavenly Father's approval and love. "All the Father has is ours by birthright as sons, simply because He loved us enough to birth us into His family, but I didn't understand that. I went from wallowing in the pigpen to working in the field, still bitter, still feeling unloved." Leif continued to lead a double life, acting out all the right clichés in church but secretly finding comfort in drugs for the emptiness and pain in his heart.

One night, Leif came home very late and very high. The doors were locked and the house was completely dark and still. Because his parents always left the door open for him, Leif was sure something strange had happened. Suddenly, a terrible dread that the rapture had occurred seized him and he fell into the snow, weeping with remorse and fear. Today, Leif believes the locked doors were arranged by God. As he lay there in the freezing snow, he experienced a powerful visitation of the Holy Spirit. That encounter with Jesus started a process of turning in Leif's life, but he continued to struggle with his image of God, the "taskmaster." Leif relates:

> In church, the message was you should be reading the Bible more. If you did that, you should be praying more. If you did that, you should be witnessing more. No matter what you did, it was never enough. You should always be doing more. I always felt like a failure who could never meet the expectations of others or of God. The Law is a terrible taskmaster.

Leif's parents sent him to a Christian college where he quickly disappointed them again by being expelled for drugs. But God had a destiny for Leif, as King David wrote, "All the days ordained for me were written in your book before one of them came to be" (Psalm 139:16). A letter came informing Leif that he had been accepted into the Covenant Players, a Christian theatrical touring group. The whole thing was a big mistake. Leif had never interviewed with them, as the letter said. Nevertheless, Leif seized the opportunity to escape and left for Germany to join the troupe, still drinking heavily.

Release into Revelation

On the night of January 5, 1985, Leif had his second major encounter with Jesus. Leslie, a Charismatic Catholic member of the group of traveling performers, discovered Leif going through the agony of detoxification, violently ill and raging with fever. As she prayed, Leif experienced the tangible presence of God in a powerful way. The sickness and fever instantly left. So did the addiction. More importantly, Leif experienced the "gift of forgiveness." In that visitation, Leif finally found freedom from the bitterness, hurt, and anger of his heart. Forgiveness and acceptance was no longer just a doctrine, but a heart revelation, experienced through a sovereign touch of God. A central theme of Leif's ministry today is the truth that "God does not treat us according to our history, but according to our destiny."

Six months later, Leif's destiny came another step closer. In Ireland, after performing at a Charismatic Catholic Renewal service, Leif responded to the altar call just so he could prove that the manifestations he was seeing were false. He says, "I ended up on the floor, with 'liquid love' pouring over me and speaking in tongues." In spite of this experience, Leif's ministry continued to be performance and achievement oriented. "I lived for the pat on the back, the compliment to what a good sermon I had preached or how many people were getting saved. In my insecurity, I needed the approval of men."

In 1988, Leif met and fell in love with Jennifer, an American from Columbus, Georgia. They married the next year. For the next ten years Leif did all the normal things a gifted young minister should do, earning his BA at Luther Rice Seminary, a Southern Baptist seminary, and taking a position as youth pastor in a Presbyterian church.

In 1991, the Hetlands had their first of four children, a son, and returned to Norway to pastor a Baptist church in Sandnes. Leif describes himself during those years as a "closet charismatic" who stopped practicing what he believed because he did not want to run the risk of losing his reputation or his church. Still, Leif does not regard that time of Holy Spirit "wilderness" as a negative for they were rich years of strengthening his foundation in the Word:

> Don't get me wrong; the Holy Spirit was still moving. God honors His Word and when the Word goes out, God sovereignly works and there will be fruit.
>
> But, by 1994, I was the classic burned-out high-achiever. I was still serving the Taskmaster who had a long to-do list. After a few years like this, I was finally so desperate for more of God that my desperation level became higher than my fear level. I was finally dry enough to pursue whatever it took to get more of God, even if it cost me my job, my home, my friends, everything around me. I looked successful on the outside, but I was miserable in many ways and I was making my family miserable. I was living *for* God, not living *from* God. That's a major paradigm shift.

In May of 1994, one of Leif's elders invited him to go with him to England to meet with some pastors who had been to Toronto. Leif was very skeptical. What he was hearing about Toronto sounded weird. The two men met the group at Queens Road Baptist Church, and then met again later at Holy Trinity Brampton (famous as the church that first produced the Alpha course). The man who prayed for Leif in that meeting had several prophetic words regarding the "elder brother" issues in his life and God began a deep healing process. When the men returned to Norway, they were shocked to find that the anointing had been imparted to them. Renewal immediately broke out in their church and many people experienced dramatic healings. The meetings often went on until twelve and one in the morning; then people had to be carried to their cars.

In November, the Hetland family went to the U.S. for four-and-a-half weeks on vacation. Sadly, when they came back, the renewal had been quenched. Leif explains:

> One of the influential elders was disturbed by some of the abuses of the gifts and began to teach that this was not of God. It was really just a lack of leadership to help the people deal with those abuses. This was hard for me. I had tasted the goodness and power of the Spirit, but now the people were afraid and didn't want it.

More Impartation

In 1995, Leif's and my paths crossed in a divine appointment. Leif describes what happened:

> In 1995, I heard Randy Clark was coming to Norway to meet with a group of 100 pastors at Haugesund Mission Church. At that meeting, my wife and I went forward for prayer. When Randy prayed for me, he began to prophesy. I don't remember every word, but I have never forgotten the gist of what he said. "You are a bulldozer . . . going into areas that have been untouched." Later, Randy came to me and said, "I want to impart to you so you can go to places no one has gone before." After that, I was flat out in the Spirit for over two hours. What felt like electricity, fire, and liquid all together seemed to be flowing up and down my body. I wept a lot! During this time, I was always conscious of others around me, especially my wife.

164

Very quickly, Leif knew a transference of anointing had taken place. He had two conferences right after that where he noticed a huge increase in healings and salvations, yet he wasn't doing anything any differently. Before, if someone got healed, it was like winning the lottery—great, but rare. Now, it was the *norm* to see people get healed, physically and also emotionally through prophetic words. Leif describes the change:

> Before, I prayed for the sick but didn't really expect God to do much. My attitude was, "Oh well, God is sovereign." Now there was a whole different expectancy as God's calling was released in my life. There was this "week of glory" shortly after Randy's impartation where *everyone* I prayed for got healed, addicts were delivered upon a single touch, and all the gifts of the Spirit were operating through me. It was actually scary! I thought I was losing my mind because I saw people through Jesus' eyes and could feel their pain when I touched them. This didn't continue but I believe God was giving me a taste of what is supposed to be the normal Christian life when we are walking in the fullness of the Spirit.

Fulfilling Destiny

Leif describes what happened concerning the prophecy he had received:

> Truthfully, I forgot about Randy's prophecy for a long time. Then, my neck was seriously injured in a pool accident, followed by a car wreck the following year. After the car accident, I was in and out of the hospital for eighteen months. During all that time in bed, the Holy Spirit reminded me of Randy's words. I began to sense a tremendous, supernatural burden for the unreached in the world. There are over 70 million people in Arab nations who have never heard the name of Jesus! I knew I was supposed to go where no one else was going.
>
> At the end of '96 a friend of mine, Bjornar Heimstad, invited me to go to Pakistan with him. I realized this was confirmation of Randy's word. That was the start of many trips to Pakistan where we have seen thousands upon thousands healed and saved. By the grace of God, I've now been in over 72 countries, many of them Muslim and some of them Communist.
>
> I know God is treating me according to His chosen destiny for me, certainly not according to my merit! He has granted me unprecedented favor with national leaders, with religious leaders, even with heads of state. He is the One opening doors no man can

shut! I have seen every kind of miracle you can imagine—tumors dropping off, creative miracles where missing parts are restored, blind eyes seeing, everything. God is revealing His glory! Through the revelation of His glory, His goodness and compassion, hundreds of thousands are coming to Christ in areas that are officially closed to the gospel.

In 2000, Leif's ministry took a dramatic turn. By this time he had been forced to resign from the Baptist Church in the U. S., primarily due to his association with the "Toronto Blessing." Wounded and hurting, Leif attended a Father-Son weekend where the ministry team included Jack Taylor, Charles Carrin, and worship leader, Dennis Jernigan. Dennis came to Leif and asked to pray for him. He ended up singing "The Father's Song" over Leif while the Holy Spirit poured out what Leif calls "a baptism of love." It had a dramatic effect:

> My whole message changed that day. My Abba Father revealed Himself to me. I was healed of my "orphan spirit" and received the "spirit of sonship." I learned that my inheritance is something I receive, not something I must achieve. My Father was giving me the nations, not because of anything I did, but because I'm his son! I went home from that weekend a changed man. I went home a lover, not a doer. Ask my wife and kids!

In the last five years, Leif has trained thousands of pastors, mostly in closed and hostile areas of the world. He gets letters every week from those to whom he has passed on the impartation he received from Randy. He explains, "The prayer of impartation is like being impregnated with what the Spirit is stirring and will bring to birth."

His message is clear. The Great Commandment—to love—must come before the Great Commission—to do. "I've stepped back from the 'work' of ministry and now I just play with my Daddy. The wonderful thing is I'm seeing more fruit than ever! God is love. When His love is released, healing comes—healing of every kind."

Leif's ministry has been an amazing conduit of God's glory. The signs, wonders and miracles worked through him and the Word proclaimed by him have brought a revelation of God's goodness to over half a million Pakistanis in recent years! Multiply that by how God is working through all his spiritual "sons" and one can get a small grasp of how God is pouring out His Spirit in these last days. But his is not the only story. . .

STEVE STEWART, VANCOUVER, BRITISH COLUMBIA

I want to finish this section with one more story—a "glory" story of fruitfulness—as told by a former Vineyard pastor, Steve Stewart, describing what happened after receiving an impartation at Toronto in 1994. Here it is in his words:

In 1994 I was pastoring the Cambridge Vineyard near Toronto. Five days into the outbreak of renewal, John Arnott called me to come over and witness what was happening. As I stood at the back of the auditorium during worship, a bit dumbfounded at what was going on, I saw John beckoning for me to come down to see something at the front. Two of my four sons, ages nine and ten, were shaking on the floor! My twelve year-old was prophesying over them! I had no frame of reference for this. The reaction going through my mind was, "We're good Presbyterian stock. We don't do this!"

John called all of us pastors into another room where he and Randy prayed for us. Now, the Vineyard didn't believe in the "falling down" stuff but the power of God fell and down we went. After about two minutes I got up, looked at the pastors out cold around me, and asked John, "What happened?" John had a sore throat so I offered to pray for him—just a simple prayer. I reached out to touch his neck. Later, people described to me what happened next. When I touched John, they said it looked like two bowling pins colliding. We both spun out and flew several feet across the room in different directions.

I stayed in that spot from 9:00 p.m. until 1:00 a.m. In those hours, EVERYTHING changed! As I lay on the floor, the power of God coursed through me in waves of electricity and light. I couldn't stand; I couldn't talk. Carol Arnott and someone, I don't know who, propped me up and began helping me lay hands on other people. As soon as I did, they would explode into various manifestations. This completely befuddled me!

The next day I had calmed down somewhat and met with the staff in my church office. No one could work. We just began to worship. Throughout the day, as others came into the office from the parking lot, they would simply fall to the floor and begin weeping.

That next night, back at Airport Vineyard, John called me up to share. I told about how I had been so dry for the past eight years. Randy laid hands on me again and, again, the power of God surged through me and I couldn't speak. For the next several months I was frequently overcome with stuttering and I still often stutter whenever the presence of God is manifesting.

The next Sunday in my church I shared my testimony. This was a church where NO ONE had ever fallen, but the whole church fell out in the 9:00 service. When the 11:00 [a.m. service] people came, they had to step over the bodies. Then they started falling out, the presence of God was so heavy. People finally started getting up to leave around 3:30 but decided to come back in the evening—even though we had never had a Sunday evening service.

A few weeks later, I left for Russia and stopped to speak for one night at a conference in Stockholm. As I stood at the podium, I felt the Holy Spirit coming on and thought, "Oh no, Lord. Not here! I only have one night with these people and I've got to preach what I have for them." I decided to stare at the ground and concentrate real hard on staying upright. Well, the translator next to me fell down! Another came up and he fell down! And the next! I finally decided to quit fighting the Holy Spirit and announced, "I guess we're done." At that moment, the Holy Spirit fell on the whole place. As I continued my trip, the same thing happened in Russia and Brazil—even though I had determined to say *nothing* about what was happening in Toronto. The Holy Spirit was showing up and we were seeing a tremendous increase in physical healings as well.

In 1995, my wife Christina and I moved to Vancouver to start a new church. We also started a ministry called Impartation Ministries International (IMI). This grew out of our realization that what Randy imparted to me that night was not just for a great one-time experience or even a few nights. It has lasted all these years and we have imparted to hundreds of others. We have traveled and ministered in healing to many nations and we keep getting testimonies from those that have been impacted. We do a lot of seminars for business people and some of these people are being used by God so powerfully that they tell me, "Steve, I don't know if I'm running a business or a ministry."

Doors continue to open for IMI that we never expected. We now run three branches of ministry—seminars for the training and equipping of leaders, mercy ministry where we send containers of relief goods to needy areas all over the world, and something called Journeys of Compassion where we send out teams on short-term-missions trips.

On April 8th, a team of twenty-five from five nations gathered in Nairobi for three days of intercession and preparation before heading into the North-East province of Kenya. The N.E. province, which formerly was part of Somalia, is 90% Muslim; its capital is Garissa, a city of about 50,000. . . .

Late every afternoon until after sunset, we held open-air healing and evangelism meetings in a large field in the middle of the city. . . . In the beginning, many Muslims came, but observed from a safe distance. As the meetings continued, more and more came forward. From the first meeting, God broke out with healing and miracles. Every night, too many healings took place to count. Near the beginning of the crusade a two-year-old who was both deaf and crippled was completely and instantly healed. News of this went all over the city so that the following afternoons, many children were brought to the meetings. . . .

Here are few of the healings that took place: A fifteen-year-old girl born deaf was completely healed. Another deaf and mute girl was healed and spoke her first word ever—Jesus! Several blind eyes were opened—including a young child who opened its eyes and began to look around (in surprise). On the last night, a twenty-year-old who had been mute his whole life was delivered of a mute spirit. His entire demeanor changed immediately; he then began to speak for the first time. A few feet away, a young boy who had been born deaf, after [receiving] prayer began to suddenly look around, because for the first time he could hear. Malaria fevers instantly left. Hundreds of people had long-standing pain leave. Hemorrhaging stopped. As the power of Christ was revealed among the Muslims and other Africans, many raised their hands to receive the Lord. Two of the team members shared the gospel with a group of about thirty children who had come early—they all prayed to ask Jesus into their lives.

After two days in Garissa, half the team went three hours further east to the refugee camps near Dadaab, while the rest carried on. There are 136,000 refugees from Somalia, Ethiopia, Sudan, Congo and Rwanda; many of them have been there for fourteen years with no opportunity to leave. The camps are 97% Muslim. . . .

From the first meeting, hundreds came forward and received healing in the name of Jesus. Some team members reported everyone they prayed for being instantly healed. A small boy with severely withered legs who could not walk or even stand was instantly healed. Like Garissa, there were hundreds of healings—more than the team could keep up with. Also like Garissa, these were the first open-air meetings by Christians ever allowed in the camps. At each meeting, more and more Muslims came close and many received prayer. Over a hundred people came forward to receive Christ. The team was able to leave funds behind to build a new church in the newest part of the camp.

It was such a privilege to witness an historic breakthrough in the Muslim dominated NE province. The good news of the kingdom was preached and demonstrated in such a way so as to begin to change the spiritual atmosphere of Garissa and the refugee camps. We are leaving behind the beginnings of several healing centers where all people in these communities can come and receive the love and power of the Lord.

What was given to me [from the impartation at Toronto] has been multiplied many, many times over. We train people and then we get out of the way and let them do the ministry. This philosophy goes all the way back to '94 when Randy imparted to me. Impartation is reproducible. That is how the kingdom of God multiplies!

This chapter's title posed the question, "Why Impartation for Signs and Wonders?" Are the signs and wonders released through impartations given to validate a message? Sometimes. But more importantly, God does good things simply because He *is* good. He works acts of love just because He *is* love. Signs and wonders, miracles and healings are just God being God, revealing His glory to a world that is desperately ignorant of His true nature. Does He need any other reason?

In the next chapter we will see how God reveals His glory through signs of love and wonders of compassion. Only through an impartation of power and love are we able to flow in signs of love and wonders of compassion, bearing the fruit which reveals the Father's nature and brings Him glory.

CHAPTER 10: IMPARTATION FOR SIGNS OF LOVE, WONDERS OF COMPASSION

"For the earth will be filled with the knowledge of the glory of the Lord, as the waters cover the sea."
Habakkuk 2:14

If signs and wonders are God's revelation of His own goodness—His love and compassion—then it makes sense that these phenomena flow most freely through people who are lined up with the Father's heart of love and compassion. No one has ever been more lined up with the Father than the Son! After all, by His own testimony, the Son did "only what pleases Him" (John 8:29) and referred to His actions as "the miracles I do in my Father's name" (John 10:25).

In the Gospels, we often read of how Jesus' own miracles were prompted by compassion. When He saw the multitudes, Matthew 14:14 tells us "he had compassion on them and healed their sick." In the next chapter, He is concerned about the wellbeing of another crowd. Matthew 15:32 says, "Jesus called his disciples to him and said, 'I have compassion for these people; they have already been with me three days and have nothing to eat. I do not want to send them away hungry, or they may collapse on the way.'" This very practical concern led to a miraculous multiplication of food. When He saw the widow of Nain, who had lost her only son, Luke 7:13 says, "his heart went out to her and he said, 'Don't cry.'" His concern for this woman prompted Him to raise her son from the dead. And what parent can miss the tenderness of Jesus in the story of the demon-possessed boy in Luke 9:42? It states, "But Jesus rebuked the evil spirit, healed the boy and gave him back to his father."

Whether Jesus was healing the sick, raising the dead, multiplying food or delivering from demons, it was always about *loving* people. Paul understood this when he wrote the familiar chapter 1 Corinthians 13, ". . . and if I have a faith that can move mountains, but have not love, I am nothing" (vs.2).

The signs and wonders that have accompanied this renewal have gotten a lot of attention. I don't think it's the miracles that are the most remarkable hallmark of this move of God. The "Toronto Blessing" and other related outpourings have born much fruit, but only because they have *first* borne the fruit of intimacy with God, then the fruit which naturally flows from intimacy—an impartation of His love and compassion.

As a result of the emphasis on intimacy and knowing the Father's heart, I believe this renewal is producing a new model of missions. I'm certainly not saying that the missionaries of the past were not motivated by love and compassion. Of course they were. But the church has traditionally tried to help out the "Lord of the Harvest" by appealing primarily to our sense of duty to the lost, our obligation to serve the Lord as faithful servants, or our call to fight the enemy as good soldiers. We have lost the sense of sonship as our *first* identity. In the past eleven and one-half years, the Holy Spirit has powerfully touched uncounted thousands of people with a profound sense of the Father's love and restored the "orphans" to their place as sons and daughters of the King. This has resulted in a new breed of missionaries—people going out who have a simple, childlike faith in their Father. The signs and wonders that have accompanied this new breed of missionary are simply the by-product of a renewed intimacy with the Father. Impartations aren't just about power they also create a new sense of intimacy with God. Signs and wonders follow the natural actions of people who, like Jesus the Son, are doing what they see the Father doing.

Leif Hetland, previously spoken of in chapter 9, has seen hundreds of thousands of Pakistanis won to Christ through his ministry. As passionate as he is about reaching the lost, he no longer does "missions" conferences. Instead, he does several "Father Loves You" conferences a year around the world. Why? As he explains it, he has seen thousands of people attend missions conferences, make commitments to serve God, and then sink right back into the same anxiety, fear and distractions that had previously kept them from stepping out in faith. But if they truly have a revelation and touch from the Holy Spirit concerning their sonship, they are able to serve the kingdom with all the joy and fearless abandonment of children who have complete trust in their Daddy.

Heidi and Rolland Baker in Mozambique are modeling this new kind of missions. While at Bethel Church in Redding, California, Heidi, to my surprise, happened to be there. I was undone by the love of God I saw in her, and the faithfulness to God that was revealed through her testimony. Only a heart that has been "transplanted" and replaced by the heart of God can minister to people in the face of such extreme hardships. The Apostle Paul, who endured such incredible hardship and persecution for the sake of the gospel, was a man of intense compassion, ministering "day and night with tears" to those he was sent to reach. Rolland and Heidi both share this same incredible passion for the lost. The motto of the Moravians, an early Protestant missionary movement, expresses their heart: "To Win For The Lamb That Was Slain The Rewards Of His Suffering."

The following excerpt is from a newsletter sent by Rolland during the disastrous floods of 2000:

> It has been more than two months since Mozambique's disastrous flooding began. . . . This terrible calamity that has beggared the capabilities of the United Nations and the world's largest relief organizations has brought a people to its knees. . . . We have a ministry team that works in the Chokwe camp, one of the most-supplied with over 70 thousand refugees in a massive sea of tents, and still we met groups who had not eaten at all in days. . . . More and more aid workers are getting tired, losing motivation and going home. Funds for aviation fuel are running out. Few organizations are even scheduling air transport flights anymore. There are only a handful of doctors to serve hundreds of thousands of flood victims. For weeks we have been flying our medical and ministry teams into completely un-served areas. The sick are walking ten and fifteen miles through water to get to our clinics. Just today the UN World Food Program and Doctors Without Borders asked Iris Ministries to go into six more areas where thousands of people have been left

desperate without aid since the floods began. . . . Without telephones and community records, and with their huts and other recognizable landmarks washed away, thousands of children are lost and wandering. We may never have an idea of how many people were drowned and swept away by strong currents. . . . Pastors at our Bible school here in Maputo are learning that their wives and children have been walking long distances to search for food. Some families have just disappeared, and there is no word from others. We have leading pastors who have no home to return to at all. . . . Every day we send them into the refugee camps by truck, helicopter, plane or boat—however we can. Identified by our Iris caps and shirts as officially registered aid workers, they are given freedom by the government to pray and minister everywhere they go. And daily they return with testimonies that we have dreamed of hearing all our lives. . . . they are thrilled to be in the King's service. They don't seem to get tired. They pray for everyone. Refugees beg them to return—with more Bibles and more teaching. *As they preach demons manifest themselves, and the pastors cast them out. The word spreads quickly: this Jesus has power!* . . . From government officials down to the smallest street children, hearts are open to Jesus on a scale we have never seen before. In the dumps, on the streets, in the refugee camps, in remote villages, among the poor and starving, a nation wants to know Jesus.

The harvest is plentiful, but the workers are few. Ask the Lord of the harvest, therefore, to send out workers into his harvest field" (Luke 10:2). Yes, the people need aid, they need food and clothes, but now they also know how much they need Jesus. They have poverty of spirit, and theirs is the kingdom of heaven. Our cry to Him is that he will supply us with all that we need to bring in the harvest—all the wisdom, energy, stamina, resources, faith, power and workers we need to please Him and to finish what He has set before us to do. . . . We are all stretched thin in many directions. But we refuse to back away and stop trusting God, for we know that His power is made perfect in our weakness. We are glad to be taken beyond ourselves, if only we can see Him at work. When all the secular agencies are gone, may the Body of Christ still be healthy, strong, bearing fruit and full of His love! May we be delighting in Him, depending on Him and glorifying Him, triumphing always as we spread everywhere the fragrance of the knowledge of Him.

Because it is difficult for us to imagine how devastating this flood was, and what an open door for ministry it created, I have included considerable material from that time period. Prior to the floods, the government was often making it hard for the Bakers, persecuting them, but a few years after the floods when I was with them for a pastors' meeting, the government attitude had changed to one of openness and affection. Much of this change came from the role of Iris Ministries during this time of great need. In another newsletter, Rolland wrote:

> But revival is blazing through the countryside. We have 350 churches now, and expect 400 by October. Our pastors are on fire with zeal. They endure any hardship to carry the Word even further. They can only be motivated by the supernatural love of God. They have raised at least five from the dead. They come streaming to our Bible school from all over the country. Another group just arrived from Beira by bus, on the way wading through waist-deep mud and water for five miles at one break in the road to get on another bus to the next break. . . . One pastor had clubfeet, and another was almost crippled, but they struggled through anyway. These are the most destitute pastors we have received yet, wearing only rags, bringing nothing with them. They are leaving their families for months in order to learn the Word of God. No one has a Bible, or a bicycle, or even a toothbrush. We spent weeks locating them, sending out messengers on foot when necessary to deliver food and bus money.

Again, he writes:

> We kept flying [in Rolland's Cessna 206] over the river, carefully studying the cultivated fields along the way. Every stand of maize was dead. The terrible floods and winds since February have taken out all the crops, even as far north as the Zambezi. The rivers have gone down, but the ground is muddy and swampy. The people have no seed for new crops, and now the dry season is here. Belongings were washed away, and families all over southern Mozambique lack even hoes to begin working their farms again. Two million landmines still in the ground make farming dangerous, and now the floods have shifted known minefields. . . . We finally coast to a stop and find ourselves surrounded by tall grass and hills—and a village. Everyone gathers around us, all excited and curious. Pastor Amori knows the local dialect and can interpret. We gather in a clearing, and soon we are preaching and having church! That's just what the villagers want. Soon they are repenting and worshipping, their hands in the air and their hearts with the King. All want Jesus. All want a church in their village. All want us to send them a pastor. Only one can read, so we give him a Bible with strict instructions to read to the

others. We will send a pastor, and we will build a church for them. They are thrilled. They can hardly believe we dropped in on them like this. And they wave and cry as we taxi back to takeoff position. May Jesus be with them richly. . . .

I have flown thousands of miles since the floods began, and I will never be the same. I have seen and felt deeper poverty than ever. I know what it feels like to lie in a cold, bare room shivering through a wintry night without a blanket or pillow—which no one else in the village has. Even our pastors have colds, coughs, and infections because they cannot keep warm. Whole families huddle together trying to survive. They have almost no utensils to eat with. They sit in the night by the light of a single candle. They are without medicine, without books, without recorded music, and often without a change of clothes. They eat a few handfuls of maize each day, not knowing what they will do next week or month. At one meeting of a dozen pastors, we bought bread, oranges and boiled eggs for their breakfast, and that was such a rare treat. Their shoes are ripped, soaked and coming apart, but they do not hesitate to walk for hundreds of miles around to carry out their ministry.

Are they discouraged? Are they depressed? No, they are overjoyed that Jesus has sent us, that we care, and that they can join our fellowship of churches. They cannot contain their enthusiasm. They are ready to preach throughout Mozambique, and then on to other countries. I visited one of our pastors in a poor town in Malawi where our staff had visited for one day last year. Now there are ten churches there, and eight thousand believers that are coming together for a conference this August! . . .

Grand cumulus clouds surround us with a heavenly wonderland. We break in and out of them, dancing to more turbulence—and get our visual senses dazzled by fresh rainbows, flashing reflections off more rivers and lakes, and the intense brilliance of cloud tops pierced by purest sunlight. We try to imagine the glories of heaven, the symphony of light, color, and sound around the throne of God, and the wonder of that love in His heart. How excellent it is to serve the King, to be His slave, and to be one with Him in spirit. . . .

Rolland and Heidi are radically in love with Jesus. Even though both are highly educated theologians, their faith is incredibly simple. Rolland once said of Heidi, "When I met Heidi, she was like a twelve-year-old child in her faith. When she was touched in Toronto, she became like a six-year-old in her simple trust in her heavenly Father." Heidi has often shared the sum of her theology as, "God's God! I'm not. Hooray!"

If they were the only "case study" of those who have been dramatically impacted by the "impartations" of this renewal, one could easily dismiss them as an anomaly. But their story is just the beginning. Testimonies continue to pour in from those who are seeing the kingdom of God come in power by "becoming as little children"— children who share their Father's heart. Let me share two stories from Europe.

HOLLY MILLER, GRAZ, AUSTRIA

Holly Miller and her husband Paul have laid their lives down for Austria as missionaries, and Holly has served with me several times in Brazil, Russia, and the Ukraine. She tells here how the outpouring of the Holy Spirit has done in her life:

My personal story has been forever changed by the outpouring of the Holy Spirit through Toronto, and later, through affiliating with Randy Clark. More importantly, what God has been able to do *through me* has expanded exponentially. Looking back on ten years ago, I can say that the following is only part of what has changed for me as a direct result of Renewal:

From being a tired missionary focused on the local situation, my awareness of and passion for the kingdom of God in the earth has expanded beyond what I thought possible. I once saw my sphere of influence as limited to a small church in southeastern Austria, but God has since expanded my territory to many other countries and other continents.

From being a person who was deeply insecure about my acceptance in The Beloved, worried about stepping over the line or offending God, I have grown to know my Father's heart in a deeper measure than ever before, and trust Him more in every situation I face. From wishing I could see at least one real miracle before I die, I have been witness to countless dramatic healings and some literal miracles— even through me! The flow of prophetic and healing power has become a part of normal ministry, rather than an abnormal event.

Best of all, I have seen countless hearts healed and countless people "ruined" by the presence of God for anything but the purposes of God, and changed forever. There is nothing I love more than being a partner with the Holy Spirit and ministering alongside Him; feeling the Father's heart, pouring it out and seeing people "get it." This is reality, this is eternal, this is worth living for and this is worth dying for. I've grown insatiably hungry to see ever more of God's kingdom manifested in the earth. It doesn't quit, folks there is always more!

Holly and Paul have been powerfully touched with fresh impartations of the Holy Spirit over the last ten years. Not only have they personally received impartations, I have numbers of testimonies from pastors whom Holly has laid hands upon that have received a powerful impartation through her ministry.

STACY AND CASEY LONG, BOSNIA-HERZEGOVINA

Now Holly Miller shares with us the story of her friends, Stacy and Casey Long, missionaries working in the predominantly Muslim culture of Bosnia-Herzegovina:

It's just past nine in the morning. I'm sitting in a (somewhat!) heated bus leaving the snowy city of Zenica in Bosnia-Herzegovina. We've just finished four days of ministry in Zenica, serving with American missionaries Stacy and Casey Long and their small band of radical Christian believers in this predominantly Muslim culture.

The Longs had been saved into a mainline evangelical church in Southern California, and it was there in 2002 they received a call from God to go to Bosnia. In May of 2003 they were at a crisis point in raising support and starting to wonder if they'd be able to go after all. Just then Randy Clark was ministering at a local Vineyard church, so they went at the invitation of a friend, who'd been trying to get them to go to renewal meetings for months.

Well, this was a divine appointment, both in prophetic confirmation of the call to Bosnia and a healing anointing that Stacy received when Randy simply laid a thumb on Stacy's left palm. Randy moved on at that point (he prayed more for him later) and Stacy was disappointed because nothing happened at first. But then the small spot started burning. This spread until his whole palm was burning intensely, and this continued with varying degrees of intensity *for days*. It comes back now and then, especially during worship. I have since been witness to at least three instant healings (and heard of more) when the manifestation was present and Stacy laid his hand on someone.

Stacy and Casey, with their four boys, left the Southern California lifestyle and moved to Zenica in September of 2003. Within the first year, everything they had come for collapsed.

Apparently, God had something else in mind because the relief organization closed. One by one, all the projects the Longs were supposed to be developing had to be dropped due to lack of funds. The orphanage leadership refused Christian help.

"The orphans basically raise themselves," Casey tells me. Jobs are not readily available, and after obligatory basic schooling they just co-exist in dormitory-like facilities not far from the Longs' home. Boys and girls are lumped together as if they were family. But they are not family. Much of the time they are without adult oversight. There are many days when the overseers they do have beat them. The law of the jungle is the law effective in this Muslim orphanage. When it's noised about that one of the girls is friendly with Christians, there are many ways for the older Muslim boys to terrorize and intimidate her. But some keep coming anyway, week after week, drawn by the taste of genuine family (Longs have four boys aged two to ten) and to soak up the atmosphere of acceptance and worship which permeates the Longs' home. Every Monday night is "worship evening," and God always shows up.

For months last year, Stacy hosted a "men's evening," when English-speaking men would gather to worship and soak in God's presence. Most were Christians but Mirko, a Muslim, liked to hang around with English speakers so he came too. One evening Stacy noticed Mirko standing motionless in the center of the room while a worship CD was playing, staring down at the floor. He stayed there quite awhile and so Stacy thought he should ask if Mirko was all right, offer prayer. . . As Stacy placed a hand on his shoulder, Mirko fell face-forward like a stone onto the floor, not breaking his fall with his hands. He lay there motionless for a few minutes and then began to shake and tremble, tried to sit up and with wild eyes shouted at the gathered men: *"What did you do to me? Where did you take me??!!"* It took awhile for the men to convince Mirko that nobody had done a thing to him, and for him to calm down. Apparently God took him into an open vision that subjectively lasted for hours. After showing him all his sins, God took him to his mother's grave and gave him a significant personal experience. This was Mirko's turning point and he gave his life to Jesus. This is only one story of those who have come to know Jesus through supernatural means—a dream or vision, a healing, a visitation.

It was a great privilege for me to enter the Longs' world, even if only for a few days, and share in their daily lives. It's *a new kind of missions:* simply living the life of Jesus in the midst of darkness. It's *empowered missions,* having something to give people besides relief goods: salvation, inner and physical healing, deliverance, word of wisdom when troubled people show up at the door, a word of knowledge for the sick or the demonized. It's *natural missions*—just being agents of God's kingdom in a nation torn by war, poverty and false religion. It works.

LOVE WITH POWER

As I write the concluding paragraphs to this chapter I am in Annapolis, Brazil. Last night at the meeting, we witnessed a dramatic skit that the local church performed. Actors were playing the part of the blind, crippled, a woman whose baby had died in the womb, diseased, elderly, weak, and sick. They were trying to see the doctor. A man who was hard-hearted was giving them tickets and treating them without love. He was arrogant and heartless. In the skit, the doctor who showed up was Jesus. As the doctor sang about his work at the cross, the blind lady took off her dark glasses, the cripples threw off their canes and calipers, a man's deformed foot righted itself, the dead baby in the mother's womb came back to life, the elderly woman threw her walker away and the neck brace came off her neck. They all leapt with joy and ran off the stage. I lost it as I watched this skit. I began to weep so hard that my shoulders were wrenching. I realized that I had personally seen all these things happen in real life except for the dead baby in the womb coming to life—but even that did happen through my friend, Carol Baerg. But why was I crying so hard? I realized it was because I had received from God not only an impartation of power for ministry, but also an impartation of love for people. I had received the Father's heart. Even as I write this, my eyes have been filled with tears—tears of gratitude that my heart of stone has become a heart of flesh. You do not get excited about healing for others unless you have concern for others.

Love for God and the love of God come *from* God, from His Spirit. Paul's great chapter on love in 1 Corinthians 13 was never meant to be the alternative to the gifts of the Holy Spirit. In context, it is clear that this chapter is to be the higher way of working in the gifts of the Spirit, motivated by the *agape*[74] love of God. It does great destruction to the context of the chapter to set this love in

180

opposition to the gifts or as an alternative to the gifts. In context, Paul was saying the "most excellent way" (1 Corinthians 13:1) to use the Spirit's gifts is when motivated by God's *agape* love for people. Indeed, it is the *only* way that is of any real value.

During times of prayer, I ask God to impart His heart to me for the people—the broken, the poor, the diseased and sick, and the demonized. I also ask God to give us His power to do something for them, because to get His heart and not have any supernatural power from Him to do something about their condition would be cruel. On the other hand, to have His power without His love makes us harsh in our ministry and makes us poor witnesses to the model of Jesus. James, the half brother of Jesus wrote:

> Religion that God our Father accepts as pure and faultless is this: **to look after orphans and widows in their distress** and to keep oneself from being polluted by the world. (James 1:27, emphasis added)

The Old Testament prophet, Isaiah, spoke this word of the Lord:

> Is not this the kind of fasting I have chosen: to loose the chains of injustice and untie the cords of the yoke, to set the oppressed free and break every yoke? Is it not to share your food with the hungry and to provide the poor wanderer with shelter—when you see the naked, to clothe him, and not to turn away from your own flesh and blood? **Then** your light will break forth like the dawn, and your healing will quickly appear; then your righteousness will go before you, and the glory of the Lord will be your rear guard. **Then** you will call, and the Lord will answer; you will cry for help, and he will say: Here am I. If you do away with the yoke of oppression, with the pointing finger and malicious talk, and if you spend yourselves in behalf of the hungry and satisfy the needs of the oppressed, then your light will rise in the darkness, and your night will become like the noonday. (Isaiah 58:6-10, emphasis added)

These passages indicate the heart of God for people. His glory is revealed in His character and His character is partially revealed in these passages that reflect His concern for people. It is out of this concern that He has equipped the church to minister to the needs of people who are in emotional, physical, mental, or spiritual distress. Some things can be ministered to out of our ability, out of our abundance, but God's compassion is so great that He has equipped us through His gifts to minister beyond our ability to reveal not only His truth, but His glory, His compassion and His love. When you cry out for an impartation I counsel you to cry out not just for His power, but also for an impartation of His love and compassion.

Now, let us turn our attention to the cost of receiving this impartation. Many believe that you can receive an impartation and continue in your everyday life as things always were. That is not the truth. There is a high price to be paid to walk in the fullness of what God has for you. There must be a commitment to lay your life down daily to walk in obedience to God. Impartations prepare us to be willing to pay that price. Let us look at the next chapter when I will talk about an impartation for the power to die.

CHAPTER 11: RADICAL OBEDIENCE – IMPARTATION FOR THE POWER TO DIE

"I tell you the truth, unless a kernel of wheat falls to the ground and dies, it remains only a single seed. But if it dies, it produces many seeds. The man who loves his life will lose it, while the man who hates his life in this world will keep it for eternal life."
John 12: 24-25

"But whatever was to my profit I now consider loss for the sake of Christ. What is more, I consider everything a loss compared to the surpassing greatness of knowing Christ Jesus my Lord, for whose sake I have lost all things."
Philippians 3:7-8

When I am preaching on the subject of impartation and know that I am going to pray for people afterwards, I always share about the experience of Heidi Baker and the wonderful fruit that has occurred since she received the impartation. Often, after asking the people, "How many of you would like to receive an impartation like Heidi Baker received?" almost everyone raises their hand. I then say, "Now, let me tell you the rest of the story." Then I tell them about all the suffering and hardships that the Bakers faced within the first year of Heidi's experience of impartation. I point out that often there is a degree of difficulty corresponding to the degree of the intensity of the impartation. I don't understand how it all works; all I am sure of is that the price of revival is high, and that impartations prepare people to be willing to pay that price.

While praying for people to receive an impartation, I don't just ask God to fill them with power, but I also ask that He will baptize them in His love. I know that it is the baptism of love that will cause them not to quit when things get hard. It is the baptism of power that gives them the ability to minister, but it is the baptism of love that gives them the motivation to minister—and keep on ministering, especially in missions.

My friend, Graham Cooke, told me about a training event he and apostolic leader Jonathan David from Indonesia conducted in the Philippines. They were training about seventy young leaders who were going into China and other places where the preaching of the gospel could result in prison and/or death. One young woman came to the two leaders having had a vision of her death as a martyr. Later a second person had a similar vision, this time it was a young man. Then another young man came with tears in his eyes, deeply burdened in his soul. He asked the question, "Is there something displeasing in my life that the Lord would not consider me worthy of being martyred for his sake?" This is the fruit of those who have had a powerful impartation from the Holy Spirit.

SOPHAL UNG, CAMBODIA

The apostolic leader Sophal Ung of Cambodia experienced deep suffering under both the Khmer Rouge and the Vietnamese. He was one of the first young Cambodians to be led to the Lord in the 1970s. He was powerfully filled with the Holy Spirit during an experience where the Holy Spirit blew open the window of the upper room where the believers were praying and filled them. They began to either speak in tongues or to prophesy. Later, almost 90% of his congregation would be killed in the killing fields or in other places by the Khmer Rouge soldiers. After being tortured himself, put in a prison dungeon, and being the only one to survive out of about 200 prisoners, he miraculously escaped and eventually made it to the United States with his wife and five children. Not long after coming to the States, his wife died of cancer. God then called Sophal Ung back to Cambodia. This was the hardest thing he had ever heard from God. He would have to leave his five children in America to be cared for by other friends and family. Sophal Ung's life is a life of miracles, a life of sacrifice and faith. Only a baptism of love and power could give someone the ability to face the prospect of torture and death, to leave behind five children, to leave the comfort of the United States to go to the war stricken and impoverished country of Cambodia.

My friend, Guy Chevreau, and I were talking one night about the cost of living our lives for Christ, and for working in this renewal/revival. We agreed that we felt like everything was worth it. Nothing really should be counted as a sacrifice in light of how He had reached down and touched us, empowered us, and sent us to the nations. Then he said to me, "That is, nothing is a sacrifice except the cost to our families. Every time the offering plate comes by, I put my hand in it and purpose in my heart that my family is placed in the offering." I agreed. We were both spending about 180 days a year away from our wives and children.

Once when flying with Rolland and Heidi Baker in Mozambique, we began to talk about what a privilege it was to get to see a revival, a people movement, a harvest of souls accompanied by miracles of healings, deliverances, and provision. As we were talking, we all mentioned the one price we counted to be the highest price—that price had been paid by our families. We all knew that at least one half of our children's lives were spent separated from us. We encouraged ourselves that God would be faithful to touch our children, and somehow redeem the time away from them.

In comparison to other periods of missionary expansion, we are living in a better time. In the nineteenth century modern missionary movement, missionaries often had to leave their children in the care of grandparents or aunts and uncles because they realized the high mortality rate for children in the country they were going to minister. Other missionaries like the Baptists Hudson Taylor and Adoniram Judson, two great pioneer missionaries to China and to Burma, buried wives and children in the soil of their mission field. Rolland's own grandparents buried two children in the remote mountains of Tibet.

I said we are living in a better time, but we cannot ignore that there is still a price. It's easy to say, "Yes, I want the anointing. I want an impartation." It is not so easy to be willing to pay the price. People see the wonderful, amazing revival going on in Mozambique and surrounding nations today through Iris Ministries.

What they rarely see are the ever-present struggles, battles, and sacrifices that are made everyday.

When Rolland's dear friend, Mel Tari, heard about the writing of this book, he urged my editor, "Please, whatever you do, don't leave people with the impression that the anointing is something you can just run down to the altar for, and bang, through one quick experience, you have a powerful ministry." Mel is right. God worked for seventeen years in the hearts of Rolland and Heidi, bringing them to a place where they were willing to be completely poured out, humble and obedient servants. Revival is not just about power. It is not even primarily about power. More importantly, it is about love and humility. Are we willing to allow the Holy Spirit to do whatever it takes to break us of our pride, our need to control, out self-seeking motives in ministry? Are we desperate enough for Him to let Him completely have His way in us?

BILL JOHNSON, REDDING, CALIFORNIA

My dear friend, Pastor Bill Johnson of Bethel Church in Redding, California, still vividly recalls the night God met him at his point of humble desperation and changed him forever. . .

> For months I had been asking God to give me more of Him. I wasn't sure of the correct way to pray, nor did I understand the doctrine behind my request. All I knew was I was hungry for God. It had been my constant cry day and night.
>
> One evening we were having meetings with a good friend and prophet, Dick Joyce. The year was 1995. At the end of the meeting, I prayed for a friend who was having difficulty experiencing God's presence. I told him that I felt God was going to surprise him with an encounter that could come in the middle of the day, or even at 3:00 a.m.
>
> In the middle of the night, God came in answer to my own prayer for more of Him, yet not in a way I had expected. I went from a dead sleep to being wide-awake in a moment. Unexplainable power began to pulsate through my body, seemingly just shy of electrocution. It was as though I had been plugged into a wall socket with a thousand volts of electricity flowing through my body. My arms and legs shot out in silent explosions as if something was

released through my hands and feet. The more I tried to stop it, the worse it got.

I soon discovered that this was not a wrestling match I was going to win. I heard no voice, nor did I have any visions. This was simply the most overwhelming experience of my life. It was raw power . . . it was God. He came in response to a prayer I had been praying for months—God, I must have more of you at any cost! When the power fell on me that night, I looked at the clock. It was exactly 3:00 a.m. I knew I had been set up.

This divine moment was glorious, but not pleasant. At first I was embarrassed, even though I was the only one who knew I was in that condition. As I lay there, I had a mental picture of me standing before my congregation, preaching the Word as I loved to do. But I saw myself with my arms and legs flailing about as though I had serious physical problems. The scene changed—I was walking down the main street of our town, in front of my favorite restaurant, again arms and legs moving about without control.

I didn't know of anyone who would believe that this was from God. I recalled Jacob and his encounter with the angel of the Lord. He limped for the rest of His life. And then there was Mary, the mother of Jesus. She had an experience with God that not even her fiancé believed, although a visit from an angel helped to change his mind. As a result she bore the Christ-child…and then bore a stigma for the remainder of her days as the mother of the illegitimate child. It was becoming clear; the favor of God sometimes looks different from the perspective of earth than from heaven. My request for more of God carried a price.

Tears began to soak my pillowcase as I remembered the prayers of the previous months and contrasted them with the scenes that just passed through my mind. At the forefront was the realization that God wanted to make an exchange—His increased presence for my dignity. It's difficult to explain how you know the purpose of such an encounter. All I can say is you just know. You know His purpose so clearly that every other reality fades into the shadows, as God puts His finger on the one thing that matters to Him.

In the midst of the tears came a point of no return. I gladly yielded, crying, "More, God, more! I must have more of You at any cost! If I lose respectability and get You in the exchange, I'll gladly make that trade. Just give me more of You!"

The power surges didn't stop. They continued throughout the night, with me weeping and praying, "More Lord, more, please give me more of You." It all stopped at 6:38 a.m. at which time I got out of bed completely refreshed. This experience continued the following two nights, beginning moments after getting into bed.

When I became the pastor of Bethel Church, in Redding, California, I came because of a cry for revival. Our church in Weaverville, California was experiencing a wonderful outpouring of the Holy Spirit. Bethel was the *mother church* of our church in Weaverville, and I accepted their invitation to come and be their Senior Pastor. When I spoke to the new congregation about my coming, I told them that I was born for revival. And if they didn't want the move of the Spirit of God, along with the messes that come from such an outpouring, then they didn't want me, because this was not negotiable! They responded positively with close to unanimous support.

The outpouring began almost immediately. Lives were changed, bodies were healed, divine encounters increased in amazing proportions, along with unusual manifestations that seem to accompany revival—and approximately 1000 people left. It was outside their point of reference, off the map of their own experience.

Few things are more devastating to pastors than when people leave the church. It feels like rejection, and those in ministry are not immune to those feelings. Pastors are a unique breed—there are times when people leave the church who hate us and we still feel bad. Yet in this strange season of exodus, my wife and I were immune to the devastation. This is only possible if you are either callous of heart to the point where no one can affect you either for good or bad, or you are in denial about the impact such a loss is causing in your heart. The only other possibility is that God has actually given you a supernatural grace to live *opposite* to your circumstances. Because of the grace given to us, not one day was spent in discouragement or questioning God, because our food really was doing His will. His will provided all the nourishment and strength we needed. Plus, His presence was the reward. The public criticisms and slander, the humiliation of decreased numbers, the daily calls of complaint to our denomination for close to a year—all had no teeth to their bite, as the need for respectability had all but disappeared on the night of my visitation.

My closest friends could rightly argue that the fear of man was never really strong in my life. And in part that is true. I had learned this from watching my Dad in my early years. He displayed the priority of obedience to God regardless of what other's thought. Yet God knew what was lying underneath it all when He asked for my respectability in exchange for the increased manifestation of His presence.

I must make it clear that it was the generosity of God that made this possible. Along with the increased manifestation of His presence, He made His will too obvious to ever miss. God often spoke to us in a dream, or a vision of the mind. Sometimes He brought forth a prophetic word that confirmed or added understanding to a direction we were to take. There was never a question. The fruit of the increased measure of His presence, along with the bounty of transformed lives, was all we needed to smile in the face of such apparent loss. And to this day, we consider it a privilege to do so.

God didn't just change Bill's life; He changed the life of his church and the church is now changing the life of their city. If you go to the church website at *www.ibethel.org*, you'll get a peek at what God is doing through this highly charged body of believers. The church ministries' listing includes such opportunities as "Neighborhood Invasion," "Nightstrike Evangelism," and "To the Streets Evangelism." All ministries are initiated by the laity, people who have been taught and equipped to continue the ministry of Jesus, preaching the gospel and healing the sick right in the streets, grocery stores and malls of Redding. I highly recommend Bill's book, *When Heaven Invades Earth: A Practical Guide to a Life of Miracles*, available through the church's website.

In April 1999 I was in Redding, California where I was to minister with Bill. Somehow Heidi and I ended up being at Bill's church at the same time. I heard that wonderful things were happening with Heidi and that she had been powerfully touched through the prophecy I gave her in January 1997. At this time, I had never been able to meet Heidi personally, nor had I really understood the magnitude of what God had been doing through her and Rolland, nor the high cost their family had paid as a result of "walking out" the prophetic word. In two years there had been over 250 churches planted! This was not accomplished with a great missionary force and an entire denomination behind them. This was a truly miraculous increase from just one church, twelve Mozambican leaders and Rolland and Heidi.

I heard Heidi's testimony for the first time as she preached a powerful sermon on walking by faith. For the first time, I understood how significant that prophetic word had been, and how much suffering the Bakers had been through in obedience to walking out the promises of that word.

It is not enough to simply have someone pray for you or prophesy over you. The word from the Lord must be met with faith, taken a hold of, and walked in. God had a destiny for the children of Israel when He led them out of Egypt. Yet, unbelief kept that generation from ever reaching the land of God's promise. Rolland, Heidi, Leif, and others like them are walking in God's promised destiny for their lives, but not simply because of a single act of impartation or prophecy. It is because they have chosen to receive by faith what God has promised, whatever the cost, and have determined to lay everything else down in reckless love for Jesus, in total submission to His every leading.

FAITH WORKING THROUGH LOVE

Heidi once told me how she picks her leadership in Mozambique. One of the things she does is to bring pastors to the orphanage to see how they minister to, play with, and love on the children. If they do not have true love for the children, and a willingness to serve them, then she feels they don't have a servant's heart enough to be considered a key leader. She looks for love and service in their hearts.

I found one of the most powerful illustrations of this type of love and servant's heart in an email from Rolland referring to a cholera epidemic that had broken out. Many children were fighting for their lives, and the medical profession believed many would die from the cholera. Read for yourself, and be touched as I was.

DANGEROUS CHOLERA OUTBREAK/God's response
Rolland and Heidi Baker
Maputo, Mozambique
28 February 2001

The rivers of central Mozambique continue to rise, cutting many thousands of our own church members off from food supplies and medical help. Upstream dams are being opened up to prevent them from overflowing and breaking. The rains continue, and now again Mozambique's government is helpless without international assistance.

Challenges to our faith in Jesus do not stop. Last week, even as we received daily reports of desperation from the flooded north, a terrible outbreak of cholera hit our center at Zimpeto near the capital city of Maputo. We now think the cholera was introduced by contaminated food brought in to a wedding in our church. The disease is wildly contagious, and within days we had taken 70 children, pastors and workers to a special cholera hospital in town. This is actually a big tent, strictly quarantined, filled with "cholera tables," bare wood beds with a hole in each and buckets underneath for nonstop diarrhea and vomiting. Every patient was on an IV drip.

Many have died in this emergency hospital. Maputo's health officials were terrified of a citywide epidemic. Maputo's Director of Health put her finger in Heidi's face and told her, "You will be responsible for killing half of Maputo!" Every day health officials came to our center, desperately trying to identify the source of the cholera and contain its spread. Soon the city police were involved, intent on shutting down our entire center and ministry. For days nothing seemed to help. We were washing and disinfecting everything. Our trucks were making hospital runs day and night. Our own clinic was filled with children on IVs. Our staff was completely exhausted.

Only Heidi was allowed to visit the tent hospital. Every day she would go in and spend hours and hours with our kids, holding them, soaking them in prayer, declaring that they would live and not die. They vomited on her, covered her with filth, and slowly grew weaker. Many were on the edge of death, their eyes sunken and rolling back. The doctors were shocked by her lack of concern for herself, and were certain she would die along with many of our children.

Our stress level was the highest ever. We remembered how we had been evicted from our first center in early 1997, and we just couldn't take that again. We had been preaching salvation and deliverance with all our hearts to these children we had rescued out of the streets and dump, and now they were slipping away right in front of us. Twenty of our pastors from the north were also in the tent and dying. Some of our weaker pastors desperately wanted to go home, certain that they would all die if they stayed with us. Heidi and I were ready yet again to quit if God did not do something.

But during all of this the Holy Spirit kept falling on our meetings. Again and again all visitors would come to Jesus and hungrily drink in His Presence. A strong spirit of intercession came over our stronger pastors, who would pray all hours, not only for our cholera victims, but also for the suffering of the whole nation. Intercessory prayer groups in the U.S. and Canada, and around the world began to pray intensely for us.

Three days ago our entire future in Mozambique was in question. No one had any more answers. Our weakness was complete. Then some of our children began coming home from the hospital, even as others were being taken there. And then there were no more new cases. Extraordinary. And then yesterday everyone was home! Just like that, the cholera is gone. And Heidi is fine.

The doctors and nurses at the hospital are in a state of shock and wonder. The Director of Health again put a finger in Heidi's face: "You! This is God! The only reason you got through this was God! You and dozens of these children should be dead!"

Eight of the medical staff there want to work with us now. "This is miraculous! You know God! We've never seen God do anything like this. We've never seen such love! We don't want to work here anymore. We want to work with you!" And so they will.

Several visitors to our center who came down with cholera did die after returning to their huts and refusing to go to the hospital. And we heard that one of our pastors had died, but that report turned out to be mistaken. We did not lose a single person who lives with us at Zimpeto.

So in a matter of days our worst crisis ever has turned into a wave of peace and joy at our center. Last night we worshiped to all hours, beholding His beauty in our hearts and enjoying His company.

At one of our recent conferences, Rolland and Heidi shared how high the attrition rate was for North American missionaries who go as long-term missionaries. Unless they have an experience of empowerment from the Holy Spirit, many do not last very long on the field. There is a great price to be paid for the pursuit of God and for the desire to be able to be a disciple who not only tries to obey God's ethical commands, but obey His commands to heal the sick, cast out demons, preach the good news to the poor, and raise the dead.

I just paused from writing to read a new email from Rolland Baker explaining his and Surpresa Sithole's recent first trip into the Congo. In the midst of describing for us the hardships of the people and the trip Rolland states:

This movement does not chase health and wealth, or manifestations, or signs and wonders. We preach Jesus and Him crucified, and the power of the Cross. Nothing counts but faith working through love, producing joy! We seek first His kingdom and His righteousness, and all these others things will chase us! We are learning how to be rich in good deeds, and blessed with godliness and contentment. We are falling in love with Him who is love, until nothing in this world attracts us like He does.

In the same email Rolland wrote:

After all these years of preaching in the bush among the poor and faraway, we realize we have seen just the beginning of what God plans for Africa. North Africa, considered almost off-limits for the Christian Gospel, is beckoning. Jesus has no competition once His reality, love, and power are known. Angola and West Africa are calling. The multitudes want what is real. Our bodies are exhausted, our time is stretched beyond endurance, our wisdom for shepherding this movement is finite, but each morning we find ourselves renewed by the power of God. These pastors in Bukavu are ready to preach all across the Congo, taking the fire of God everywhere they go. We must encourage them; we must do our part; we must obey. Our lives are worth nothing to us, if only we may finish the race and complete the task the Lord Jesus has given us—the task of testifying to the gospel of God's grace (Acts 20:24).

What is this Revival all about? Sacrifice being made? Yes. Joy being present? Yes. Love reaching out to others? Yes. Intimacy with God in the secret place? Yes. I can hear the pleas of Heidi as I write, "Lower still, lower still, lower still, the river flows to the lowest place, lower still, lower still." She is ever crying out for a greater willingness to lay down her life, her pride, her desires. What are the twin engines that have driven this move of God? Intimacy with God and humility before God. These two engines have been fueled by love and power, impartations and gifts. I used impartations in the plural on purpose for I know of at least four impartations Heidi has received and one that Rolland has received since

193

the initial prophecy I gave her in Toronto. It is not a one-time experience, but one that will need to be repeated as we pour ourselves out on His behalf to those in need. We who are willing to "spend and be spent" for the salvation of souls need to occasionally have our own lives renewed by a fresh impartation of the Holy Spirit.

Do you want to be part of this new missionary movement? I have given you the keys to being used by God: intimacy and humility, faith, and hunger to ask God for a powerful impartation of the Holy Spirit. Some of you may never have had the experience of being filled with or baptized in the Holy Spirit. Others may have had this experience but you need a fresh new filling of the Holy Spirit. Others have had this experience but need an impartation for certain gifts to increase your fruitfulness in His kingdom. Perhaps you need the gifts of healings or the gift of faith for miracles, or the gift of word of knowledge, etc. Actually these gifts often come in tandem. For example the gifts of healings are often connected to the gift of a word of knowledge, the gift of working of miracles is connected to the gift of faith, the gift of prophecy to the gift of discernment, and the gift of tongues to the gift of interpretation of tongues. So I encourage you to ask, and keep on asking, knock and keep on knocking, seek and keep on seeking. I remind you of the words of the Apostle Paul, "But eagerly desire the greater gifts. . . . Follow the way of love and eagerly desire spiritual gifts, especially the gift of prophecy" (1 Corinthians 12:31, 14:1).

Come join us in the nations. Perhaps you will find meaning for your life as you lay it down for Him. First I counsel you with the words of Jesus to "stay in your city until you have been clothed with power from on high." This was after he promised them, "I am going to send you what my Father has promised." This was the promise of the Holy Spirit. I believe the reference here is not to the Spirit's work of regeneration, or sealing the believer, but the ministry of the Holy Spirit to "come upon" them and fill them with power from on high. If you are a Christian you have already been baptized by the Spirit into the body of Christ. But, I am counseling you to desire the mighty promise of the Father for the Spirit to come upon you and fill you with power for service.

So Phal Ung, who in my opinion is the greatest apostle in the nation of Cambodia, returned to Cambodia, leaving his five children in the United States. This was just after barely escaping from the killing fields when he first came to the United States. His heart burns for the salvation of his nation. When he visited Toronto Airport Christian Fellowship he experienced such a powerful new baptism of the Holy Spirit that it affected his body. He shook and trembled under the power. He said it made his body do similar movements to what it did when the Vietnamese tortured him with electrical prods, but instead of bringing weakness and pain the power of God brought joy, strength, and boldness. He then encouraged any Cambodians in the United States who were considering coming back to Cambodia to work with him to first go to Toronto and receive from God.

Oh, Holy Spirit, work in our hearts today to produce a love that is extravagant for God. Give us a love so extravagant that we are willing to "waste" our lives on Him, poured out as costly perfume. Only You can produce this kind of sacrificial love for Jesus and the Father. We confess that we cannot crucify our flesh; this must be your work. So come, come Holy Spirit and create in us the life of Christ.

We have just seen how God can use any one of us if we are willing to pay the price. In the next chapter I want to share how God has used the "little ol' mes" in ways that are almost beyond imagination. Read ahead and you will see how God clothes people with power. Nobody is safe when God begins to move!

CHAPTER 12: CLOTHED WITH POWER – NOBODY'S SAFE

Before January of 1994, I had heard several times through different speakers at various conferences:

> A revival is coming. It will be a nameless, faceless revival where there will be no "God's man of power for the hour" superstars but rather the emphasis will be upon the equipped saints of the church. So many will be touched that, at large events where many healings and miracles were happening, reporters won't be able to find out who prayed for someone who just received a major miraculous healing. Why not? Because the saints have been equipped and the old distinction between clergy and laity has been replaced from understanding it to be the role of the clergy to pray for the sick, to understanding that the role of the clergy and all five-fold offices is to "equip the saints for the work of the ministry."

I believe the outpourings in Toronto and later in Pensacola, Florida, in several evangelical colleges, and earlier through Rodney Howard-Browne are a fulfillment of this prophetic word.

I have written a small book called *God Can Use Little Ol' Me*. That title sums up my testimony and my basic message to the church. I look at my past, my limitations, things that I considered failures, and I have a whole new appreciation for what Paul wrote in Ephesians 3:20, 21: "Now to him who is able to do immeasurably more than all we ask or imagine, according to **his power that is at work within us**, to him be glory in the church and in Christ Jesus throughout all generations, for ever and ever!" (Emphasis added). God is to be glorified in and through His church! He is glorified when we finally believe that it is not about what we can do, but all about what He will do through us by His power, if we will let Him. Let me share several testimonies from people who thought of themselves as just a "little ol' me" until they received a powerful touch from the Holy Spirit and realized that God had a lot more for them than anything they had ever thought to "ask or imagine."

JOHN GORDON, ILLINOIS

There was a man who had attended our church for years and was even on the board for several years by the name of John Gordon. Even though he had been serving on the board for years, he hadn't had a true experience with Christ—he would tell you in his own words that he had a "false conversion." But just a few nights before what I am about to tell you took place, he had a true conversion to Christ for the first time. John was upset with me over all this healing stuff that was going on and that was being taught in our church. In John's mind, it wasn't of God.

John came late to the meeting at the church and was standing in the back, leaning with his hand on the wall. The speaker, Blaine Cooke, said, "God's going to commission some of you tonight to begin to pray for the sick. This is how He'll do it. You're going to have a feeling of electricity or heat in your hands."

John was back there muttering, "That's a bunch of bull! What's Randy getting us into now? This is bogus. I don't believe this." While he was standing there, his hand started tingling. He figured it had gone to sleep because he had been holding it up against the doorframe. Moments later John came down the aisle weeping profusely, with his hands shaking rapidly. He told me later, "I felt like my fingers were going to blow off of my hands!"

John came up to me crying, "Randy, I've got to take my contact lens out! I've been crying so hard, my left eye is killing me!"

I piped up, "John! That could be a word of knowledge!"

He said, "Oh, you and those words of knowledge. I don't believe in them. It's not a word of knowledge. I've just been crying too much."

Right behind John stood a young girl in our church who was 14 years old at the time. Her name was Tammy Ferguson. Tammy had come forward because she had been to the ophthalmologist that day for her left eye, which was severely crossed. They told her the only way it would ever be corrected would be through surgery.

So I said, "John, look! It's Tammy!"

So he didn't take his contact out and we started to pray for her. John told her to open her eyes, she did, but it was still crooked. He told her to close her eyes and we would pray again. We did that four times, and on the fifth time her eye was totally straight. She was healed and to this day has never had a problem with it. There were no words to express the excitement we felt.

About a week or two later John and I were asked to pray for a woman who was having grand mal seizures. Her family had recommended we pray for her because one of the family members had been delivered from demons just a few days earlier. The formerly demonized woman and her husband believed it was probable that this woman was also demonized. This was because she was not a Christian and when they had gone to pray for her she began to have a grand mal seizure. I had told them not to jump to conclusions too quickly and think it was a demon. I suggested they wait and, if it happened the next time they prayed, then we should meet with her again. Sure enough, the next time they prayed, she had another grand mal seizure. I was very nervous when we met to pray for her because this was only the second person I had ever prayed for who was demonized. The woman was thirty-nine years old and had to use a walker; she was losing her eyesight, and was eaten up with arthritis. Before we began to pray for her, we prayed for ourselves to be more receptive to the leading of the Spirit. As we were praying for ourselves, we knelt at a distance from the demonized woman but she still fell to the floor in a grand mal seizure.

When this happened, John went up to her and said, "You tried to kill me last night. I know who you are, and I know all about you."

Then He said, "What about Mike?" and, "What about Benton?"

Both times she went into much stronger manifestations that were obviously demonic. Then he commanded two demons by their names to come out of her, and they did!

I found out that the night before we were to do the deliverance, John had been attacked by an evil spirit while in his sleep. He felt like he was being choked and was overcome with great fear. He was barely able to utter the name, "Jesus." But once he did, immediately the stranglehold around his neck left, as well as the fear.

Then God took him into an open vision where he saw that this demonized woman had been raped when she was sixteen years old, twenty-three years earlier. The only other person who knew about this was the woman's mother who told her to never share with anyone what happened to her. In the open vision, John knew the rapist's name, the make of the car in which she had been raped, the name of the town where she was raped, and the names of the two demons that had entered her as a result of this traumatic experience. Ever since this experience, John has had the gift of "discerning of spirits." He can literally feel a twisting of the muscles in his chest when he gets around the demonic.

John's impartation took place in March of 1994, but he is still living out the fruit of the impartation to this day. Several years later he was driving by the Bethesda Cancer Institute in southern Illinois. As he passed it he said, "I would like the opportunity to pray for one hundred cancer patients." A brief time passed and John received a call from his secretary. She said, "John, the director from the Bethesda Cancer Institute is on the line and wants to talk to you." John took the call and heard the director say, "I have heard that you like to pray for the sick and I was wondering if you would participate in a study we are doing on the effects of prayer upon our patients. Would you be willing to pray for one hundred of our patients?" John immediately answered, "Yes!"

Later, I asked John about the results of this opportunity. He told me there were several healings as a result of prayer, but the most dramatic happened this way. He entered the room of a large African-American man and prayed for him. The power of God came upon this man and he was healed! What was dramatic was the rest of the story: The man receiving prayer had had a dream of John—

whom he had never met—the night before John entered his hospital room. In the dream, the man saw John enter his room wearing a white coat and ask to pray for him, after which the man experienced the power of God go through his body and he was healed. When John actually did enter the room and offered to pray, the faith of the man exploded. He said to John, "I knew I was going to be healed. There was not one doubt!"

John's impartation was now twenty-one years ago, and he is still one of the most on fire people in that part of the state in praying for healing and deliverance.

ANNE STEPANEK, CHARLOTTE, NORTH CAROLINA

A very recent impartation story is that of Anne Stephaek. Here is her own testimony as to what happened to this "little ol' me":

> I attended the first Healing School in Everett, Washington in May of 2004 with a friend of mine. I'd been praying for the sick for about nine years with very minimal results and had never seen anyone instantly healed while I prayed for them. Well, the Healing School that I attended changed all that! On the last day of the school, I prayed for a woman with knee and back injuries, and she was instantly healed! The day we arrived back home in N.C., my friend prayed for a woman over the phone who was suffering with knee pain, and she was instantly healed! We continued to pray for the sick and saw more and more healings.
>
> We were so excited that we trained up people in our church using your Ministry Training Manual.[75] During the practice sessions of the training, people started getting healed! A six-year-old boy was prayed for at two practice sessions for a hole in his heart. The next week, at his doctor's appointment, the hole was totally gone! We saw an increase in healings in our church services, and also people began to pray for the sick in their workplaces and in stores, parks and doctors' offices. God miraculously healed many, some instantly and many within just a few days of receiving prayer.
>
> It's just amazing what God's doing. I can't believe that God can use a little ol' home school mom to release His healing power into the people I encounter as I just go about my day!

Many ask if the fruit of impartation is lasting. Listen to this "first fruit" (her words) tell the story of how one "little ol' me" went in 1994 from dying to a life of fruitfulness:

It was January, 1994, when my friends literally dragged me into a meeting at the Toronto Airport Vineyard. These dear friends had prepared a room in their house so I could stay with them during the last few weeks of my life. The doctors said there would only be six to twelve of them! I had been in so much pain for the past twenty years I was looking forward to the end. My life consisted of months at a time in the hospital—sometimes months I couldn't even remember. I lived on painkillers just to keep from going insane. Even though I was a nurse by profession, I had never seen symptoms like mine. This started in 1974, before the days of AIDS, so doctors knew very little about severe immune deficiencies. Although they suspected bone cancer, I couldn't be treated because I had no immunities. Any chemo would have killed me instantly. I had severe pain in all my extremities, severe headaches, lived on oxygen treatments, and had lost track of the times I'd been told I was dying. Every day was a struggle to live. At the age of fifty-four, I was ready to die!

When the ministry time came at the end of the service, my friends led me to Randy for prayer. When he laid his hands on me, I heard him say, "There is enough sadness in the church and you have been sad long enough!" When he said that, I hit the deck, instantly 'drunk' with joy! There's just no other way to describe it. I don't remember much of the next two weeks, except that I was totally intoxicated with the love and joy of the Lord. My friends carried me to and from the meetings since I could rarely walk on my own. One night, sitting up front, I just couldn't close my mouth. Randy came by and "poured more" into my mouth. This was only a symbolic gesture, but I realized the word spoken was "Open your mouth and He will fill it." (Psalm 81:10). I was so drunk on the Holy Spirit it took me three days to realize all my pain was gone!

After two weeks, I was asked to share my story at a women's conference. I was amazed to discover that as I tried to share, I could not speak because I was so overtaken with the Holy Spirit. I was helped to my seat! Later, many ladies came and asked if there was any way they could have what I had. What a shock to discover that I could "pass it on" to others!

Friends in ministry asked me to share and so I began to travel with them a bit. One of the trips took us to Minneapolis. Well, the Holy Spirit touched so many—healings, refreshing and lots of fun in the Holy Spirit. A team of pastors came from Europe in October of 1994 and we prayed over them. When the top leader got off the floor, he asked if we would come to Belgium and share at the opening of his ministry center there. That's how I started going to Europe. From there it has been by word of mouth. When I first started to travel, it was such a surprise because I thought "women do not do this!!"

I know what it is to feel like my hands and feet are on fire! Sometimes I've even had to take my shoes off because it felt like my feet were going to melt. In those first meetings, Randy called all those who had burning hands to come up. So, up I went. The next year, when I was in Belgium, a woman came to me with her daughter who was eight to nine months pregnant. The baby was dead. Doctors had told her to wait another week for labor to deliver the dead fetus. I panicked! I thought, *"I can't do this!"* I began to look around frantically with another thought, *"Where are the men of God?"* There was no one but "little ol' me" to pray for this woman. The grandmother had such faith but I was terrified.

"Does she speak English?" I asked my interpreter.

"No."

That brought me a little relief. These women wouldn't know what I was praying. I started, "Father, I have no faith for this..."

Now, Randy had touched my hands many times in past meetings and imparted a flaming heat, so I thought, "Something's got to start happening! This woman is expecting something!"

Well, I couldn't tell if anything happened that day but three years ago, when I was in Belgium again, a young boy ran to me and threw his arms around me, crying, "I'm the miracle baby!" I met the grandmother and, sure enough, that boy was the one that I had prayed for!

I am still discovering the gift that Randy has imparted to me. In September of 2004, I was in a service when the pastor's wife walked a very elderly man with severe asthma up to the front row and asked me to pray for him. I took one look at this frail man with his gray, bloodless skin and raspy, wheezy breathing and thought, "Oh God, somebody call an ambulance!" Then I found out he had a badly damaged heart. This guy was on his way out! What was I supposed to pray? I said, "Well, maybe God will give him a new heart." I prayed for him that night but had to leave town before the end of the conference.

A few days later, a friend called me, really excited. "Do you remember the eighty-year-old with the bad heart and asthma? Well, he's got a new heart! Last night he was dancing on the stage and running around the room, telling us about his new heart!"

On a recent plane flight, as I was thinking about what has happened to me, I suddenly realized I am a sort of "first fruits" of this revival. I think I was the first major healing in Toronto. The inheritance of this revival is healing and I am walking in that inheritance. This realization has caused a new level of faith and authority to rise in me. It's been over eleven years, and I'm still growing in this! I believe we are going to see more healings and more profound healings.

I'm sixty-four now and travel regularly in twelve countries, mostly in Europe. How have all these doors opened up? The Holy Spirit touches one in Switzerland and she tells her friend in Cologne, Germany. Then I get invited to share in churches and in "church around the kitchen table." It keeps multiplying beyond me. A woman I prayed for in Holland was healed of leukemia. Now she's a missionary overseas.

I have a BURNING in me to see people passionate about life and in love with Jesus, especially the young people. I am seeing so much fear and depression healed. I think I've been given much ministry to youth because they are so preoccupied with death and that breaks my heart.

I prayed for a young girl about six weeks ago. (June 2005) I don't know what they call it these days, but she had multiple personalities and was under the influence of demons. I covered her eyes and declared the glory of God over her. Her eyes suddenly opened and they were totally focused. Her countenance completely changed. She was delivered! It's the love of Jesus! He shows us the Father. The women in that church are now praying with authority! They saw how simple it is and just started doing it themselves.

I just got back from Germany where God opened doors to minister to refugees from Kyrgyzstan. One of the pastors saw a deaf woman get healed and asked me, "Can God do that for me too?" I prayed for this deaf pastor and God healed him too! The most awesome thing was going back into the Bavarian forest and finding people with an incredible hunger and humility. They are now eager to go into their own communities, ignited for Jesus!

I once thought of what I'm doing now as something only leaders and pastors and their wives could do. But God's using me and it's a lot of fun! This revival is about grabbing ahold of what God has spoken for you. It's about not saying, "Oh no, not me," but saying, "Let the glory fall!"

Twenty years ago I was ready to die. Now I'm more full of life and joy than I've ever been. I have a great sense of security in my Father. He loves me! The words Randy spoke over me are the message of my life and the message I carry, "Church, you've been sad long enough!"

THE CHILDREN OF MOZAMBIQUE

The only thing "little" about a "little ol' me" is one's perception. And man's perception is certainly not God's perception! In the rotting, smoldering dumps of Maputo, in the disease-ridden flood plain of the Zambezi river, in the slums, in abandoned fields still littered with mines, Iris Ministries finds the "least of these"—little ones discarded, unwanted and forgotten by the world. Their own families see no value in them, except perhaps as a body that can be sold on the streets. Many in the West see them as a burden to the earth's resources, better to have never been born. How we need the eyes of God! Truly, He is El-Roi, the God who sees (Genesis 16:13). He sees past the damage inflicted by the sins of man, He sees past the work of the enemy, for He sees according to His promise through eyes of love.

Today, nine years after Rolland and Heidi's arrival in Mozambique, many of the first rescued children are serving as leaders and pastors in a national revival that now numbers over 6,000 churches! These children are now young adults, transformed and empowered by the love of God. They form God's "search and rescue" parties, loving and healing the ones who now sit in the garbage and gutters as they once did. The Spirit of the Lord is on them, and they can say "He has anointed me to preach good news to the poor. He has sent me to proclaim freedom for the prisoners and recovery of sight for the blind, to release the oppressed, to proclaim the year of the Lord's favor" (Luke 4:18-19).

Today, Iris Ministries operates seven children's centers with over 3,000 children in their care. In addition, each of Iris's affiliated pastors is asked to take up to ten children into his family's or church's personal care. These children, with their simple, humble faith, are being used of God to preach, to work healings and miracles, and to bring deliverance from demonic powers—to literally transform a nation!

What a reminder this should be to us in the West who put so much value on our intellect, our talent and our resources. How many of us can say, "I touched a blind beggar in the name of Jesus and now he can see!" Lest we put too much stock in things that are not nearly as important to God as we think, we have the words of Paul, "But God chose the foolish things of the world to shame the wise; God chose the weak things of the world to shame the strong. He chose the lowly things of this world and the despised things—and the things that are not—to nullify the things that are, so that no one may boast before him" (1 Corinthians 1:27-29).

THE PASTORS OF MOZAMBIQUE

When Heidi first returned to Mozambique, after being powerfully impacted by the prophetic word and experience of the power of God in Toronto, she immediately began preparing a three-month Bible school curriculum. Rolland was a great help in this area, being such a man of the Word and so well trained and educated. They understood that unless there was a grounding of the leaders in the Word of God, the fruit of their labors could be lost. This was what happened to the fruit of John G. Lake's ministry in Africa. Today the movement he began is basically a cult. Solid Bible training would be a high priority for the Bakers, with a key emphasis on recognizing cultish beliefs or practices. There is a real concern on Rolland and Heidi's part to avoid heresy and to keep the movement within the tracks of orthodoxy.

Twelve men were invited to the first school where Rolland and Heidi would teach the essentials of the Christian faith. These men would later become the leaders of what was to become one of the most powerful church planting movements on the earth today. But, these men didn't just receive teaching and information; they also received an impartation.

There were many times during the prayer meetings when the power of God would come down in their midst. The men would be laid out under the power of the Holy Spirit. They received visions and heard God speak to them about things they would later do in the power of the Spirit of God. On occasions, Heidi was given prophecies for these men. God had told her to prophesy to these key leaders everything that I had prophesied to her when she was first touched in Toronto. She told them, "God wants to give us the nation of Mozambique. You are going to see the blind see, the lame walk, the deaf hear, and the dead raised." Then God revealed to Heidi the men who would raise the dead. She prophesied, "Rego, you're going to raise the dead. Joni, you're going to raise the dead." Within the next three years these men and others would raise the dead.

When I visited Mozambique for the first time, I saw these men living some of the most sacrificial lives I had ever seen. I asked them why they were doing what they were doing. Each told me the same thing, "When I was in the Bible school, I had an experience with God. I was shown in a vision what I was going to be doing. I have been living out what God showed me to do in the vision." These visions have played a large role in how God has led this church planting movement. Much like the Apostle Paul's experience in Acts 16 where he was instructed to go to Macedonia through a vision, God's Holy Spirit has led these men.

By the end of the first year (1997-98) there were 400 churches. By the end of the second year, there were 1000 churches, 2000 in the third year, and 4000 in the fourth year. These numbers are from the annual pastors' meeting where a careful count of churches and people are taken. Today, 6,000 churches have been started that are connected to Rolland and Heidi's ministry.

At the time of my first visit, I had been leading renewal meetings around the world for six years and had seen a lot of physical manifestations. It is important to know that there is a lot more happening to people during a physical manifestation of God's presence than just an emotional or even temporary spiritual experience.

What God has done in Mozambique through the weakness of those first twelve men and Rolland and Heidi is evidence of this. Their testimonies, and the testimonies of other volunteer workers at Maputo with Rolland and Heidi, have had a profound impact on my life. It causes me to wonder, "How many more people are there scattered around the world that are serving the King and His kingdom on the mission field because they too were impacted in this time of renewal?"

SURPRESA SITHOLE, MOZAMBIQUE

Surpresa Sithole is a co-director of Iris Ministries, along with Rolland and Heidi Baker. I'll let Rolland tell you about him through this excerpt from a story in "Spread the Fire Magazine" dated 2003:

> Surpresa became our Mozambican national director and is a powerful encouragement everywhere he goes. Both his father and mother were witch doctors in his hometown of Morrumbala out in the bush of a remote province. When he was fifteen the audible voice of Jesus told him to get out of his house or he would die within a week. He didn't know anything about the cross and salvation then, but he did know that from then on his life belonged to this amazing Jesus. He fled down the road and learned later that his parents were murdered within the week. He survived out in the rough like a refugee, and eventually a pastor in Malawi explained the gospel of Jesus Christ to him.
>
> Surpresa never looked back, and has been living a life of signs and wonders ever since. He speaks fourteen languages, ten given to him supernaturally. Fasting and prayer are a way of life for him, and he sees visions regularly. But Surpresa's most impressive quality is that he is filled with love and joy. He is virtually incapable of a negative thought, laughing easily and often in all circumstances. He still travels with me preaching all over Mozambique and surrounding countries to our churches, which now number in the thousands.
>
> I remember when he first told me about praying for a little girl who was raised from the dead. It had happened months earlier, but Surpresa had forgotten to mention it. Our pastors are so extremely understated and not hungry for publicity. In February of 2001 Surpresa was holding a crusade in the community hall of Komatipoort, a small town [in South Africa] on the border of Mozambique. On a Wednesday morning the area chief came to him

208

and said that the meetings would have to be stopped. A girl had died of malaria the night before in a nearby house and people wanted quiet so they could mourn.

Surpresa responded by going to the house and praying for the family of the little six-year-old Shansha. Her father was gone, trying to find transport to take her body to the mortuary. She was still in her bed, cold and stiff, and had begun to smell of decay. Surpresa began to pray at ten o'clock in the morning with her mother and six ladies present in her room. According to Surpresa, he didn't know what else to do so he kept praying for the family.

"After awhile," he said smiling, "I prayed with such power that they fell asleep on grass mats on the cement floor." Not knowing what else to do, he kept praying. His fingers were resting on the mat beside the dead girl. Suddenly, after about another hour of prayer, the little girl grabbed Surpresa's finger and sat up as though she had been in a deep sleep.

"I nearly jumped out of my skin!" Surpresa says.

The little girl asked for a drink, and Surpresa poured a glass of Coke for her. Surpresa had to wake up her mother and the ladies in the hut. . . . In shock, they began weeping, laughing and jumping with joy and ran screaming the news into the village. For the next two weeks, Surpresa says, they held meetings in that village to packed audiences and many were saved.

As far as we know, at least eight people have been raised from the dead in this revival between 2000 and 2002, and maybe fourteen since 1998. Several of these resurrections took place in heavily Moslem areas, and many Moslems have come to Jesus as a result. Surpresa and the pastors involved are absolutely shocked by God's graciousness in allowing them to experience such power in spite of their inferiority. But they know that we as Christians live by faith, looking not at our sin and weakness, but into His face. He has given us a commission: "As you go, preach this message: 'The kingdom of heaven is near.' Heal the sick, raise the dead, cleanse those who have leprosy, drive out demons. Freely you have received, freely give." (Matt. 10:7-8 NIV)

As Surpresa says, if you wait for miracles to take place, the miracles will only wait for you to move. But if you go, they will follow you. Signs and wonders are behind your back, pushing you forward so that you will experience breakthrough. Don't wait for the world to bring dead people into the church. Instead, the church has to go where dead people are. All of this is waiting for you! [76]

CORPORATE IMPARTATIONS

We have just read powerful stories of impartations to individuals. Our amazing God even gives impartations to whole churches. Let us look at examples that I have personally witnessed.

Redding, California

In the introduction to this book, Pastor Bill Johnson talked about the increase of anointing that happened in his church in Redding, California. This is what I call an impartation for a corporate anointing. Over eight days of meetings, with training on how to have words of knowledge and an activation clinic, and teachings on how to pray for the sick, we saw about 400 people healed. This was something that only God could do; it was a grace release, a sovereign impartation. It was more than the method of the teaching and activation clinics that produced such an outpouring of healings. It was more than the material taught—there was an impartation that the people received.

I remember teaching on words of knowledge and immediately following up with an activation clinic. A woman stood up and gave her first word of knowledge.

She said, "Water bottle."

I thought, "Now what do I do? What kind of a word of knowledge is that?" Since I didn't know how to interpret it I asked, "Does that word make sense to anyone?"

A woman raised her hand, overcome with faith and excitement. She had her saliva glands destroyed and had to carry a water bottle with her all the time. She knew the word was for her and she was totally healed.

Bill told me that even though his church was already moving in a strong anointing for healing, there was a 25% increase of healings in their church after the corporate impartation the church received, and it has never gone back to the earlier level. This occurred in 1998.

210

Two other times that a strong corporate impartation came upon an entire church and not just a few individuals happened close to the same time, one in Brazil, and the other in the Ukraine.

Goinia, Brazil

I went to Goinia, Brazil to minister to the Videira Church. We taught three or four sermons to equip the church for healing. When I went back the next year, I met with all the staff and had a chance to interview them and I was blown away by their reports. When I asked them if this was the fruit of the last time we ministered in their church they responded, "Before you came we were a good church, noted for our strong teaching ministry, but we never had healings. After you left we have not had one Sunday go by without healings occurring. Every week in our cell groups we now have healings, whereas before healings were very rare." They continued, "We personally did not expect God to use us for healing, but now we are expectant, and we now pray regularly for the sick."

A few years later, at this same church, we experienced a major breakthrough for healing the blind. In one night alone there were six blind people healed. This was the first time the pastor had successfully prayed for a blind person. One man had come in with white corneas and pupils. Three days after receiving prayer, he experienced a creative miracle as he slept and woke up with new corneas and pupils. The church had not experienced healings like these before receiving an impartation.

Kiev, Ukraine

The other church that received a corporate anointing was in Kiev, Ukraine. The pastor is a powerful man of God. (Due to security issues with ministering in a Muslim nation, that pastor has asked that his name not appear in print. We will refer to him as Pastor.) The first time I ministered in Pastor's church, the words of knowledge I received were so frequent and powerful that I couldn't concentrate on my message. This was the most powerful meeting that I had experienced up to that

211

point in my ministry. In three days, over 2,000 people were healed. It was obvious that there was a powerful and distinct anointing in those meetings. Once again, the focus of those meetings was to equip the saints for the work of ministry.

When I returned a little less than a year later I asked Pastor, "What has been the fruit of our last visit to your church?"

He told me how he had previously been given a plan to evangelize the cities of Europe by the Holy Spirit. He was instructed by God to do it the way Jesus had done, by sending out disciples two by two with the message that the "kingdom of God is at hand." The kingdom's demonstration would be through healing the sick and casting out of demons. However at the time of that vision Pastor did not possess the faith to begin this ministry, nor did he feel his people were ready to embark upon such a ministry. He shared that the first time I ministered in his church, the people were so impacted that they immediately began to go out and pray for the sick. He also said that he watched how God used me and was so faithful to me that it encouraged his faith to believe God would use him as well. He too received an impartation when I prayed for him.

His vision was to extend this message beyond his own city. He sent out about one hundred people from his church to share the message of the kingdom of God, heal the sick and cast out demons. These people would go two weeks prior to Pastor's visit to a particular city to preach and minister in the gifts of the Spirit in the marketplace. They would go to the streets, to the hospitals, anywhere to heal the sick, cast out demons and preach the gospel with power. This was replicated in three different cities on three different occasions. In each city, about 20,000 people were saved, usually as a result of personally being healed or delivered. Or, they came to hear Pastor preach because a family member or friend had been healed or delivered.

The fruit of this church made it obvious that they had received a corporate anointing during the impartation service. Now, not just a few, but the majority of the people were actively ministering. Pastor has continued to do these types of evangelistic outreaches throughout his part of the world. Hundreds of thousands have been saved as a result.

Raleigh, North Carolina

The last example of a church receiving a corporate anointing occurred in Raleigh, North Carolina. While ministering there, a "glory cloud" appeared while I was preaching. This cloud was visible for everyone to see. If you got close or stepped into it, you could feel intense peace. That night many were healed. The most outstanding healing occurred to a man who had been almost totally deaf in his ears since the Korean War. He was healed as he sat on the front row, right in front of the glory cloud. The pastor, Rev. John Sanger, told me that this phenomenon had never happened before in the church, but it has happened three more times in the last three years since our visit.

IMPARTATION FOR ADVANCEMENT

For many years now, I have observed the practice of impartation and studied the Scriptures on this vital grace. God sovereignly chooses to anoint someone with the grace to lay hands on others. The person prayed for receives an impartation of power for healings, miracles and/or deliverances. Some receive an impartation through corporate or individual prayer, without the "laying on of hands." Regardless of the method that they receive, people who receive an impartation are then mightily used to advance the kingdom of God.

I noticed that during the early days of Pentecostalism, many of the men and women who went out and pioneered churches around the world were first touched by a powerful impartation of the Holy Spirit. Let us take the outpouring of the Spirit at Azusa Street for example. Many received their unusual power through going to Azusa Street and either through "praying through" in the upper room for the baptism in the Holy Spirit, or by having someone lay hands upon them for this experience. Regardless of which of the two biblical ways of bestowing power, the issue is that they did receive power. As they went around the world with this

213

restoration message, many others were built up in faith through their words. The Pentecostal message was the answer to a half century of expectant prayer that went up from the church around the world. That prayer was based on the belief that God was about to restore to the church the gifts and power of the first century apostolic church. This message created a desire for the impartation of new power, or an impartation for gifts of healing and miracles.

Nearly forty years after the Azusa Street revival, the church experienced another visitation of the Holy Spirit (1946-49), often referred to as the Latter Rain movement. Once again, hearts were set on fire, and once again revival would go quickly around the world. There was a strong emphasis again upon healing, and especially upon impartation and prophecy. This movement, like the earlier Pentecostal movement, was the catalyst for a new round of missionary outreach around the world. About forty years later (1992-96) another movement began. This movement is again emphasizing and restoring to the church the ability to receive renewing power for ministry. Once again, people are coming from around the world to receive an impartation and take it back to their countries. This movement, with its various streams that contribute to the river of outpouring, is producing a new missionary expansion in the world. Again, thousands of new churches are being started.

This kind of empowered ministry is most needed if we are to see a revival of Christianity in Western Europe. Western Europe has lots of preachers and pastors working in its respective countries, but it has a very small percentage of practicing Christians. I have read statistics for most of their nations that indicate only between 3%-6% attend church regularly. Western Europe needs another Patrick from Ireland to raise up a missionary movement that is characterized not only by the preaching of the gospel, but also by the faithful obedience to the Lord's command, "Heal the sick, cleanse the leper, cast out demons, and raise the dead" (Matthew 10:8).

214

The largest churches in most European countries are churches that do believe in the continuation of the ministry of our Lord Jesus. Many of these churches were started at the beginning of the last century, following the outbreak of the Pentecostal movement that restored the message of the kingdom with power to the church. Many of the other largest churches, in both Western and Eastern European countries, have been started in the last 15-25 years by Africans who believe in the continuation of the ministry of healing. Pastor Sunday from Nigeria, and a pastor from Zimbabwe pastor the two largest churches in the Ukraine with over 25,000 and 10,000 believers respectively. While I was in England there was a special on television about a rather new church that had been started by a man that I believe is from Africa. This church has rapidly grown to be the largest church in all of Great Britain. Rev. Colin Dye pastors one of the other largest churches in Great Britain. It is a Pentecostal church and was part of the network of churches started as a result of the powerful healing ministries of the Jeffrey brothers.

Advancement in missions has always followed periods of revival. This was true of the First and Second Great Awakenings, the 1858 Prayer Revival, the Welsh Revival, the Pentecostal Revival, the Latter Rain Revival, and it is true of the outpouring of the Spirit in the 1990s. A fresh impetus for missions is characteristic of true revival because true revival renews people's first love and motivates them to go to the nations because they love what God loves.

When I think of the key leaders who participated in the meetings in Toronto or wherever this "Blessing" was taken, and what has happened since then, I see this evidential characteristic of true revival. Rolland and Heidi Baker are on fire for the nations of Africa. I think of Leif Hetland, who has ministered in over seventy countries since his impartation. I think of Wesley Campbell who burns with his concern for children at risk among the nations, and his efforts to raise money to help them and be used of God to call others to go and minister to them. I think of the apostolic leader, Che Ahn, who was so powerfully touched in Toronto and who has been used to start an apostolic network of churches with a very strong commitment to planting churches around the world, particularly in Asia. I think of the hundreds of "little ol' mes" who have taken vacation time and spent their savings to go on short term missions trips around the world.

While preaching in Toronto the last few times I asked the question, "How many of you have been to a nation since you were touched in Toronto?" I was shocked to see how many had gone from that congregation—at least half! Now I know that is not normal for the average congregation. Global Awakening has been sending 12-19 teams a year to the nations with 20-120 on each team. Just in the last three years we have seen about 2,000 people go with us to the nations. As I write this from the airport lounge, I am on my way to Sao Paulo to join 299 young people for our annual Youth Power Invasion. These young people, all 13-29 years old, will be the teachers, preachers, and the ministry team. Two weeks ago we sent out two of our interns to join Rolland and Heidi Baker for long-term work in Mozambique. Two more of our interns are leaving in five months to join Leif Hetland, to help him in his missionary work.

When I made my first trip to Mozambique five years ago, I was exhausted by the time I got there. Heidi asked me to lead devotions for her team that evening. I felt so tired, I thought an easy way to do this would be to interview each one at the meeting and ask them why they had become a missionary and why they were in Mozambique. Every person there was white in the middle of an all black nation. They had come from Israel, Great Britain, Canada, United States, Australia, and New Zealand. Each gave me the same answer. They had been touched by the Renewal either in Toronto or by someone who came to their area, carrying the anointing from Toronto. The touch of God had led them to the mission field.

Today, some five years later, Heidi's personal assistant is a woman who was in that team of visitors. Before she returned home to Nebraska, this average housewife, who had no experience with missions work, was touched by a sermon on impartation and God's ability to use the "little ol' mes" of this world. She believed it and is now a valuable servant with the Bakers. Another man I met while on my first trip to Mozambique was Steve Lazar. Steve was an educator that came from New Zealand. He too was so touched that he returned to Mozambique and established a school for the orphans. In its first year, those students had the highest scores of any school in the nation. One church from North Carolina sent about twelve on that trip with me and six of them ended up going back as long-term missionaries to help the Bakers.

In the spring of 2004 I was in Mozambique with a team. During that trip I received three independent, prophetic words within twenty-four hours which were all in agreement. The words came from Heidi Baker; Lesley-Ann Leighton, Heidi's spiritual twin; and Prophetess Jill Austin. The word was, "Randy, God wants to know if you are willing to be the father of a new missionary movement?" Each time I said, "Yes!" But I felt several things about this word. First, I felt unqualified to lead a new missionary movement. I felt like God must be calling several other leaders in the church to also become fathers in this new missionary movement. Secondly, I sensed a total awareness of my inability to know what to do to accomplish this word. A year later, I now have the peace of knowing what I have learned from my new friend Leif Hetland. "This is a promise, not a problem. If it is a promise it must be received; if it is a problem it must be achieved." I realize this is way beyond my ability to achieve so I am going to rest and watch God give it to me as a promise.

I want to address you, the reader. Don't tell yourself that you couldn't be used of God on the mission field or in a ministry of mercy. I want to tell you that there are people who are shocked at how God is using them in major ways. Just be open to the supernatural power of God to enable you to live a transformed life of ministry. Like Carole Baerg described in her testimony early in the chapter, this is about not saying, "Oh no, not me," but about receiving the promise of the Father, the promised Holy Spirit, and saying "yes" to the inheritance that is ours through Jesus. "Ask of me, and I will make the nations your inheritance, the ends of the earth your possession." (Psalm 2:8)

PEOPLE MOVEMENT

I will always remember my first trip to Mozambique in August of 2000. I was prepared for the long flight, having made three previous trips to neighboring South Africa. The travel would take almost forty hours to get from my house to the Bakers' home. Though I was prepared for the trip, I was not prepared for what I would experience in Mozambique.

Upon arriving at the orphanage compound, Heidi asked us if we wanted to go on a trip with her into the city where she would be ministering to people on the streets. We all said yes, we wanted to go and minister to the people on the street.

Heidi took me to places I never imagined experiencing. We met young people living on the streets. She knew their hangouts, and took bread for them to eat. Heidi takes an evangelistic team with her made up of older youth from the orphanage, young people who have been touched themselves by the grace and power of God. These young people used to be prostitutes, on drugs, abused, throw-away children, but now are mighty evangelists for the kingdom. They began singing, which gathered a crowd. Then they gave testimonies of the grace of God in their lives. Finally, a short invitation was given by one of the young evangelists. Everyone responded by kneeling on the sidewalk, repenting for their sins, and giving their lives to Jesus. People who walked up to this scene of grace, who had not heard the singing, or the testimonies, or the invitation, still came under conviction, dropped to their knees and gave their lives to Jesus also.

Then Heidi took me to a block of the city that had become a living dump. I remember her warning me and the team to, "Watch out for the rats in this place; they are as big as cats." She took me to visit "one of her friends." I was not prepared for this. I had traveled the world since Toronto, and had seen many of the slums where the poor lived in huts made out of discarded tin, cardboard, and plastic. But, I had always seen these shanties from the safety of a bus, plane or car. Now I found myself sitting in this little hovel of a home in the middle of a dump, infested with rats, without water, sewers or electricity. I looked around at my surroundings. The home consisted of a half-bed, one little wooden chair where I was seated, and a small lamp stand with a candle for light. There was enough room in this home for one other person to sit right next to the half-bed, but there was no chair. I thought, "Most of our bathrooms are larger than this home." The woman Heidi was visiting was sick, so Heidi prayed for her.

We left this home and walked through the garbage to the next. This one was a little larger. I stepped into this lean-to type of dwelling. There were two half-beds, a little couch and two chairs. Again the light of two candles dimly lighted it. Around me sat about five young women; all had become prostitutes to earn money to live. The hostess had been a prostitute, but had responded to the gospel when she met Heidi. She began to cry as Heidi talked with her, feeling she had not lived as close to God as she should have. Heidi showered her with love and then began to present the gospel to the other young women, not in Portuguese, but in the local dialect. Before long, all of the young women were crying and gave their lives to this God of love, mercy, and grace. Before we left, everyone had accepted Jesus.

Next we went to another "home." Outside they were preparing their meager food on an open charcoal fire; there are no kitchens in these shanties. Heidi began to talk to a very young woman in her teens. This young woman opened up her skirt to Heidi showing how terribly she was afflicted with some type of sexually transmitted disease. Heidi asked me to pray with her for the healing of the woman and then we took her to the clinic to get treatment.

At one of our stops Heidi found a young boy who had been thrown away by the new man who moved in with the boy's mother. (This is a too-common practice in Mozambique.) She took the boy to her orphanage and saw that he got cleaned up and was given some clothes and food.

I dropped into bed and lay there amazed at the capacity to love that I had witnessed in Heidi. I was totally exhausted and overwhelmed emotionally by what I had just experienced. I remember Heidi telling me that she and Rolland had been in Mozambique for **four years prior to the flood**. They had not had this kind of responsiveness to the gospel. She told me that this was very different, now it seemed that almost everyone was hungry for God, and ready to accept the gospel.

What is happening in Mozambique today can be defined as a "people movement." While in college, I read a book by Dr. Donald McGavarn called *Church Growth*. Dr. McGavarn related how, in India, he witnessed the greatest lost opportunity of his fifty years of missionary service. India had been a very gospel resistant land. Missionaries could work for years with very few converts. In one of the states of India, a people movement began. A "people movement" is when the Holy Spirit is working in a very special way and it seems like everyone in the state is ready to accept Jesus. The mistake was in the missionary agency not calling other missionaries stationed around India to come help reap the harvest. Instead, they were left in their gospel resistant stations, and the missionaries in the state where the people movement was occurring were overwhelmed. They were not able to reap the harvest, and in time the season of opportunity passed, resulting in the people once again becoming difficult to lead to Christ.

When I read that story, I made a commitment to myself that if I was ever privileged to witness a true "people movement" that I would do all I could to try and get the people to the harvest field to reap the harvest before it was lost. That is one of the purposes of this book—to sound the call that a people movement is now happening in Mozambique. Help is needed. Don't ignore the call of God if you are sensing His call to reap the harvest fields of the nations.

During the writing of this book, Rolland Baker flew to meet me in Washington State where I was conducting meetings so we could go over the details and facts of the manuscript. When we came to this section of the manuscript Rolland told me, "We are very much in the situation that MacGavern spoke of in India. Help is desperately needed. The nets are breaking!" Unless more help comes to the Mozambican people, many converts will be lost. The few workers are becoming exhausted. Hands are becoming limp from the burden of the weight of the harvest. In light of this, I ask you the reader to bring this situation to your pastor or to your mission board. I ask you to pray to the Father that He would send forth laborers into His harvest. Literally millions of souls are at stake.

I want to encourage you to consider going with us to Mozambique. Already several people who have gone with us are now going to Mozambique as short-term missionaries, and several other churches have become partners with the Bakers as a result of going and seeing what God is doing through them.

But first I want to lay a solid foundation on how to receive an impartation. In the next chapter I will give some practical insights and suggestions on how to prepare your heart and place yourself in a posture to receive from God.

Chapter 13: How To Receive An Impartation

These are exciting days. We are seeing the Holy Spirit build the kingdom through a church that is increasingly more unified as we acknowledge that God can and does work through a diversity of experience. Since I went to Toronto Airport Christian Fellowship almost eleven-and-a-half years ago, I have been privileged by God's grace to meet key leaders of both Evangelical and Pentecostal streams. I find Pentecostals open to working with me, knowing that I don't believe one must speak in tongues to be baptized in the Spirit. (Though I have had a prayer language since 1971, my receiving it did not coincide with my baptism in the Holy Spirit.) At the same time, I am finding Evangelicals who are open to working with me, knowing that I do believe in the gifts of the Spirit and the baptism of the Spirit occurring both simultaneously with conversion but, much more often, subsequent to conversion. I am finding Evangelicals who admit they were baptized in the Holy Spirit after their conversion, and I am meeting Pentecostals who admit that they believe one can be baptized in the Holy Spirit before receiving one's prayer language, at the time one receives it, or after one receives it. In summary, the traditional walls are beginning to fall. I am finding that there is much more openness to diversity of spiritual experiences than there was twenty years ago. Why? Because there has arisen a desperation in the hearts of many to experience *all* the Bible speaks of, rather than be satisfied with a tidy, supposedly theologically correct understanding of the baptism in the Spirit or other types of impartations.

Within all this diversity of experience, the question still arises: How do we receive the fullness of the Spirit, be it the impartation of a specific anointing or a "baptism" of the Spirit? Can the ways of the Spirit even be narrowed down to a question of "how"? The question implies there is some kind of formula or proscribed process. Unfortunately, church traditions tend to reduce the ways of

God to steps and stages that leave little room for God to pour out His multi-faceted grace in ways uniquely suited to each of His children.

Before proceeding, I'd just like to make clear that, while this chapter attempts to deal with the "how" of impartation, there will be frequent use of the term "baptism in the Spirit." These terms are not quite synonymous, but "baptism" certainly is an impartation. So even if you would classify yourself as a "Spirit-baptised" believer, what I have to say regarding "baptism" would apply equally to any further impartation you may be seeking.

In the history of the church, there have been two basic approaches to receiving impartations. The first is to try to pursue holiness as a matter of conquering sin in one's life. *When one has become "sanctified," then one is eligible for a powerful impartation.* This can be traced back to the asceticism of the "desert fathers"—the monks who deprived their fleshly desires for basic needs. This conquering of the flesh or subjecting of the flesh to the Spirit is seen in the writings of the "Holiness" groups from John Wesley until today, but especially in the 1700s to the early 1900s. It was John Wesley, known as the "father of Pentecostalism" who first taught on a "second definite work of grace" experience of the Holy Spirit subsequent to and distinct from the indwelling of the Spirit that occurs at salvation.

This "holiness" view became the model for "three-stage" Pentecostals who believe in (1) salvation, (2) consecration of one's life which leads to sanctification (defined as victory over all *known* sin) as an instantaneous, second definite work of grace, and (3) baptism in the Spirit evidenced by speaking in tongues. A more "Baptist" stream of Pentecostals also developed; they hold to a "two-stage" view that believes in (1) salvation, and (2) baptism in the Holy Spirit. For these groups, experiencing sanctification is a process throughout one's life while "positional" sanctification is ours through the finished work of Christ. Both groups of traditional Pentecostals hold to the doctrine of "initial evidence of speaking in tongues." In the early 1900s, this became the divisive element that caused half of

224

the numerous Holiness groups to reject the Pentecostal movement. For non-Pentecostals, the work of sanctification *was* the baptism of the Holy Spirit, and the evidence of being Spirit-filled was a holy life, not speaking in tongues.

The second approach to receiving impartations is simply to put one's faith in the "finished work" of Jesus. This view holds that *Jesus has already made me holy and He is my sanctification.* What I need to do is to reckon this as truth in my life. Then I receive my sanctification, baptism in the Spirit, and impartation of gifts by faith. Striving is removed and resting in faith takes its place.

This second approach is the more Calvinistic perspective within the Holiness movement. This view would have been exemplified by Phoebe Palmer who pioneered a form of "confess what the word says is yours and then claim this experience by faith in the word of God." The Keswick Movement also represented this view of sanctification as a finished work, but still emphasized the need to confess any known sin prior to receiving the baptism in the Holy Spirit. This last approach, receiving by faith in order to receive an impartation, seems to be the one that has allowed more people to enter into or receive their experience of impartation.

However, there is truth in the first approach mentioned above. Some of the men and women who crucified their flesh and sought God for both purity and power did become very anointed for healing. But, in my opinion, it wasn't because of their asceticism or piety that they moved in this power, but because of their hunger for God and His power, and their intimacy with God.

Why so much discussion over these differing views? I simply want the reader to understand the great degree of diversity even within the traditions that value and appropriate impartations. God has poured out His Spirit in the context of many traditions and theologies. There is truth to be found in all of them. Can sanctification be a process? Yes. In one area or another, I think we have all experienced the process of transformation into His likeness, from glory to glory. Well then, can sanctification be an instantaneous work of grace? Yes. Many have experienced an immediate and glorious release from some besetting sin, bondage, or addiction. Does one need to achieve some degree of maturity or sanctification before one is eligible for an impartation or baptism in the Spirit? In general—and I emphasize "in general"—those who have sought to honor God through a consecrated life seem to be the most frequent recipients of an impartation. Is this always the case? No. Sometimes God seems to delight in rattling our self-righteous cages by sovereignly pouring out His Spirit on the least "holy" among us. I believe this is to remind us that His gifts are about grace, not our works.

Regardless of one's theological tradition, the point is we all need an impartation or "baptism" of the Holy Spirit. I am more concerned that we have the experience than I am with having the best, most theologically correct way of talking about the experience.

I have given much thought to the prerequisites of receiving an impartation of the Holy Spirit. There does not seem to be any pat theology or one-two-three-step formula that adequately encompasses all the workings of the Spirit. If we try to define God's ways in terms of steps or formulas, we leave no room in our faith to receive anything beyond that step or outside our formula. What if I believe that I received all God has for me at the moment of salvation? There is no faith for more if I'm convinced this is all there is. Likewise, what if I believe that the "baptism of the Holy Spirit" is a one-time step to some new level? Now, years after my "baptism" experience, I feel burned-out, discouraged and powerless. I have little faith for more if that experience was supposed to be the answer to all my spiritual needs. Pretty discouraging. The church is full of discouraged, disillusioned Christians wondering, "Is this all there is?"

I believe it is time to move beyond the divisive walls of denominational semantics and arguments over terminology and process. Where we can all meet is in our common need. We need the Holy Spirit!

The only true prerequisites to receiving more of the Holy Spirit are really quite simple. I believe there are three.

The first prerequisite is to be aware of the personal inadequacy in our Christian life. We must recognize how our lives are characterized by too much defeat, indifference, lack of power, lack of love, and lack of faith. We must come to the place of facing our weakness and our inability to affect the work of the kingdom. We may be well-trained to do church work, run committees, preach or teach, administrate, counsel—all done through our training and education. But that is not the same as the ability to heal the sick, cast demons out, raise the dead, and preach with the anointing to break through to hard hearts with such conviction that people are brought to Jesus. These things need the anointing, the grace, and the gifts of the Holy Spirit. So the first condition is to recognize our need, our spiritual poverty.

Second, we must earnestly desire for this condition to change. By this I mean we allow the Holy Spirit to develop within us a serious desire to be victorious Christians. Some people do not even believe a victorious life is possible. This is because they have interpreted Paul's statement in Romans 7 as a declaration of defeat to be expected as the norm. This Calvinistic viewpoint is counterproductive to any hope of living victoriously. I highly recommend the chapter by Dr. Gordon Fee in my book *Power, Holiness, and Evangelism.* Dr. Fee takes the opposite viewpoint—the understanding that Paul taught we could live a life of victory rather than defeat by the power of the Holy Spirit. The same Holy Spirit that can develop the desire for such a victorious lifestyle can also provide the faith for such an experience and continued lifestyle. This material can be a great help in building your faith upon the word of God and not just upon your experience.

Third, we must want our lives to honor God and be used in His service and for His glory. So, we do not ask for a spiritual high to make us feel good, or for an experience that can boost our ego or spiritual pride. Rather, we ask for power and gifts to make us commensurate to the task before us of binding the "strong man" of Matthew 12:29 and plundering his home. The task is that of "breaking down the gates of hell." For in our victory God is glorified, honored and pleased. This empowering enables our faith to express itself in love.

Billy Graham said:

> I think it is a waste of time for us Christians to look for power we do not intend to use; for might in prayer, unless we pray; for strength to testify, without witnessing; for power unto holiness, without attempting to live a holy life; for grace to suffer, unless we take up the cross; for power in service, unless we serve. Someone has said, "God gives dying grace only to the dying."[77]

We all need to be filled or baptized with the Holy Spirit. Since the idea of being filled or baptized in the Holy Spirit is not an issue for those within the Pentecostal or Holiness traditions, but poses more of a problem for those in the Evangelical position, especially the Cessationist Evangelical, I am going to draw insights from two famous Evangelicals, Dr. Billy Graham and Dr. Harold Lindsell.

I trust all know who Billy Graham is, but not all may know of Dr. Harold Lindsell's reputation. Dr. Lindsell, at the time he wrote the book from which I will be quoting, *The Holy Spirit in the Latter Days*, was the editor emeritus of *Christianity Today*. He received his Ph.D. in history from New York University and his D.D. from Fuller Theological Seminary. For more than twenty years he served on the faculties of Bible colleges and seminaries. He was a prolific author and editor.

Billy Graham places an extremely high value on being "filled with the Spirit." He said it this way:

> I am convinced that to be filled with the Spirit is not an option, but a necessity. It is indispensable for the abundant life and for fruitful service. The Spirit-filled life is not abnormal; it is the normal Christian life. Anything less is subnormal; it is less than what God wants and provides for His children. Therefore, to be filled with the Spirit should never be thought of as an unusual or unique experience for, or known by, only a select few. It is intended for all, needed by all, and available to all. That is why the Scripture commands all of us, "be filled with the Spirit."[78]

In Billy Graham's book, *The Holy Spirit,* he devotes chapter 9 to the subject of "How to Be Filled with the Holy Spirit." He lists three truths of the Bible that we must understand as conditions to being filled. First, we must know that God has given us His Holy Spirit and He indwells us. For conversion to be genuine, this indwelling must occur at conversion.

Billy Graham lists the second truth we must understand. It is that "God *commands* us to be filled with the Spirit. That means it is His will for you to be filled—and to refuse to be filled with the Spirit is to act contrary to the will of God. It is his command, and therefore it is His will. Just to make it even clearer—God *wants* to fill us with His Spirit" (Italics Graham's). [79]

The third understanding is in regard to the presence of sin in our lives. "What is it that blocks the work of the Holy Spirit in our lives? It is sin. *Before we can be filled with the Holy Spirit we must deal honestly and completely with every known sin in our lives. . . .* There will be no filling by the Holy Spirit apart from cleansing from sin, and the first step in cleansing from sin is awareness of its presence" (Italics Graham's). [80]

Over the next several pages it becomes clear that Dr. Graham is not referring to a quick sentence confession such as, "Father, I ask you to forgive me of my sins for Jesus sake." No, he instead means to thoroughly allow the Holy Spirit to search our hearts and bring to us every sin that we are walking in and to confess it specifically. He writes:

> That is why the Bible is so vital in this matter. We must not be content with a casual examination of our lives, thinking that only the sins which seem to give us the most trouble are worthy of being confessed. Instead, as we prayerfully study the Word of God, the Holy Spirit—who is, remember, the author of Scripture—will convict us of other areas of sin which need confessing to God. We must confess not only what we think is sin, but what the Holy Spirit labels as sin when we really listen to His voice from the Word of God. "All Scripture is inspired by God and profitable for teaching, for reproof, for correction, for training in righteousness" (2 Timothy 3:16). [81] . . . There is one other point we need to make about confession of our sins. We must not only be honest about the various

sins in our lives, but we must get down to the deepest sin of all—our failure to let Christ rule our lives. *The most basic question any Christian can ask is this: Who is ruling my life, self or Christ? . . .* It is amazing how many Christians never really face this issue of Christ's Lordship, and yet the New Testament is full of statements about Christ's demand for our full commitment.[82] (Italics Graham's)

I include here some of Dr. Lindsell's observations on how to be "filled with the Holy Spirit." He believes that:

[A]ll believers are sealed, indwelt, and experience the sanctifying grace of the Spirit in them. But not every believer is, at the time of the new birth or even later, necessarily filled or controlled by the Holy Spirit. The filling of which we speak is certainly the believer's birthright. It belongs to him or her because he or she is a child of God and a joint heir with Jesus Christ. It is the Father's wish that all of His children be filled with the Spirit. It is a **blessing that must be claimed.**[83] (Emphasis added)

Lindsell writes concerning the believer's attitude toward receiving the infilling of the Spirit:

This may be summarized by six statements: (1) The Spirit's fullness is the Christian's birthright. It belongs to him or her by way of promise in the covenant of redemption. (2) The promise of the Spirit was made available to all believers once Pentecost had come. (3) Every believer knows whether he or she has the Spirit's fullness. If one does not know if one has the Spirit's fullness, then one does not have it. (4) The Scripture makes it evident that no one can secure the fullness of the Spirit by one's own efforts. Nor can it be bought. . . . (5) Every sincere believer should obtain the Spirit's fullness, whatever the price may be. (6) The believer can be certain that if he or she meets the conditions set down for receiving the fullness of the Holy Spirit, he or she is sure to receive it, because God always keeps His word.[84]

He further states:

The believer who asks God to fill him or her with His Holy Spirit should do so with certain biblical facts in mind and heart. The first is that it is the will of God for each believer to be filled with the Spirit. If this is so, then it is something that can be prayed for without contingency [with confidence, *clarification mine*], because whatever is the will of God can be asked for with the certitude of faith. [He then quotes 1 John 5:14-15] "Now this is the confidence that we have in Him, that if we ask anything according to His will, He hears us. And if we know that he hears us, whatever we ask, we know that we have the petitions that we have asked of Him."[85]

Dr. Lindsell summarizes his thoughts by saying:

Every believer who serves Christ as Lord, who has repented of and confessed all known sin, and who has asked to be filled with the Holy Spirit can claim the promise of God in faith. . . . The Promise of God is kept even when there may be no sign at all. We are not to look for an experience. We are simply to accept the promise by faith, and begin to thank God for what He has already done.[86]

As I reflect upon the positions of Dr. Graham and Dr. Lindsell, I am aware that I have seen things that didn't fit their "conditions." Though I think their positions are noble and generally correct, I have to admit that I don't agree 100% with the issue of conditions. There are exceptions to the conditions position, especially "every known sin confessed and repented of" prior to receiving the infilling or baptism of the Spirit. The exceptions are "signs" that this is not about performance, but about grace-based gifts appropriated through faith. Even as I wrote the last sentence I realized that sometimes impartations are totally sovereign visitations where there is still need of confession and repentance, and where there is no or little faith. I have seen people who had not confessed every known sin receive impartations for power and gifts that came solely by grace. I agree that the three things Dr. Graham mentions are important to growing in our relationship with God, but sometimes God sovereignly touches someone in the church who everyone knows doesn't have their spiritual life together. The reason He does this is to remind us that we all receive by grace. As I have said previously, His gifts are "charismata" not "worksmata." This helps us stay in the place of gratitude and praise for His grace to us. In other words, when you are in a meeting where someone is being used of God for impartation, "Nobody is safe!" God could pour out His Spirit upon anyone. Though this is true, the *norm* is that He generally touches in public those who have been crying out in private for His impartation. The *norm* is that He touches those who genuinely desire to live, no longer for self, but for His glory.

Billy Graham concludes his book, *The Holy Spirit* with this illustration:

> Over 100 years ago, two young men were talking in Ireland. One said, "The world has yet to see what God will do with a man fully consecrated to Him." The other man meditated on that thought for weeks. It so gripped him that one day he exclaimed, "By the Holy Spirit in me I'll be that man." Historians now say that he touched two continents for Christ. His name was Dwight L. Moody.[87]

Ironically, today Moody Bible Institute is a bastion of Cessationism, even though its first two presidents, Dwight L. Moody and R.A. Torrey, clearly believed in the impartation of the Spirit as an experience distinct from and subsequent to one's salvation.

In summary, I do not believe the Bible fits any denominational system, either Pentecostal or Evangelical, regarding the baptism in the Holy Spirit or how one receives other types of impartations. Both are too narrow.[88]

John Wesley's contemporary and associate, John Fletcher, taught that one could have many effusions (pouring outs) of the Holy Spirit. By accepting the possibility of multiple experiences, we should not confine God to a set pattern or method, but be open to as many as needed for the work God has planned for us. By loosing the tight order and making room for diversity, we can find room to validate others' experiences that are different from our own. I believe, had we listened to what Fletcher was saying, the church could have avoided much of the current division that arises from the terminology and formulas that we use. By allowing God to be bigger than our doctrinal traditions, I believe we find faith for Him to bring us into the fullness of what He wants us to be.

The same God Who did not make two fingerprints or two snowflakes alike did not intend our experience of His Spirit to be the same for everyone. When we look back at the biblical passages, especially in Acts, we find sometimes the people were baptized/filled in the Holy Spirit at a prayer meeting with tongues (Acts 2), and at another prayer meeting in Acts, this time without tongues (Acts 4:31). Sometimes the Spirit came after water baptism with the laying on of hands and no tongues occurred (Acts 8). At other times, we are not told the particulars of how or when someone received an impartation of the Spirit (Acts 9). Impartations of the Spirit can occur at the time of conversion, before water baptism, with tongues and prophecy accompanying it (Acts 10). It can also occur after water baptism with the laying on of hands accompanied by tongues and prophecy (Acts 19). What we see here is the work of a God who likes diversity, and I suggest we need to learn to like diversity. In fact, I believe if we could learn to appreciate this biblical diversity, it would enable us to appreciate the diversity within the body of Christ that Satan has used to divide us.

In my former church we honored and welcomed people who had had experiences reflecting this New Testament diversity. We did not try to convince them that their experience was not valid, or was not normative. Rather, we emphasized that God was free to baptize us and fill us with His Spirit or impart gifts to us in whatever way He might choose. In this manner, we found unity in the midst of diversity.

As a matter of fact, my emphasis in ministry hasn't been so much on the experience of receiving an impartation of the Spirit as it has been on the fruit of having an intimate relationship with Jesus Christ. I have encouraged the people of my church not to ask someone if they have been baptized in the Spirit because the answer doesn't really tell one much. What do I mean by this? Well, it's like asking someone if they have had a wedding. They may answer, "Yes," but you don't know anything about the relationship. They may be living in hell in the marriage. They may be living in marital bliss. They may have had a wedding, but are now divorced, or widowed, or separated. So, one doesn't really know much about the relationship by asking someone if they have had a wedding. Rather, ask them

233

about how intimate they are with their mate and if they love him/her more today than when they first married.

In like manner, people could have had an experience, call it baptism in the Holy Spirit, or some kind of impartation of the Spirit, years ago but now they are cold, or lukewarm, or backslidden. Or, they may be passionately in love with God. Focus on the relationship. In this way people can't hide behind an experience of the past. It is not enough to have had a baptism in the Holy Spirit; we must continue to be filled with the Holy Spirit. It is not enough to have had an impartation of the Spirit; we need to live in the continuing power of the Spirit.

Jesus told us the evidence of the Holy Spirit would be the reception of power (Luke 24:49 and Acts 1:8). When I read the history of the church, I find men who received power and who then had a powerful influence upon the church and society. Some of these people, like Francis of Assisi, Ignatius Loyola, and Mother Teresa, were Roman Catholic. Others like George Whitefield and Billy Graham were/are Reformed; others like John Wesley, E. Stanley Jones, and Charles Finney were Armenians; and still others like Maria Woodworth Etter, John G. Lake, Smith Wigglesworth, T. L. Osborn, Oral Roberts, Omar Cabrera, Carlos Annacondia, Claudio Freidzon, Luis Palau, and David Yonggi Cho are Pentecostals. I cannot believe that the non-Pentecostals mentioned above were not baptized with the Holy Spirit or had never received an impartation of the Holy Spirit because they did not speak in tongues. Nor can I believe that others who have spoken in tongues, but who have had little impact upon the church and society, have received a baptism in the Holy Spirit. If power is a major purpose and evidence of the presence and work of the Holy Spirit, then I must acknowledge that church history and the Bible both indicate that people can be baptized or receive an impartation in the Holy Spirit with diverse experiences in how they received this baptism or impartation.

Let me conclude with some very practical instructions regarding receiving different types of impartations. I will begin and end with a note of caution. Do not take this advice, these insights, and turn them into rules. Do not limit God to my limited insights. However, I do hope these insights will give you a starting place to begin to better understand how to enter into the presence of God and/or receive an impartation from God.

I started out listing three of what I have called "prerequisites" only because they seem to be the normal characteristics seen in people prior to their being "filled or baptized in the Holy Spirit." First, we must be aware of our desperate need for more of the presence of God in our lives, our spiritual inadequacy. Second, we must desire for this condition to be changed; we must want to have the "more" that is available. And, third, we must want our lives to honor God and be used in His service and for His glory. It is the third characteristic—desiring our lives to bring glory to His name—where I find common ground with Graham's and Lindsell's language of "conditions." If there is a genuine desire in someone to live a life that glorifies God, there will naturally be a renouncing of sinful habits because they do not bring honor to God. And again, where I diverge from their view is that I see this attitude of consecration as the "norm" but not necessarily an absolute requirement. There are exceptions; I have seen the Spirit poured out in a powerful way on people who had no preexisting desire for holiness. Their sanctification was the *fruit* of the Spirit's touch, not a precursor to it.

So, "prerequisites" aside, let me get practical.

In hopes of helping people who have difficulty in receiving, let me share some insights on how to receive. There are several aspects of receiving because sometimes the impartation will deal with receiving power, other times peace, other times healing. Sometimes a person will receive all or several of these blessings at one time.

I learned a lot from John Arnott who had found it difficult to receive himself. Both John and I have sympathy for those who are left standing in ministry times. We've both had similar experiences and out of our experience we feel for those who find it more difficult to receive. What I have learned is to not try and stop anything. Don't try to stop trembling or shaking, don't try to keep standing by tightening up all the muscles in your back and move your feet to keep standing, don't try to stand and don't try to fall.

Now I do not want to limit or categorize falling or shaking or laughing or some other type of movement to mean any specific thing. It would be foolish to try to limit God in such a manner. However, I would be less than honest if I did not share that there are some things that have occurred often enough to say there are some common patterns in how many people respond to the Holy Spirit.

For example, when people are receiving blessings of peace, they often have a tendency to become weak and fall. On the other hand, those who are receiving blessings of power often feel power in their hands or some other part of the body. They often shake as a result of this power. Sometimes they will bounce up and down for long periods of time. Sometimes the power is so strong they will fall and shake on the ground. When anointing for healing comes, they often feel heat or electricity in their body. Other times they simply feel the pain alleviate.

When it came to healing we often had to tell the people, after the first wave of power had come upon them, to stay focused, that often God came in waves with pauses between them to allow the person receiving prayer a breather. This is something you appreciate because often the intensity of the experience is so powerful and demonstrative that a rest or pause is needed. Helping them stay focused or in an atmosphere of receptivity was important. Too many people are used to quick prayers of pronouncements that they are to believe or stand for, and they are not used to waiting upon the Holy Spirit to actually affect the healing they have asked for.

In meetings, I often instruct people with the following, "We are not desiring any courtesy drops tonight. That would be the flesh. However, if you try to stand, that is the flesh also. Don't try to fall; don't try to stand up. Both are flesh."

One of the problems many people have is that of analysis. Borrowing from John Arnott, I instruct people to "get out of analysis and into romance.

Experiencing God is a thing of romance, not analysis. Analysis ruins it. For example, did you know that the human mouth has more germs in it than any other part of the human body? Why would two adults put their mouths together with all those germs? Because they are not into analysis, but are caught up in romance. What you need to do is quiet your spirit and pucker." Humor often helps lift the pressure that people put on themselves.

Another area that deals with receiving is what to do after you have fallen. I find that too many people get up too quickly. Sometimes the anointing is so strong, a person can't move. Other times it is not that strong. However, people quench the Spirit by getting up when He is resting on them with His peace. I instruct people to continue to lie on the floor until it is not difficult to move; to stay on the floor until they do not feel heavy, and it takes no more willpower than normal to get up.

One of the most difficult things to do is to get people to stop praying when they are being prayed for. This is especially true for those who have been in the church longer, and certain types of people who feel it is important to pray in tongues when receiving or to say something like, "I believe, I believe, I receive, I receive." I have found it much more difficult for people to receive while they are praying and claiming. I am referring to receiving impartations of power for ministry that may include certain gifts.

Obviously, if someone desires the gift of tongues I would not discourage them from praying or being willing for the Spirit to move them to pray. But, my preference is when the gift of tongues just comes without any instruction on what to do to "prime the pump" so to speak. I don't encourage anyone to start saying the names of Japanese cars to get started. I take the pressure off of them and tell them it may happen when I pray for them or it may happen sometime as they are driving down the highway or mashing potatoes, or in worship. The point is to ask, believe, rest, and receive.

I hope what I have written in this chapter is of help to you. I caution you against turning my observations into rules rather than leaving them as observations. At best, I consider them to be principles. I admit that God uses other people in a way that is very different from what I have talked about, and it really is God. So don't make my observations and suggestions "Saul's armor" for a young David. If God has blessed you in the use of the sling, then use it. I was just sharing how I use my sling. My counsel to people when ministering to them works with the use of the sling God has given me. It could prove counterproductive if God has equipped you to minister in a different manner. So do not hear me saying I have something better than you. What I have written is just the sharing of what works for me.

God bless you as you begin or continue the exciting ministry of cooperating with the Holy Spirit. Through Him we are enabled to become co-laborers with Christ.

Let the name of Jesus Christ be held in high honor in our cities when people witness healing and deliverances as the gospel is being shared.

CONCLUSION

I thank God for the way he made it possible for me to receive a good education for ministry. I thank God for the Baptists who helped me go through college and seminary and for my seminary class on revivals. Because of it, I learned so much about historical revivals. Dr. Lewis Drummond's class at The Southern Baptist Theological Seminary prepared me to be able to recognize revival. In those classes I had been exposed to almost all the phenomena that occurred in Toronto through my reading of the historic revivals in America.

However, the greatest revival in Christian history was not talked about in my college and seminary classes. In fact, it was totally ignored. That was the great Pentecostal Revival. But God in His providence saw that this blind spot was removed from my eyes. He created divine appointments for me to begin to learn about the great revivals of the Pentecostals. Because of these studies, I learned that not too many were saved in the great Azusa Street Revival that lasted about three years—yet, this was truly a revival.

The fruit from the Azusa Street Revival was in what happened to the people who came to the meetings. They were baptized in the Holy Spirit, and with this impartation they returned to their region of the United States or the world. Those places were where the salvations began. From these revived churches, or the newly formed Pentecostal churches, would come a world revival with the greatest mission's outreach of the century.

In less than one hundred years, Pentecostals and Charismatics would become the largest group of Protestant Christians in the world, numbering more than all other Protestants combined. Where other Protestant works had been going for 500 years, the Pentecostal movement would sweep past them in numbers of adherents, conversions, and workers in one hundred years.

I hope, as you read of the revival that has broken out in Mozambique and around the world, that you will hunger for the outpouring of God in your own life and church. I hope you are hungry for an "impartation" from God. I hope you will not be afraid of the manifestations of God's Holy Spirit. I hope those who sell "fear" through their radio program and/or books will not mislead you. These detractors of revival can only see the extremes, and paint the moves of God by those extremes. Furthermore, they only communicate the worst fruit, which occurs when pastors and/or their parishioners do not use wisdom in handling the power of God. You never get to hear of the good fruit that is a result of these moves of God.

Now you've heard about some of the real and lasting fruit in the preceding pages. I hope that I've laid out enough of the biblical and historical foundation for what we are experiencing, that it is no longer a cause for fear and rejection. I don't know if it is too late for the United States and Europe to get into what we came to call this move of God, "The River." The opportunity has come and may now be gone. I hope not. I pray for another visitation of God's presence for our country. This time, I hope there is enough information about true revival, and its accompanying phenomena that people will not respond in fear or fight the move of God, but will instead respond in faith and embrace the move of God. I hope they will desire to be among the first to receive a fresh "impartation" of the new thing God will be doing.

I hope this book has made you hungry for more—hungry for an impartation of apostolic love and compassion, hungry for an impartation of the gifts needed to be more fruitful in your ministry. I believe you are hungry; otherwise you probably wouldn't have bought this book and read it to this point. I believe God sees your hunger and wants to touch you. I believe some of you will become missionaries. Others will become church planters, pastors and key leaders in the church. It has been my experience that those who have received an impartation are those who are most ready to serve in the kingdom of God and have the most joy while serving.

I will be the first to admit that not everyone is called to go to the nations. But, everyone is called to go somewhere. The question is where? Perhaps to a distant land—another nation like Mozambique, Cambodia, Ukraine, or Brazil. Others are called to go to the slums, to the poorest of the poor, whether in ours or another nation. Others are called to reach their neighborhood, their block, their town or their city. Others are called to minister to the prostitutes on the streets or the drug addicts. The point is we are all called to go. Even those of us who give our lives in serving the local church must model this sense of being "sent ones." I am inviting you to become a part of this great new missionary expansion that is growing around the world. Come join us in the streets of our nation and in the nations of the world!

I am also extending two specific invitations that will build up your faith and give you and an opportunity to receive an impartation of the Holy Spirit. The first invitation is to come with us on a short-term mission trip to somewhere like Brazil, Argentina, Columbia, Russia, Ukraine, or Korea.

The second invitation is to enroll and attend one of our four-day Schools of Healing and Impartation. It is best to attend the School 1 before School 2, but in both there are three to four sessions given to "laying on of hands for impartation" following a teaching that is faith building for such an experience.

If we want to be more successful in our going—to whatever place or group— we need more of the anointing. We need a fresh "impartation" from heaven. I remind you of the concern of Mel Tari in his council to not lead people into thinking that all they need is someone to lay hands on them and receive an impartation. No, you need much more than this. You need humility, character, integrity, as well as intimacy with God. What you receive in an impartation must be lived out in faithful obedience even when it involves suffering. What you receive must be guarded through maintaining a personal relationship with God. You must guard your heart against pride, bitterness, unforgiveness, broken relationships or covenants, and the lust for fleshly or material things. Always "seek first His kingdom and His righteousness and all these other things *[author: your needs, not desires]* will be added to you." (Matthew. 6:33)

Let me pray for you:

> *Father, in the name of Jesus I ask that You would meet the faith and hunger of the person holding this book. I bless them in the name of Jesus and ask for Your Holy Spirit's fire to come upon them. I ask that You would release Your compassion and love into their hearts right now. I ask that You would especially impart the gifts of word of knowledge, healings, prophecy and the working of miracles through them. As they wait in Your presence Father, with their hands out before them with their palms raised, I ask that Your power would touch their hands. MULTIPLY Your power. INCREASE Your power. BAPTIZE them in Your Holy Spirit and fill their souls with the love and the peace of the Prince of Peace, in Jesus' name. Amen.*

I encourage you to pray this prayer and then wait upon the Lord to come and touch you. You may find yourself waiting as long as ten minutes—but I counsel you to wait upon the Lord. I believe many of you will be touched and refreshed, and that a smaller number will receive a commission from God with an impartation so strong that you will become a "history maker in the land." If you experience a powerful touch from God after praying and waiting upon the Lord, please contact our office by email at *goglobal@globalawakening.com* and send us your testimony.

God bless and strengthen each of you with His mighty power.

Randy Clark

September 6, 2005

FURTHER INFORMATION:

If you are interested in becoming a missionary, pastor, or church planter and would desire training, contact our office by email or phone. We plan to start a training school for equipping people for ministry in September 2006.

Global Awakening
1-866-AWAKENING
www.globalawakening.com

Note: The **Endnotes** *contain bibliographic and contact information useful for obtaining the books and articles referenced in this volume.*

ENDNOTES

[1] The articles written by Jon Ruthven may be obtained from his website. Go to *home.regent.edu/ruthven/disciple.html.*

[2] Fee writes:

> In Galatians 3:1-5, when [Paul] encourages them to stay with "faith in Christ" and not get entangled with "works of law," he first appeals not to the truth of the gospel, but to their experience of the Spirit by which they started on the path of Christian discipleship. This is not an appeal to feelings but to something common to them all—the *experienced* reality of their conversion to Christ through the coming of the Spirit....The solution lies with the role of the Spirit in Paul's understanding. Indeed, the experience of the promised eschatological Spirit, not righteousness by faith, forms the core of Paul's argumentation in the one letter (Galatians) devoted primarily to this issue. The death of Christ brought an end to the curse of the law—that one had to live by "doing the law" and thus not "by faith" (Gal. 3:10-14). The gift of the Spirit makes the law's function of identifying God's people obsolete. "Those who are led by the Spirit," Paul says, "are not under Torah" (5:18). For those in whom the fruit of the Spirit is growing "there is no law" (v. 23). For Paul the Spirit thus marks the effective end of Torah. How so? Because the Spirit is sufficient to do what Torah was not able to do in terms of righteousness, namely to "fulfill in us who walk by the Spirit the righteous commandment of Torah" (Romans 8:4)." Gordon Fee, *Paul, the Spirit, and the People of God,* pp. (Peabody, Massachusetts: Hendrickson Publishers, Inc. 1996) pp. 84, 102-103.

[3] If you want to learn more about how to receive words of knowledge, see my book *Words of Knowledge.* It explains the five ways to receive words of knowledge that Lance gave me that day. Since that time, I've discovered a few more ways to receive words which are also included. To order it call our office at 1-866-292-5364 or go online to our website at *www.globalawakening.com.*

[4] If you would like to read the 11 page case study of the effects of this experience, and what it felt like, I have recorded it in my book, *Baptism in the Holy Spirit* along with several others experiences. It is available for purchase. To order call 1-866-292-5364 or go online to our website at *www.globalawakening.com.*

[5] Joe McIntyre's book on E.W. Kenyon has corrected a lot of my misunderstandings of the "Word of Faith Movement." Its great historical analysis corrects much misunderstanding and places the roots of the movement's message not in Kenneth Hagin and Ken Copeland, but in the brilliant Baptist pastor A. J. Gordon, the Dutch Reformed pastor Andrew Murray, and the Presbyterian pastor who became the founder of the Christian and Missionary Alliance, A. B. Simpson. It is available for purchase through our bookstore. To order call 1-866-292-5364 or go online to our website at *www.globalawakening.com.*

[6] If you would be interested in reading more about how God prepared me this information is in my book, *Lighting Fires*. It is available for purchase. To order call 1-866-292-5364 or go online to our website at *www.globalawakening.com*.

[7] A N.T. Greek word, "a fixed or definite period, a season, sometimes an opportune or seasonable time," see Vine, W., & Bruce, F. *Vine's Expository dictionary of Old and New Testament words*. (Old Tappan NJ: Revell, 1981, [Published in electronic form by Logos Research Systems, 1996])

[8] David Hilborn, *'Toronto' in Perspective. Papers on the New Charismatic Wave of the Mid 1990's* Evangelical Alliance Policy Commission Report (ACUTE), (Carlisle, UK: Paternoster Press, 2001) p. 14

[9] While not the *primary* function (to demonstrate the Father and the kingdom) the miraculous can be evidential, but needs to be seen so within a "kingdom" context See Jesus' statement in John 10:37-38.

[10] If you prefer (at this book's date of publication), you can review a condensed summary of the topic contained in our *School of Healing and Impartation 2* workbook and/or the workbook's accompanying recorded lectures. See our website at *www.globalawakening.com* for more information.

[11] A N.T. Greek word, "a fixed or definite period, a season, sometimes an opportune or seasonable time," see Vine, W., & Bruce, F. *Vine's Expository dictionary of Old and New Testament words*. (Old Tappan NJ: Revell, 1981, [Published in electronic form by Logos Research Systems, 1996])

[12] 1 Corinthians 15:52, (NKJV/NASB)

[13] Matthew 24:14.

[14] The works of Dr. Jon Ruthven are very important to develop what I have been speaking about in this paragraph. I believe Dr. Ruthven, a professor at Regent University at Virginia Beach, VA, is one of the most insightful religious professors of our time. See his articles: On the Cessation of Charismata, and Can a Charismatic Theology be Biblical? The first article is from his excellent book, *On the Cessation of the Charismata: The Protestant Polemic on Postbiblical Miracles*. The latter article is an urgent call for Protestants to become more biblical in the way they interpret the Scriptures, not seeing them through the glasses of 16th century context, but allowing them to say what the writers in their context intended. Only by allowing the Bible to speak for itself can we develop a more biblical theology to base our church practices upon.

[15] Morton's book, *Healing and Christianity* is now in its third edition as *Healing and Christianity: A Classic Study*. While I am not in agreement with the latter part of his book which analyzes healing from a Jungian psychological framework, I highly recommend it for its thorough historical, documentation of healing ministry accounts in Church history.

[16] Morton Kelsey, *Healing and Christianity: A Classic Study*, Augsburg Fortress edition, (Minneapolis, MN: Augsburg Fortress, 1995) p. 108, quoting Justin Martyr, *Second Apology: To the Roman Senate*, 6.

[17] Ibid., p. 118, quoting The Shepherd of Hermas, III.X.4 in *The Apostolic Fathers,* trans. Archbishop William Wake, (1909), 1:299.

[18] Ibid., p. 118-119

[19] Ibid., p. 109

[20] Ibid.

[21] Ibid., quoting Tertullian, *To Scapula* 4

[22] Ibid., p. 119

[23] Ibid., p. 108, referring to Cyprian, *Epistle* 75.15-16.

[24] Ibid., pp.119-120

[25] Ibid., p. 120

[26] Ibid., p. 119

[27] Ibid., p. 146 citing *De Vera Religione*, cap. 25, nn. 46,47

[28] Ibid., citing Saint Augustine, *The City of God* XXII.8 (1954), p. 445.

[29] Ibid., p. 172

[30] Guy Chevreau, *Catch the Fire* (Toronto, Canada: HarperCollins Publishers, Ltd. 1995) p. 77, quoting from *The Works of Jonathan Edwards,* I.lxiva

[31] Ibid., footnote 1, p. 177

[32] Ibid. Chevreau's citation "I.lxiva" references *The Works of Jonathan Edwards.*

[33] Ibid., pp. 78-79

[34] Ibid. Chevreau's citation "I.377b" references *The Works of Jonathan Edwards.*

[35] Ibid. Chevreau's citation "I.1378a" references *The Works of Jonathan Edwards.*

[36] Ibid. Chevreau's citation "I.lxviiib" references *The Works of Jonathan Edwards.*

[37] Ibid., pp. 86-88

[38] Ibid., p. 90

[39] Ibid., p. 92, quoting from *The Works of Jonathan Edwards,* I.lxiva

[40] Clare George Weakley, Jr. *The Nature of Revival* p. 79 quoting Nehemiah Curnock, ed., *The Journal of the Reverend John Wesley* (London: Charles H. Kelly, 1909), entry dated March 8, 1739

[41] Ibid., p. 83, quoting *The Journal of the Reverend John Wesley,* entry dated April 21, 1739

[42] Ibid., quoting *The Journal of the Reverend John Wesley,* entry dated April 26, 1739

[43] Ibid., quoting *The Journal of the Reverend John Wesley,* entry dated April 30, 1739

[44] Ibid., quoting *The Journal of the Reverend John Wesley,* entry dated May 1, 1739

[45] Ibid., quoting *The Journal of the Reverend John Wesley,* entry dated May 2, 1739

[46] Ibid., quoting *The Journal of the Reverend John Wesley,* entry dated July 7, 1739

[47] John Havlik and Lewis Drummond, *How Spiritual Awakenings Happen,* (Nashville, Tennessee: The Sunday School Board of the Southern Baptist Convention, 1981) p.15

[48] Paul K. Conkin, *Cane Ridge: America's Pentecost*, (Madison, Wisconsin: The University of Wisconsin Press, 1990) p. 19

[49] Ibid., p. 23

[50] Ibid., p. 24

[51] Lewis Drummond, *The Awakening That Must Come,* (Nashville, Tennessee: Broadman Press, 1978)
p. 17

[52] John Havlik and Lewis Drummond, *How Spiritual Awakenings Happen*, (Nashville, Tennessee: The Sunday School Board of the Southern Baptist Convention, 1981)

[53] Notes from my class with Dr. Drummond. I have to admit that Dr. Lewis Drummond had a profound impact and influence upon me to have a great hunger to experience revival.

[54] Charles L. Wallis, *Autobiography of Peter Cartwright*, (Nashville, Tennessee: Abingdon Press, 1856)   p. 12.

[55] Ibid., p. 45

[56] Ibid., p. 46

[57] This was Dr. Lewis Drummond's opinion.

[58] Charles Finney, *Charles G. Finney: An Autobiography,* (Old Tappan, New Jersey: Fleming H. Revell Company, 1876, renewed 1908) pp. 20-21

[59] Vinson Synan, *In The Latter Days: The Outpouring of the Holy Spirit In The Twentieth Century* (Fairfax, Virginia: Xulon Press, 2001) p.31

[60] Ibid., p. 32

[61] Ibid., p. 35, Synan quoting from *Spurgeons Sermons* (Grand Rapids, Michigan, reprint from 1857), pp.129-130

[62] Most present scholarship regarding Kenyon attributes some of the origins of his beliefs to the New Thought heresy of New England, (p. 374 of *The Dictionary of Pentecostal and Charismatic Movements*, edited by Stanley Burgess and Gary McGee). However, this is based upon the faulty research of D.R. McConnell, *A Different Gospel* (Peabody, Mass.: Hendrickson Publishers, 1988). The excellent book *E.W. Kenyon and His Message of Faith: The True Story* by Joe McIntyre, thoroughly disproves this theory based upon faulty conjectures and faulty time lines of Kenyon's life. McIntyre's book is a must read for anyone who wants to understand the true source of the Word of Faith origins. Time does allow me to prove his point which McIntyre does so completely, but let me just state that the origins of Kenyon's thought were in great evangelical leaders of the day; men like, A. J. Gordon, the Baptist pastor who read the Bible every morning for devotions from the Greek text; A. B. Simpson, Presbyterian and founder of the Christian Missionary Alliance, A. T. Pierson, D. L. Moody, R. A. Torrey, Andrew Murray, et. al.

[63] Timothy L. Smith, *Called Unto Holiness: The Story of the Nazarenes: The Formative Years* (Kansas City, Missouri: Nazarene Publishing House, 1962) p. 97

quoted from E. A. Girvin, P. F. Bresee, *A Prince in Israel*, New York, NY: Garland Publishing, 1984) pp. 82-83

[64] This is very interesting because on this same day was the first time tongues as the initial evidence of the Holy Spirit's baptism occurred in Topeka, Kansas with students in Parham's bible school.

[65] Vincent M. Walsh, *What is Going On: Understanding the Powerful Evangelism of Pentecostal Churches* (Philadelphia, Pennsylvania: Key of David Publications, 1995) pp. 158-162

[66] Ralph Martin, *The Catholic Church at the End of an Age: What is the Spirit Saying?*(San Francisco, California, Ignatius Press,1994) p.110-111 quoting from John Paul II, *Encyclical Veritatis Splendor (The Splendor of Truth),* section 108.

[67] Ibid., p. 111

[68] The details of this great outpouring of the Holy Spirit among Chinese orphans may be read in H.A. Bakers' book *"Visions Beyond The Veil."* You can order this book by contacting Iris Ministries, Inc. of Ohio at *www.irismin.com.*

[69] *Chasing the Dragon* by Jackie Pullinger with Andrew Quicke, is another "must read.")

[70] A future book is planned which will include many more testimonies called, *Stories of Impartations.*

[71] If you want to read more about Gary's eyes being opened you can get *Open My Eyes, Lord* by Gary Oates by contacting our ministry. To order it, call our office at 1-866-292-5364 or go online to our website at *www.globalawakening.com.*

[72] See Jon Ruthven's article *The "Imitation of Christ" in Christian Tradition: Its Missing Charismatic Emphasis.* It can be found on his website located at *home.regent.edu/ruthven/disciple.html.*

[73] Jon Ruthven, On *the Cessation of the Charismata: The Protestant Polemic on Postbiblical Miracles* Journal of Pentecostal Theology Supplement Series 3 (Sheffield, England: Sheffield Academic Press Ltd, 1993, 1997) p. 206

[74] Under entry for *agape* (derived from the verb, *agapaō*): "as used of God, it expresses the deep and constant love and interest of a perfect Being towards entirely unworthy objects, producing and fostering a reverential love in them towards the Giver, and a practical love towards those who are partakers of the same, and a desire to help others to seek the Giver." Vine, W., & Bruce, F. *Vine's Expository dictionary of Old and New Testament words.* Old Tappan NJ: Revell, 1981, [Published in electronic form by Logos Research Systems, 1996].)

[75] The full title is *Ministry Team Training Manual.* It is available for purchase. To order call our office at 1-866-292-5364 or go online to our website at *www.globalawakening.com.*

[76] Rolland Baker and Surpresa Sithole, "Raising the Dead", *Spread the Fire Magazine*, February 21, 2003, p. 13. The original story version was contained in an electronic newsletter emailed by Rolland Baker from Iris Ministries. This expanded version was published as noted.

[77] Billy Graham, *The Holy Spirit* (Waco, Texas: Word Books, 1978) p. 107

[78] Ibid., p. 108

[79] Ibid., p. 110

[80] Ibid.

[81] Ibid., p. 112

[82] Ibid., pp. 112-113

[83] Harold Lindsell, *The Holy Spirit in the Latter Days* (Nashville, Tennessee: Thomas Nelson, 1983) p. 111

[84] Ibid., p. 120

[85] Ibid.

[86] Ibid., p. 121

[87] Billy Graham, *The Holy Spirit* (Waco, Texas: Word Books, 1978) p. 220

[88] I am planning on writing a booklet on this subject that deals with the Holiness and Pentecostal history, traditions, experiences, and doctrinal formulation of those experiences. Readers interested in knowing more about the basis for positions outside the teachings of their own denomination might be interested in this. The title is going to be *A New Theology of Impartation: A Basis for Christian Unity Instead of Division.*